Lecture Notes in Computer Science   9889

Commenced Publication in 1973
Founding and Former Series Editors:
Gerhard Goos, Juris Hartmanis, and Jan van Leeuwen

More information about this series at http://www.springer.com/series/7408

Fernando Castor · Yu David Liu (Eds.)

Programming Languages

20th Brazilian Symposium, SBLP 2016
Maringá, Brazil, September 22–23, 2016
Proceedings

 Springer

Editors
Fernando Castor
Universidade Federal de Pernambuco
Recife
Brazil

Yu David Liu
State University of New York
Binghamton, NY
USA

ISSN 0302-9743   ISSN 1611-3349 (electronic)
Lecture Notes in Computer Science
ISBN 978-3-319-45278-4   ISBN 978-3-319-45279-1 (eBook)
DOI 10.1007/978-3-319-45279-1

Library of Congress Control Number: 2016948600

LNCS Sublibrary: SL2 – Programming and Software Engineering

Printed on acid-free paper

This Springer imprint is published by Springer Nature
The registered company is Springer International Publishing AG Switzerland

Preface

This volume contains the proceedings of the 20th Brazilian Symposium on Programing Languages (SBLP 2016), held during September 22–23, 2016, in Maringá, Brazil. SBLP is a well-established symposium, promoted by the Brazilian Computer Society since 1996, and provides a venue for researchers and practitioners interested in the fundamental principles and innovations in the design and implementation of programming languages and systems. Since 2010, SBLP has been organized in the context of CBSoft (Brazilian Conference on Software: Theory and Practice), co-located with a number of other events on computer science and software engineering.

The Program Committee of SBLP 2016 was formed by 41 members from 10 countries. The symposium received 29 submissions, including 2 short papers, with authors from 9 different countries. Each paper was reviewed by at least three reviewers and most of them by four. Papers were evaluated based on their quality, originality, and relevance to the symposium. The final selection was made by the program co-chairs, based on the reviews and Program Committee discussion. The final program featured a keynote talk by co-chair Yu David Liu (State University of New York, Binghamton), 12 papers in English, and 3 papers in Portuguese. The latter were presented at the conference but are not included in these proceedings.

We would like to thank the authors, the reviewers, and the members of the Program Committee for contributing to the success of SBLP 2016. We also want to thank the members of the Organizing Committee of CBSoft 2016, for all their help and support, and EasyChair, for once again making the paper submission process smooth and for the invaluable help in organizing these proceedings. We do not want to conclude without expressing our gratitude to Alberto Pardo, chair of the SBLP Steering Committee and chair of the previous edition of SBLP, for all his support at the different stages of the organization of the symposium.

September 2016

Fernando Castor
Yu David Liu

Organization

Program Committee

Luis Barbosa	University of Minho, Portugal
Thiago Bartolomei	LogicBlox, USA
Mariza Bigonha	Federal University of Minas Gerais, Brazil
Roberto Bigonha	Federal University of Minas Gerais, Brazil
Christiano Braga	Fluminense Federal University, Brazil
Carlos Camarão	Federal University of Minas Gerais, Brazil
Francisco Carvalho-Junior	Federal University of Ceara, Brazil
Fernando Castor	Federal University of Pernambuco, Brazil
Marcelo d'Amorim	Federal University of Pernambuco, Brazil
Fernando Pereira	Federal University of Minas Gerais, Brazil
João Fernandes	University of Beira Interior, Portugal
João F. Ferreira	Teesside University, UK and HASLab/INESC TEC, Portugal
Ismael Figueroa	Pontifical Catholic University of Valparaíso, Chile
Alex Garcia	Military Institute of Engineering, Brazil
Rodrigo Geraldo Ribeiro	Federal University of Ouro Preto, Brazil
Roberto Ierusalimschy	Pontical Catholic University of Rio de Janeiro, Brazil
Rafael Lins	Federal University of Pernambuco, Brazil
Yu David Liu	State University of New York at Binghamton, USA
Hans-Wolfgang Loidl	Heriot-Watt University, UK
Marcelo Maia	Federal University of Uberlândia, Brazil
Manuel A. Martins	University of Aveiro, Portugal
Fabio Mascarenhas	Federal University of Rio de Janeiro, Brazil
Sérgio Medeiros	Federal University of Rio Grande do Norte, Brazil
Ana Milanova	Rensselaer Polytechnic Institute, USA
Alvaro Moreira	Federal University of Rio Grande do Sul, Brazil
Martin Musicante	Federal University of Rio Grande do Norte, Brazil
Bruno C.D.S. Oliveira	The University of Hong Kong, China
Zachary Palmer	Swarthmore College, USA
Alberto Pardo	University of the Republic, Uruguay
Gustavo Pinto	Federal Institute of Pará, Brazil
Louis-Noel Pouchet	Ohio State University, USA
Zongyan Qiu	Peking University, China
Andre Rauber Du Bois	Federal University of Pelotas, Brazil
Sandro Rigo	University of Campinas, Brazil
Noemi Rodriguez	Pontifical Catholic University of Rio de Janeiro, Brazil
João Saraiva	University of Minho, Portugal

Doaitse Swierstra   Utrecht University, The Netherlands
Leopoldo Teixeira   Federal University of Pernambuco, Brazil
Simon Thompson   University of Kent, UK
Varmo Vene   University of Tartu, Estonia

Additional Reviewers

Annamaa, Aivar   Fonte, Victor   Viera, Marcos
Apinis, Kalmer   Lins, Rafael   Vojdani, Vesal
Cruz, Marco   Proenca, Jose
de Moraes, Camila   Tavares, Carlos

Contents

Language Support for Generic Programming in Object-Oriented Languages: Peculiarities, Drawbacks, Ways of Improvement

Julia Belyakova[✉]

I. I. Vorovich Institute of Mathematics, Mechanics and Computer Science,
Southern Federal University, Rostov-on-Don, Russia
julbel@sfedu.ru
http://mmcs.sfedu.ru/~juliet/

Abstract. Earlier comparative studies of language support for generic programming (GP) have shown that mainstream object-oriented (OO) languages such as C# and Java provide weaker support for GP as compared with functional languages such as Haskell or SML. But many new object-oriented languages have appeared in recent years. Have they improved the support for generic programming? And if not, is there a reason why OO languages yield to functional ones in this respect? In this paper we analyse language constructs for GP in seven modern object-oriented languages. We demonstrate that all of these languages follow the same approach to constraining type parameters, which has a number of inevitable problems. However, those problems are successfully lifted with the use of the another approach. Several language extensions that adopt this approach and allow to improve GP in OO languages are considered. We analyse the dependencies between different language features, discuss the features' support using both approaches, and propose which approach is more expressive.

Keywords: Generic programming · Object-oriented languages · Programming language design · Type parameters · Constraints · Interfaces · Concepts · Type classes · Concept pattern · Multi-type constraints · Multiple models · C# · Java · Scala · Ceylon · Kotlin · Rust · Swift · Haskell

1 Introduction

Most of the modern programming languages provide language support for generic programming (GP) [13]. As was shown in earlier comparative studies [4,7,8,14], some languages do it better than others. For example, Haskell is generally considered to be one of the best languages for generic programming [4,7], whereas mainstream object-oriented (OO) languages such as C# and Java are much less expressive and have many drawbacks [1,3]. But several new object-oriented languages have appeared in recent years, for instance, Rust, Swift, Kotlin. Have they improved the support for generic programming? To answer this question,

© Springer International Publishing Switzerland 2016
F. Castor and Y.D. Liu (Eds.): SBLP 2016, LNCS 9889, pp. 1–15, 2016.
DOI: 10.1007/978-3-319-45279-1_1

we analyse seven modern OO languages with respect to their support for GP. It turns out that all of these languages follow the same approach to constraining type parameters, which we call the "Constraints-are-Types" approach. This approach is specific to object-oriented languages and has several inevitable limitations. The approach and its drawbacks are discussed in Sect. 2.

Section 3 provides a survey of the existing extensions [2,3,17,24,25] for object-oriented languages that address the limitations of OO languages [1] and improve the support for generic programming: all of them add new language constructs for constraining type parameters. We call the respective approach "Constraints-are-Not-Types". The advantages and shortcomings of this approach as compared with the basic one used in OO languages are discussed; yet we outline the design issues that need further investigation.

In conclusion, we argue that the "Constraints-are-Not-Types" approach is more expressive than the "Constraints-are-Types" one. Table 1 is a modified version of the well-known table [7,8] showing the levels of language support for generic programming. It provides information on all of the object-oriented languages and extensions considered, introduces some new features, and demonstrates the relations between them.

```
interface IPrintable { string Print(); }

void PrintArr(IPrintable[] xs)
{ foreach (var x in xs) Console.WriteLine("{0}\n", x.Print()); }

string InParens<T>(T x) where T : IPrintable
{ return "(" + x.Print() + ")"; }
```

Fig. 1. An ambiguous role of C# interfaces

2   Object-Oriented Approach to Constraining Type Parameters

We have explored *language constructs for generic programming* in seven modern object-oriented languages: C#, Java 8, Ceylon, Kotlin, Scala, Rust, Swift. As we will see, all of these languages adopt the same approach to constraining type parameters, which we call the "Constraints-are-Types" approach [3]. In this approach, interface-like constructs, which are normally used as types in object-oriented programming, are also used to constrain type parameters. By "interface-like constructs" we mean, in particular, interfaces in C#, Java, Ceylon, and Kotlin, traits in Scala and Rust, protocols in Swift. Figure 1 shows a corresponding example in C#: IPrintable is an interface; it acts as a *type* in the array parameter xs in the PrintArr function, i.e. xs is an array of arbitrary values convertible to string, whereas in the InParens<T> function IPrintable is used to *constrain* the type parameter T. This example is not of particular interest, but it shows a common pattern of how constructs such as interfaces are used for generic programming in OO languages. Section 2.1 provides a survey of similar constructs for GP in the modern object-oriented languages mentioned above. The main problems and drawbacks of the approach are discussed in Sect. 2.2.

2.1 Language Constructs for Constraining Type Parameters in Object-Oriented Languages

Interfaces in C#, Java and Kotlin. A classical interface describes methods and properties of a type that implements/extends the interface. In C# and Java 7 only signatures of instance methods are allowed inside the interface. Kotlin and Java 8 also support *default method implementations*. This is a useful feature for generic programming. For instance, one can define an interface for equality comparison that provides a default implementation for the inequality operation. Figure 2 demonstrates corresponding Kotlin definitions: the Ident class implements the interface Equatable<Ident> that has two methods, equal and notEqual; as long as notEqual has a default implementation in the interface, there is no need to implement it in the Ident class.

Note that the Equatable<T> interface is generic: it takes the T type parameter that "pretends" to be a type implementing the interface, and this is indeed the case for the function contains<T> due to the "recursive" constraint T : Equatable<T>. The type parameter T is needed to solve the so-called binary method problem [5]: the equal method of the interface is expected to operate on two values of the same type (thus, equal is a "binary method"), with the first value being a receiver of equal, and the second value being a parameter of equal. T is an actual type of the other parameter, and it is supposed to be a type of the receiver.

Interfaces in Ceylon. Ceylon interfaces are much similar to the Java 8 and Kotlin ones, but the Ceylon language also allows a declaration of a type parameter as a *self type*. An example is shown in Fig. 3. In the definition of the Comparable<Other> interface the declaration "of Other" explicitly requires Other to be a self type of the interface, i. e. a type that implements this interface. Because of this the reverseCompareTo method can be defined: the other and this

```
interface Equatable<T> {
   fun equal (other: T) : Boolean
   fun notEqual(other: T): Boolean { return !this.equal(other) }
}
class Ident (name : String) : Equatable<Ident> {
   val idname = name.toUpperCase()
   override fun equal (other:Ident): Boolean { return idname == other.idname }
}
fun <T : Equatable<T>> contains(vs : Array<T>, x : T): Boolean
{ for (v in vs)      if (v.equal(x)) return true;
   return false; }
```

Fig. 2. Interfaces and constraints in Kotlin

```
interface Comparable<Other> of Other
           given Other satisfies Comparable<Other> {
  formal Integer compareTo(Other other);
  Integer reverseCompareTo(Other other) { return other.compareTo(this); } }
```

Fig. 3. The use of "self type" in Ceylon interfaces

values have the type `Other`, with the `Other` implementing `Comparable<Other>`, so the call `other.compareTo(this)` is perfectly legal. Without "`of Other`" the `Other` type can only be *supposed* to be a type of `this`, but this cannot be verified by a compiler, so the `reverseCompareTo` method cannot be written in Java 8 and Kotlin.

Scala Traits. Similarly to advanced interfaces in Java 8, Ceylon, and Kotlin, Scala traits [14,15] support *default method implementations*. They can also have *abstract type* members, which, in particular, can be used as *associated types* [11, 16]. Associated types are types that are logically related to some entity. For instance, types of edges and vertices are associated types of a graph.

Just as in C#/Java/Ceylon/Kotlin, type parameters (and abstract types) in Scala can be constrained with traits and supertypes (upper bounds): the latter constraints are called *subtype constraints*. But, moreover, they can be constrained with subtypes (lower bounds), which are called *supertype constraints*. None of the languages we discussed so far support supertype constraints nor associated types. Another important Scala feature, implicits [15], will be mentioned later in Sect. 2.2 with respect to the Concept design pattern.

Rust Traits. The Rust language is quite different from other object-oriented languages. There is no traditional `class` construct in Rust, but instead it suggests structs that store the data, and separate method implementations for structs. An example is shown in Fig. 4[1]: two `impl Point` blocks define method implementations

```
struct Point { x: i32, y: i32, }
...
impl Point {
  fn moveOn(&self, dx: i32, dy: i32) -> Point
  { Point {x: self.x + dx, y: self.y + dy } }}
...
impl Point {
  fn reflect(&self) -> Point { Point {x: -self.x, y: -self.y} }}
...
let p1 = Point {x: 4, y: 3};
let p2 = p1.moveOn(1, 1);    let p3 = p1.reflect();
```

Fig. 4. `Point` struct and its methods in Rust

---

[1] Some details were omitted for simplicity. To make the code correct, one has to add `#[derive(Debug,Copy,Clone)]` before the `Point` definition.

```
trait Equatable { fn equal(&self, that: &Self) -> bool;
    fn not_equal(&self, that: &Self) -> bool { !self.equal(that) } }
trait Printable { fn print(&self); }
...
impl Equatable for i32 {
    fn equal (&self, that: &i32) -> bool { *self == *that } }
...
struct Pair<S, T>{ first: S, second: T }
...
impl <S : Equatable, T : Equatable> Equatable for Pair<S, T> {
    fn equal (&self, that: &Pair<S, T>) -> bool
    { self.first.equal(&that.first) && self.second.equal(&that.second) } }
```

Fig. 5. An example of using Rust traits

for the Point struct. If a function takes the &self[2] argument (as moveOn), it is treated as a method. There can be any number of implementation blocks, yet they can be defined at any point after the struct declaration (even in a different module). This gives a huge advantage with respect to generic programming: any struct can be *retroactively* adapted to satisfy constraints. "Retroactively" means "later, after the point of definition". Constraints in Rust are expressed using traits. A trait defines which methods have to be implemented by a type similarly to Scala traits, Java 8 interfaces, and others. Traits can have *default method implementations* and *associated types*; besides that, a *self type* of the trait is directly available and can be used in method definitions. Figure 5[3] demonstrates an example: the Equatable trait defining equality and inequality operations. Note how support for self type solves the binary method problem (here equal is a binary method): there is no need in extra type parameter that "pretends" to be a self type, because the self type Self is directly available.

Method implementations in Rust can be probably thought of similarly to .NET "extension methods". But in contrast to .NET[4], types in Rust also can *retroactively implement traits* in impl blocks as shown in Fig. 5: Equatable is implemented by i32 and Pair<S, T>. The latter definition also demonstrates a so-called *type-conditional implementation*: pairs are equality comparable only if their elements are equality comparable. The constraint <S : Equatable... is a shorthand, it can be declared in a where section as well.

There is no struct inheritance and subtype polymorphism in Rust. Nevertheless, traits can be used as types, and due to this, a dynamic dispatch is provided. This feature is called trait objects in Rust. Suppose i32 and f64 implement the Printable trait from Fig. 5. Then the following code demonstrates creating and

---

[2] The "&" symbol means that an argument is passed by reference.
[3] Some details were omitted for simplicity. The following declaration is to be provided to make the code correct: #[derive(Copy, Clone)] before the definition struct Pair<S : Copy, T : Copy>. Yet the type parameters of the impl for pair must be constrained with Copy+Equatable.
[4] Similarly to .NET, Kotlin supports extending classes with methods and properties, but interface implementation in extensions is not allowed.

use of a polymorphic collection of values of the &Printable type (the type of the polyVec elements is a reference type):

```
let pr1 = 3; let pr2 = 4.5; let pr3 = -10;
let polyVec: Vec<&Printable> = vec![&pr1, &pr2, &pr3];
for v in polyVec { v.print(); }
```

Swift Protocols. Swift is a more conventional OO language than Rust: it has classes, inheritance, and subtype polymorphism. Classes can be extended with new methods using extensions that are quite similar to Rust method implementations. Instead of interfaces and traits Swift provides protocols. They cannot be generic but support *associated types* and *same-type* constraints, *default method implementations* through protocol extensions, and explicit access to a *self type*; due to the mechanism of extensions, types can *retroactively* adopt protocols. Figure 6 illustrates some examples: the Equatable protocol extended with a default implementation for notEqual (pay attention to the use of the Self type); the contains<T> generic function with a protocol constraint on the type parameter T; an extension of the type Int that enables its conformance to the Printable protocol; the Container protocol with the associated type ItemTy; the allItemsMatch generic function with the same-type constraint on types of elements of two containers, C1 and C2.

```
protocol  Equatable { func equal(that: Self) -> Bool; }
extension Equatable { func notEqual(that: Self) -> Bool
{ return !self.equal(that) }}
func contains<T : Equatable> (values: [T], x:T) -> Bool { ... }

protocol Printable { func print(); }
extension Int : Printable { ... }

protocol Container { associatedtype ItemTy ... }
func allItemsMatch<C1: Container, C2: Container
                   where C1.ItemTy == C2.ItemTy, C1.ItemTy: Equatable> ...
```

Fig. 6. Protocols and their use in Swift

2.2   Drawbacks of the "Constraints-are-Types" Approach

The Problem of Multi-type Constraints. Constructs such as interfaces or traits, which are used both as types in object-oriented code and constraints on type parameters in generic code, describe an interface of a *single* type. And this has inevitable consequence: *multi-type constraints* (constraints on several types) cannot be expressed naturally. Consider a generic unification algorithm [12]: it takes a set of equations between terms (symbolic expressions), and returns the most general substitution which solves the equations. So the algorithm operates on three kinds of data: terms, equations, substitutions. A signature of the algorithm might be as follows:

```
interface ITerm<Tm> { IEnumerable<Tm> Subterms(); ... }

interface IEquation<Tm, Eqtn, Subst>           where Tm : ITerm<Tm>
     where Eqtn : IEquation<Tm, Eqtn, Subst>
     where Subst : ISubstitution<Tm, Eqtn, Subst>
{ Subst Solve();
  IEnumerable<Eqtn> Split(); ... }

interface ISubstitution<Tm, Eqtn, Subst>       where Tm : ITerm<Tm>
     where Eqtn : IEquation<Tm, Eqtn, Subst>
     where Subst : ISubstitution<Tm, Eqtn, Subst>
{ Tm SubstituteTm(Tm);
  IEnumerable<Eqtn> SubstituteEq (IEnumerable<Eqtn>); ... }
```

Fig. 7. The C# interfaces for the Unification algorithm

```
Subst Unify<Tm, Eqtn, Subst> (IEnumerable<Eqtn>)
```

But a bunch of functions have to be provided to implement the algorithm:

Subterms : Tm $\rightarrow$ IEnumerable<Tm>, Solve : Eqtn $\rightarrow$ Subst,

SubstituteTm : Subst $\times$ Tm $\rightarrow$ Tm,

SubstituteEq : Subst $\times$ IEnumerable<Eqtn> $\rightarrow$ IEnumarable<Eqtn>,

and some others. All these functions are needed for unification at once, hence it would be convenient to have a single constraint that relates all the type parameters and provides the functions required:

```
Subst Unify<Tm, Eqtn, Subst> (IEnumerable<Eqtn>)
     where <single constraint>
```

But in the languages considered in the previous section the only thing one can do[5] is to define three different interfaces for terms, equations, and substitution, and then separately constrain every type parameter of the Unify<> with a respective interface. Figure 7 shows the C# interface definitions. To set up a relation between mutually dependent interfaces, several type parameters are used: Tm for terms, Eqtn for equations, and Subst for substitution. The parameters are repeatedly constrained with the appropriate interfaces in every interface definition. Those constraints are to be stated in a signature of the unification algorithm as well:

```
Subst Unify<Tm, Eqtn, Subst> (IEnumerable<Eqtn>)
     where Tm : ITerm<Tm>
     where Eqtn : IEquation<Tm, Eqtn, Subst>
     where Subst : ISubstitution<Tm, Eqtn, Subst>
```

There is one more thing to notice here — interfaces are used in both roles in the same piece of code: the IEnumerable<Eqtn> interface is used as a type, whereas other interfaces in the where sections are used as constraints. So the semantics of the interface construct is *ambiguous*.

The Lack of Language Support for Multiple Models. For simplicity, in this part of the paper we call "constraint" any language construct that is used

---

[5] The Concept design pattern can also be used, but it has its own drawbacks. We will discuss concept pattern later, in Sect. 2.2.

to describe constraints, while the way in which types satisfy the constraints we call "model". All of the object-oriented languages considered earlier allow having only one, unique model of a constraint for the given set of types. And indeed this makes sense for the languages where "Constraints-are-Types" philosophy works, because it is not clear what to do with types that could implement interfaces (or any other similar constructs) in several ways. But how does this affect generic programming? It turns out that sometimes it is desirable to have multiple models of a constraint for the same set of types. For instance, one could imagine sets of strings with case-sensitive and case-insensitive equality comparison; another common example is the use of different orderings on numbers, yet different graph implementations, and so on. Thus, with respect to generic programming, the absence of multiple models is rather a problem than a benefit. Without extending the language the problem of multiple models can be solved in two ways:

1. Using the Adapter pattern. If one wants the type `Foo` to implement the interface `IEquatable<Foo>` in a different way, an adapter of `Foo`, the `Foo1` that implements `IEquatable<Foo1>` can be created. This adapter then can be used instead of `Foo` whenever the `Foo1`-style comparison is required. An obvious shortcoming of this approach is the need to repeatedly wrap and unwrap `Foo` values; in addition, code becomes cumbersome.
2. Using the Concept pattern, which is considered below.

Concept Pattern. The Concept design pattern [15] eliminates two problems:

1. First, it enables *retroactive modeling* of constraints, which is not supported in languages such as C#, Java, Ceylon, Kotlin, or Scala.
2. Second, it allows defining *multiple models* of a constraint for the same set of types.

The idea of the Concept pattern is as follows: instead of constraining type parameters, generic functions and classes take extra arguments that provide a required functionality — "concepts". Figure 8 shows an example: in the case of the Concept pattern the constraint `T : IComparable<T>` is replaced with an extra argument of the type `IComparer<T>`. The `IComparer<T>` interface represents a concept of comparing: it describes an interface of an object that can compare

---

```
// Type Parameter Constraints
interface IComparable<T> { int CompareTo(T other); }
void Sort<T>(T[] values) where T : IComparable<T> { ... }
class SortedSet<T> where T : IComparable<T> { ... }

// Concept Pattern
interface IComparer<T>  { int Compare(T x, T y); }
void Sort<T>(T[] values, IComparer<T> cmp) { ... }
class SortedSet<T> { private IComparer<T> cmp; ...
   public SortedSet(IComparer<T> cmp) { ... } ... }
```

Fig. 8. The use of the Concept design pattern in C#

values of the type T. As long as one can define several classes implementing the same interface, different "models" of the IComparer<T> "concept" can be passed into Sort<T> and SortedSet<T>.

This pattern is widely used in generic libraries of mainstream object-oriented languages such as C# and Java; it is also used in Scala. Due to implicits [14, 15], the use of the Concept pattern in Scala is a bit easier: in most cases an appropriate "model" can be found by a compiler implicitly, so there is no need to explicitly pass it at a call site[6]. Nevertheless, the pattern has two substantial drawbacks. First of all, it brings *run-time overhead*, because every object of a generic class with constraints has at least one extra field for the "concept", while generic functions with constraints take at least one extra argument. The second drawback, which we call *models-inconsistency*, is less obvious but may lead to very subtle errors. Suppose we have s1 of the type HashSet<String> and s2 of the *same* type, provided that s1 uses case-sensitive equality comparison, s2 — the case-insensitive one. Thus, s1 and s2 use different, inconsistent models of comparison. Now consider the following function:

```
static HashSet<T> GetUnion<T>(HashSet<T> a, HashSet<T> b)
{ var us = new HashSet<T>(a, a.Comparer); us.UnionWith(b); return us; }
```

Unexpectedly, the result of GetUnion(s1, s2) could differ from the result of GetUnion(s2, s1). Despite the fact that s1 and s2 have the same type, they use different comparators, so the result depends on which comparator was chosen to build the union. Comparators are run-time objects, so the models-consistency *cannot* be checked at *compile time*.

3 The "Constraints-are-Not-Types" Approach to Constraining Type Parameters

In contrast to object-oriented languages discussed in Sect. 2, type classes [10] in the Haskell language are not used as types, they are used as *constraints only*. Inspired by the design of type classes, several language extensions for C# and Java have been developed. For defining constraints all these extensions suggest *new language constructs* that have *no self types* and *cannot* be used as types. They describe requirements on type parameters in an external way; therefore, retroactive constraints satisfaction (*retroactive modeling*) is automatically provided. Besides retroactive modeling, an integral advantage of such kind of constructs is that *multi-type constraints* can be easily and naturally expressed using them; yet there is no semantic ambiguity which arises when the same construct, such as a C# interface, is used both as a type and constraint, as in the example below:

```
void Sort<T>(ICollection<T>) where T : IComparable<T>;
```

Here ICollection<T> and IComparable<T> are generic interfaces, but the former is used as a type whereas the latter is used as constraint.

---

[6] Scala is often blamed for its complex rules of implicits resolution: sometimes it is not clear which implicit object is to be used.

JavaGI Generalized Interfaces. JavaGI [24] provides *multi-headed* generalized interfaces that adopt several features from Haskell type classes [23] and describe interfaces of several types. There is no self type in such interface, it cannot be used as a type. An example of multi-headed interface is shown in Fig. 9: the UNIFY interface contains all the functions required by the unification algorithm considered in Sect. 2.2; the requirements on three types (term, equation, substitution) are defined at once in a single interface. Note how succinct is this definition as compared with the one in Fig. 7.

```
interface UNIFY [Tm, Eqtn, Subst] {
   receiver Tm    { IEnumerable<Tm> Subterms(); ... }
   receiver Eqtn  { IEnumerable<Eqtn> Split();   ... }
   receiver Subst { Tm SubstituteTm(Tm); ...              }}
 Subst Unify<Tm, Eqtn, Subst>(Enumerable<Eqtn>)
   where [Tm, Eqtn, Subst] implements UNIFY {...}
```

Fig. 9. Generalized interfaces in JavaGI

Language G and C++ Concepts. Concept as an explicit language construct for defining constraints on type parameters was initially introduced in 2003 [19]. Several designs have been developed since that time [6,20,21]; in the large, the expressive power of concepts is rather close to the Haskell type classes [4]. Concepts were designed to solve the problems of unconstrained C++ templates [1,18]. A new version of concepts, Concepts Lite (C++1z) [22], is under way now. The language G declared as "a language for generic programming" [17] also provides concepts that are very similar to the C++0x concepts. Similarly to a type class, a concept defines a set of requirements on one or more type parameters. It can contain *function signatures* that may be accompanied with *default implementations*, *associated types*, nested *concept-requirements* on associated types, and *same-type constraints*. A concept can *refine* one or more concepts, it means that the refining concept includes all the requirements from the refined concepts. Refinement is very similar to multiple interface inheritance in C# or protocol inheritance in Swift. Due to the concept refinement, a so-called *concept-based overloading* is supported: one can define several versions of an algorithm/class that have different constraints, and then at compile time the most specialized version is chosen for the given instance. The C++ advance algorithm for iterators is a classic example of concept-based overloading application.

It is said that a type (or a set of types) *satisfies* a concept if an appropriate model of the concept is defined for this type (types). Model definitions are independent from type definitions, so the modeling relation is established *retroactively*; models can be generic and *type-conditional*.

C# with Concepts. In the C#[cpt] project [3] (C# with concepts) concept mechanism integrates with subtyping: type parameters and associated types can be

```
concept CEquatable[T] { bool Equal(T x, T y);
   bool NotEqual(T x, T y) { return !Equal(x, y); }}

interface ISet<T> where CEquatible[T] { ... }

model default StringEqCaseS for CEquatable[String] { ... }
model StringEqCaseIS for CEquatable[String] { ... }

bool Contains<T>(IEnumerable<T> values, T x)
   where CEquatable[T] using CEq {... if (cEq.Equal(...) ...}
```

Fig. 10. Concepts and models in C#^{cpt}

constrained with *supertypes* (as in basic C#) and also with *subtypes* (as in Scala). In contrast to all of the languages we discussed earlier, C#^{cpt} allows *multiple models* of a concept in the same scope. Some examples are shown in Fig. 10: the CEquatable[T] concept with the Equal signature and a default implementation of NotEqual, the generic interface ISet<T> with concept-requirement on the type parameter T, and two models of CEquatable[] for the type String — for case-sensitive and case-insensitive equality comparison. The first model is marked as a *default* model[7]: it means that this model is used if a model is not specified at the point of instantiation. For instance, in the following code StringEqCaseS is used to test equality of strings in s1.

```
ISet<String> s1 = ...;
ISet<String>[using StringEqCaseIS] s2 = ...;
s1 = s2; // Static ERROR, s1 and s2 have different types
```

Note that s1 and s2 have *different types* because they use different models of CEquatible[String]. Models are compile-time artefacts, so the models-consistency is checked at compile time. One more interesting thing about C#^{cpt}: concept-requirements can be named. In the Contains<T> function (Fig. 10) the name cEq is given to the requirement on T; this name is used later in the body of Contains<T> to access the Equal function of the concept. It is also worth mention that the interface IEnumerable<T> is used as a type along with the concept CEquatable[T] being used as a constraint; thus, the role of interfaces is not ambiguous any more, interfaces and concepts are independently used for different purposes.

Constraints in Genus. Like G concepts and Haskell type classes, constraints in Genus [25] (an extension for Java) are used as constraints only. Figure 11 demonstrates some examples: the Eq[T] constraint, which is used to constrain the T in the Set[T] interface; the model of Eq[String] for case-insensitive equality comparison; the multi-parameter constraint GraphLike[V, E], and the type-conditional generic model DualGraph[V,E]. Methods in Genus classes/interfaces can impose additional constraints:

```
interface List[E] { boolean remove(E e) where Eq[E]; ... }
```

---

[7] The default model can be generated automatically for a type if the type conforms to a concept, i.e. it provides methods required by the concept.

```
constraint Eq[T] { boolean T.equals(T other); }
constraint GraphLike[V, E] { V E.source(); ... }

interface Set[T where Eq[T]] { ... }

model CIEq for Eq[String] { ... } // case-insensitive model

model DualGraph[V,E] for GraphLike[V,E] where GraphLike[V,E] g
{ V E.source() { return this.(g.sink)(); } ... }
```

Fig. 11. Constraints and models in Genus

Here the List[] interface can be instantiated by any type, but the remove method can be used only if the type E of elements satisfies the Eq[E] constraint. This feature is called *model genericity*.

Just as C#cpt, Genus supports *multiple models* and automatic generation of the *natural* model, which is the same thing as the default model in C#cpt. Models-consistency can also be checked at compile time. In Genus this feature is called *model-dependent types*. As well as in C#cpt, constraint-requirements in Genus can be named; the example is shown in Fig. 11: g is a name of the GraphLike[V,E] constraint required by the DualGraph[V,E] model.

Table 1. The levels of support for generic programming in OO languages

	Haskell	C#	Java 8	Scala	Ceylon	Kotlin	Rust	Swift	JavaGI	G	C#cpt	Genus
Constraints can be used as types	○	●	●	●	●	●	●	●	◐	○	○	○
Explicit self types	—	○	○	◐	●'	○	●	●	◐	—	—	—
Multi-type constraints	●	✳	✳	✳	○	✳	○	○	●	●	●	●
Retroactive type extension	○	●	○	○	○	●	●	●	○	○	○	○
Retroactive modeling	●	✳	✳	✳	○	✳	●	●	●	●	●	●
Type conditional models	●	○	○	○	○	○	●	○	●	●	●	●
Static methods	●[a]	○	●	○	●	●	●	●	●	●[a]	●[a]	●[a]
Default method implementation	●	○	●	●	●	●	●	●	◐	●	●	○
Associated types	●	○	○	●	○	○	●	●	○	●	●	○
Constraints on associated types	◐	—	—	●	—	—	●	●	—	●	●	—
Same-type constraints	◐	—	—	●	—	—	●	●	—	●	●	—
Subtype constraints	—	●	●	●	●	●	—	●	○	○	●	○
Supertype constraints	—	○	○	●	○	○	—	○	○	○	●	○
Constraints refinement	●	●	●	●	●	●	●	●	●	●	●	●
Concept-based overloading	○	○	○	○	○	○	●	○	○	◐[b]	○	○
Multiple models	◐[c]	✳	✳	✳	✳	✳	○	○	○	◐[d]	●	●
Models-consistency (model-dependent types)	—[e]	○	○	○	○	○	—[e]	—[e]	—[e]	—[e]	●	●
Model genericity	—	✳	✳	✳	✳	✳	●	○	○	○	○	●

[a] Constraints constructs have no self types, therefore, any function member of a constraint can be treated as static function.
[b] C++ 0x concepts, in contrast to G concepts, provide full support for concept-based overloading.
[c] Partially supported with OverlappingInstances extension.
[d] G supports lexically-scoped models but not really multiple models.
[e] If multiple models are not supported, the notion of model-dependent types does not make sense.

4   Conclusion and Future Work

Taking into consideration what we have found out in Sects. 2 and 3, we draw a conclusion that there are merely two language features concerning generic programming that cannot be incorporated in an object-oriented language *together*:

1. the use of a construct both as a type and constraint;
2. natural support for multi-type constraints.

Using the "Constraints-are-Types" approach, the first feature can be supported, but not the second; using the "Constraints-are-Not-Types" approach, vice versa. Can we choose one feature that is more important? The answer is yes. It was shown in the study [9] that in practice interfaces that are used as constraints (such as `IComparable<T>` in C# or `Comparable<X>` in Java) are almost never used as types: authors had checked about 14 millions lines of Java code and found only one such example, which was even rewritten and eliminated. At the same time, multi-type constraints, which can be so naturally expressed under the "Constraints-are-Not-Types" approach, have rather awkward and cumbersome representation in the "Constraints-are-Types" approach. Furthermore, the Concept design pattern used in OO languages to provide the support for multiple models has serious pitfalls, whereas with the "Constraints-are-Not-Types" approach models-consistency can be ensured at compile-time if multiple models are allowed. All other language facilities we discussed could be supported under any approach. Therefore, we claim that *the "Constraints-are-Not-Types" approach is preferable*.

   Without sacrificing OO features, object-oriented languages can be extended with new language constructs for constraining type parameters to improve the support for generic programming. Nevertheless, further study is needed to identify an effective design and implementation of such extension. The existing designs that support multiple models, C#^{cpt} and Genus, have at least one essential shortcoming: constraints on type parameters are declared in "predicate-style" rather than "parameter-style". In Haskell, G, C#, Java, Rust, and many other languages, where only one model of a constraint is allowed for the given set of types, constraints on type parameters are indeed predicates: types either satisfy the constraint (if they have a model that is unique) or not. But in Genus and C#^{cpt} constraints *are not predicates*, they are actually *parameters*, as long as different models of constraints can be used. Unfortunately, the "predicate-style" syntax does not correspond to this semantics. It misleads a programmer and makes it more difficult to write and call generic code. Features such as multiple dynamic dispatch, concept variance, and typing rules in presence of concept parameters are also to be investigated.

   Table 1 provides a summary on comparison of the OO languages and language extensions considered: each row corresponds to one property important for generic programming; each column shows levels of support of the properties in one language. Black circle ● indicates full support of a property, ◑ — partial support, ○ means that a property is not supported at language level, ✳ means that a property is emulated using the Concept pattern, and the "–"

sign indicates that a property is not applicable to a language. Related properties are grouped within horizontal lines; some of them, such as "using constraints as types" and "natural language support for multi-type constraints" are mutually exclusive. The major features analysed in the paper are highlighted in bold. The purpose of this table is to show dependencies between different properties and to graphically demonstrate that the "Constraints-are-Not-Types" approach is more powerful than the "Constraints-are-Types" one. There are some features that can be expressed under any approach, such as static methods, default method implementations, associated types [11], and even type-conditional models.

Acknowledgment. The authors would like to thank Artem Pelenitsyn, Jeremy Siek, and Ross Tate for helpful discussions on generic programming.

References

1. Belyakova, J., Mikhalkovich, S.: A support for generic programming in the modern object-oriented languages. Part 1. Anal. Probl. **2**(2), 63–77 (2015). Transactions of Scientific School of I.B. Simonenko (in Russian)
2. Belyakova, J., Mikhalkovich, S.: A support for generic programming in the modern object-oriented languages. Part 2. Rev. Mod. Solutions **2**(2), 78–92 (2015). Transactions of Scientific School of I.B. Simonenko (in Russian)
3. Belyakova, J., Mikhalkovich, S.: Pitfalls of C# generics and their solution using concepts. Proc. Inst. Syst. Program. **27**(3), 29–45 (2015)
4. Bernardy, J.P., Jansson, P., Zalewski, M., Schupp, S., Priesnitz, A.: A comparison of C++ concepts and haskell type classes. In: Proceedings of the ACM SIGPLAN Workshop on Generic Programming, WGP 2008, New York, NY, USA, pp. 37–48. ACM (2008)
5. Bruce, K., Cardelli, L., Castagna, G., Leavens, G.T., Pierce, B.: On binary methods. Theor. Pract. Object Syst. **1**(3), 221–242 (1995). http://dl.acm.org/citation.cfm?id=230849.230854
6. Dos Reis, G., Stroustrup, B.: Specifying C++ concepts. In: Conference Record of the 33rd ACM SIGPLAN-SIGACT Symposium on Principles of Programming Languages, POPL 2006, New York, NY, USA, pp. 295–308. ACM (2006)
7. Garcia, R., Jarvi, J., Lumsdaine, A., Siek, J., Willcock, J.: An extended comparative study of language support for generic programming. J. Funct. Program. **17**(2), 145–205 (2007)
8. Garcia, R., Jarvi, J., Lumsdaine, A., Siek, J.G., Willcock, J.: A comparative study of language support for generic programming. SIGPLAN Not. **38**(11), 115–134 (2003). http://doi.acm.org/10.1145/949343.949317
9. Greenman, B., Muehlboeck, F., Tate, R.: Getting F-bounded polymorphism into shape. In: Proceedings of the 35th ACM SIGPLAN Conference on Programming Language Design and Implementation, PLDI 2014, New York, NY, USA, pp. 89–99. ACM (2014)
10. Hall, C.V., Hammond, K., Peyton Jones, S.L., Wadler, P.L.: Type classes in haskell. ACM Trans. Program. Lang. Syst. **18**(2), 109–138 (1996). http://doi.acm.org/10.1145/227699.227700

11. Järvi, J., Willcock, J., Lumsdaine, A.: Associated types and constraint propagation for mainstream object-oriented generics. In: Proceedings of the 20th Annual ACM SIGPLAN Conference on Object-oriented Programming, Systems, Languages, and Applications, OOPSLA 2005, New York, NY, USA, pp. 1–19. ACM (2005)
12. Martelli, A., Montanari, U.: An efficient unification algorithm. ACM Trans. Program. Lang. Syst. **4**(2), 258–282 (1982). http://doi.acm.org/10.1145/357162.357169
13. Musser, D.R., Stepanov, A.A.: Generic programming. In: Gianni, P. (ed.) ISSAC 1988. LNCS, vol. 358, pp. 13–25. Springer, Heidelberg (1989). http://dl.acm.org/citation.cfm?id=646361.690581
14. Oliveira, B.C., Gibbons, J.: Scala for generic programmers: comparing haskell and scala support for generic programming. J. Funct. Program. **20**(3–4), 303–352 (2010)
15. Oliveira, B.C., Moors, A., Odersky, M.: Type classes as objects and implicits. In: Proceedings of the ACM International Conference on Object Oriented Programming Systems Languages and Applications, OOPSLA 2010, New York, NY, USA, pp. 341–360. ACM (2010)
16. Pelenitsyn, A.: Associated types and constraint propagation for generic programming in scala. Program. Comput. Softw. **41**(4), 224–230 (2015)
17. Siek, J.G., Lumsdaine, A.: A language for generic programming in the large. Sci. Comput. Program. **76**(5), 423–465 (2011). http://dx.doi.org/10.1016/j.scico.2008.09.009
18. Stepanov, A.A., Lee, M.: The standard template library. Technical report 95–11(R.1), HP Laboratories, November 1995
19. Stroustrup, B.: Concept checking – a more abstract complement to type checking. Technical report N1510=03-0093, ISO/IEC JTC1/SC22/WG21, C++ Standards Committee Papers, October 2003
20. Stroustrup, B., Dos Reis, G.: Concepts – design choices for template argument checking. Technical report N1522=03-0105, ISO/IEC JTC1/SC22/WG21, C++ Standards Committee Papers, October 2003
21. Stroustrup, B., Sutton, A.: A concept design for the STL. Technical report N3351=12-0041, ISO/IEC JTC1/SC22/WG21, C++ Standards Committee Papers, January 2012
22. Sutton, A.: C++ Extensions for Concepts PDTS. Technical Specification N4377, ISO/IEC JTC1/SC22/WG21, C++ Standards Committee Papers, February 2015
23. Wadler, P., Blott, S.: How to make ad-hoc polymorphism less ad hoc. In: Proceedings of the 16th ACM SIGPLAN-SIGACT Symposium on Principles of Programming Languages, POPL 1989, New York, NY, USA, pp. 60–76. ACM (1989). http://doi.acm.org/10.1145/75277.75283
24. Wehr, S., Thiemann, P.: JavaGI: the interaction of type classes with interfaces and inheritance. ACM Trans. Program. Lang. Syst. **33**(4), 12:1–12:83 (2011). http://doi.acm.org/10.1145/1985342.1985343
25. Zhang, Y., Loring, M.C., Salvaneschi, G., Liskov, B., Myers, A.C.: Lightweight, flexible object-oriented generics. In: Proceedings of the 36th ACM SIGPLAN Conference on Programming Language Design and Implementation, PLDI 2015, New York, NY, USA, pp. 436–445. ACM (2015). http://doi.acm.org/10.1145/2737924.2738008

JetsonLeap: A Framework to Measure Energy-Aware Code Optimizations in Embedded and Heterogeneous Systems

Tarsila Bessa[1], Pedro Quintão[1], Michael Frank[2],
and Fernando Magno Quintão Pereira[1(✉)]

[1] UFMG, Avenida Antônio Carlos 6627, Belo Horizonte, MG 31270-010, Brazil
{tarsila.bessa,fernando}@dcc.ufmg.br, pedrohquintao@gmail.com
[2] San Jose Lab, LG Mobile Research,
2540 North 1st Str., San Jose, CA 95131, USA
michael.frank@lge.com

Abstract. Energy-aware techniques are becoming a staple feature among compiler analyses and optimizations. However, the programming languages community still does not have access to cheap and precise technology to measure the power dissipated by a given program. This paper describes a solution to this problem. To this end, we introduce Jetson-Leap, a framework that enables the design and test of energy-aware code transformations. JetsonLeap consists of an embedded hardware, in our case, the Nvidia Tegra TK1 System on a Chip Device, a circuit to control the flow of energy, of our own design, plus a library to instrument program parts. We can measure reliably the energy spent by 400.000 instructions, about half a millisecond of program execution. Our entire infra-structure – board, power meter and circuit – can be reproduced with about $500.00. To demonstrate the efficacy of our framework, we have used it to measure energy consumption of programs running on ARM cores, on the GPU, and on a remote server. Furthermore, we have studied the impact of OpenACC directives on the energy efficiency of high-performance applications.

1 Introduction

Compiler optimizations improve programs along three different directions: speed, size or energy consumption. Presently, advances in hardware technology, coupled with new social trends, are bestowing increasing importance on the latter [15]. This importance is mostly due to two facts: first, large scale computing - at the data center level - has led to the creation of clusters that include hundreds, if not thousands, of machines. Such clusters demand a tremendous amount of power, and ask for new ways to manage the tradeoff between energy consumption and computing power [1]. Second, the growing popularity of smartphones has brought in the necessity to lengthen the battery life of portable devices. And yet, despite this clear importance, researchers still lack precise, simple and affordable technology to measure power consumption in computing devices. This deficiency

© Springer International Publishing Switzerland 2016
F. Castor and Y.D. Liu (Eds.): SBLP 2016, LNCS 9889, pp. 16–30, 2016.
DOI: 10.1007/978-3-319-45279-1_2

provides room for inaccuracies and misinformation related to energy-aware programming techniques [14,19,22].

Among the sources of inaccuracies, lies the ever-present question: how to measure energy consumption in computers? Given that the answer to such question does not meet consensus among researchers, conclusions drawn based on potential answers naturally lack unanimity. For instance, Vetro et al. [20] have described a series of patterns for the development of energy-friendly software. However, our attempt to reproduce these patterns seem to indicate that they are rather techniques to speedup programs; hence, the energy savings they provide are a consequence of a faster runtime. This strong correlation between energy consumption and execution time has already been observed previously [22]. As another anecdotal case, Leal et al. [9,10] have used a system of image acquisition to take pictures each one second of a energy display, in order to probe energy consumption on a smartphone. Such creativity and perseverance would not be necessary, had they access to more straightforward technology. In our opinion, such divergences happen because the programming languages community still lacks low-cost tools to measure energy reliably in computing devices.

The goal of this paper is to fill up this omission. To this end, we provide an infra-structure to measure energy in a particular embedded environment, which can be reproduced with affordable material and straightforward programming work. This infra-structure – henceforth called *JetsonLeap*[1] – consists of an NVIDIA Tegra TK1 board, a power meter, a simple electronic circuit, plus a code instrumentation library. This library can be called directly within C/C++ programs, or indirectly via native calls in programs written in different languages. We claim that our framework has three virtues. First, we measure actual – physical – consumption, at the device's power supply. Second, we can measure energy with great precision at the granularity of about 400,000 instructions, e.g., 100 µs of execution. Contrary to other approaches, such as the *AtomLeap* [11], this granularity does not require synchronized clocks between computing processor and measurement device. Finally, even though our infra-structure has been developed and demonstrated on top of a specific device, the NVIDIA Jetson board, it can be reused with other gadgets that provide general Input/Output (GPIO) ports. This family of devices include FPGAs, audio codecs, video cards, and embedded system such as Arduino, BeagleBone, Raspberry Pi, etc.

To validate our apparatus, we have used it to carry out experiments which, by themselves, already offer interesting insights about energy-aware programming techniques. For instance, in Sect. 4 we compared the energy consumption of a linear algebra library executing on the ARM CPUs, on the Tegra GPU, or remotely, in the cloud. We have identified clear phases on programs that perform different tasks, such as I/O, intensive computing or multi-threaded programming. Additionally, we have analyzed the behavior of sequential programs, written in C, after been ported to the GPU by means of OpenACC directives. We could, during these experiments, observe situations in which the faster GPU code was not more energy-friendly than its slower CPU version. The recipe to

---

[1] LEAP (Low-Power Energy Aware Processing) is a name borrowed from McIntire [6].

reproduce these experiments is, in our opinion, one of the core contributions of this work.

2   Overview

Power, Energy and Runtime. Computer programs consume energy when they execute. Energy – in our case electric power dissipated on a period of time – is measured in watts (W). The instantaneous power consumed by any electric device is given by the formula:

$$P = V \times I \tag{1}$$

where V measures the electric potential, in volts, and I measures the electrical current passing through a well-known resistance. Therefore, the energy consumed by the electrical device on a given period of time $T = e - b$ is the integral of its instantaneous consumption on T, e.g.:

$$E = \int_b^e V_f I(t)dt = V_f \int_b^e I(t)dt = V_f \int_b^e \frac{V_s(t)}{R_s}dt = \frac{V_f}{R_s} \int_b^e V_s(t)dt \tag{2}$$

Above, V_f is the source voltage, which is constant at the power source. To obtain I we utilize a shunt resistor of resistance R_s. Thus, by measuring V_s at the resistor, we get, from Ohm's Law, the value of $I = V_s/R_s$. One of the contributions of this work is a simple circuit of well-known R_s, plus an apparatus to measure V_s with high precision in very short intervals of time. This circuit can be combined with different hardware. In this paper, we have coupled it with the NVIDIA TK1 Board, which we shall describe next.

The NVIDIA TK1 Board. All the measurements that we shall report on this paper have been obtained on top of an NVIDIA "Jetson TK1" board, which contains a Tegra K1 system on a chip device, and runs Linux Ubuntu. Tegra has been designed to support devices such as smartphones, personal digital assistants, and mobile Internet devices. Moreover, since its debut, this hardware has seen service in cars (Audi, Tesla Motors), video games and high-tech domestic appliances. We chose the Tegra as the core pillar of our energy measurement system* due to two factors: first, it has been designed with the clear goal of being energy efficient [18]; second, this board gives us a heterogeneous architecture, which contains:

- four 32-bit quad-core ARM Cortex-A15 CPUs running at up to 2.3 GHz.
- a Kepler GPU with 192 ALUs running at up to 852 MHz.

Thus, from a research standpoint, this board lets us experiment with several different techniques to carry out energy efficient compiler optimizations. For instance, it lets us offload code to the local GPU or to a remote server; it lets us scale frequency up and down, according to the different phases of the program execution, and it gives ways to send signals to the energy measurement apparatus, as we shall explain in Sect. 3.

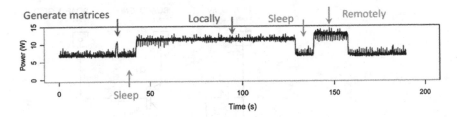

Fig. 1. Example showing the energy consumed at different phases of a matrix multiplication program.

JetsonLEAP in one Example. Before we move on to explain how our energy-measurement platform works, we shall use Fig. 1 to illustrate which kind of information we can produce with it. Further examples shall be discussed in Sect. 4. That figure shows a chart that we have produced with JetsonLeap, for a program that performs three different tasks: (i) it initializes two 3000×3000 matrices; (ii) it multiplies these matrices locally; and (iii) it sends these matrices to a remove server, and reads back the product matrix, which was constructed remotely. Notice that phases (ii) and (iii) represent the same operation, except that in the former case the multiplication happens locally, and in the latter it happens remotely.

We have forced the main program thread to sleep for 10 s in between each task. In this way, we have made it visually noticeable the beginning and the ending of each phase of the program. These marks, e.g., a 10 s low on the energy chart, lets us already draw one important conclusion about this program: it is better, from an energy perspective, to offload matrix multiplication, instead of performing it locally. However, this modus operand is far from being ideal. Its main shortcoming is the fact that it makes it virtually impossible to measure the energy consumed by program events of very small duration. Additionally, this modus operandi bestows too much importance on visual inspection. We could, in principle, apply some border detection algorithm to detect changes in the energy pattern of the program. However, our own experience has shown that at a very low scale, border detection becomes extremely imprecise. One of the main contributions of this paper is to demonstrate that it is possible to mark – in an unambiguous way – different moments in the execution of a program.

3 The Infra-Structure of Energy Measurement

The infra-structure of energy measurement that we provide consists of two parts: on the hardware side, we have an electric circuit that enables or disables the measurement of energy, according to program signals; on the software side, we have a library that gives developers the means to toggle energy acquisition; plus a program that reads the output of the power meter, and produces a report to the user. In this section we describe each one of these elements.

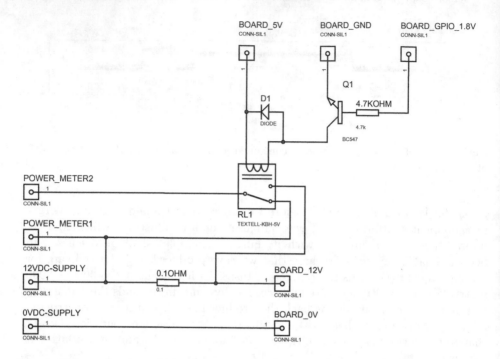

Fig. 2. Schematic view of the circuit that we use to measure energy in the Jetson board.

Hardware. Figure. 2 shows the electric circuit that we use to control the measurement of energy. This circuit enables or disables the power measurement, once it links or not the power meter's probes to the shunt resistor edges. This measurement is controlled by signals which are issued from the target program, in such a way that only regions of interest within the code are probed. The circuit is formed by the following components: 1 relay of 5 V[2], a resistance of 0.1 Ω and 5 W, a resistance of 4.7 KΩ and 0,25 W, a transistor BC547, 1 flyback diode, 10 mini electric cables, 2 connectors with sockets to feed the board, and a protoboard. All in all, these components can be acquired with less than \$ 20.00. Figure 3 (Left) shows how the circuit looks like in practice.

The measurement of power spent by the circuit is controlled by the General Purpose I/O (GPIO) pin of the Jetson board. The GPIO port can be activated from any software that runs on the board. Each hardware defines GPIO ports in different ways. In our particular case, the Jetson has eight such ports, which we have highlighted in Fig. 3 (Right). Besides, the 5 V supply and the Ground pins, can be found in the same figure. According to the Jetson's programming sheet, these ports are installed on the pins: 40, 43, 46, 49, 52, 55 and 58, in J3A2, and 50, in J3A1[3]. Each port can be signalled independently.

---

[2] http://voron.ua/files/pdf/relay/JQC-3F(T73).pdf.
[3] http://elinux.org/Jetson/GPIO.

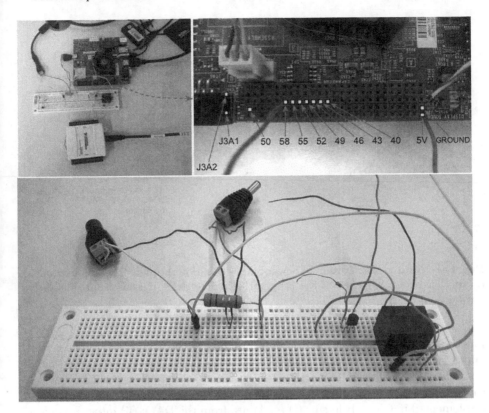

Fig. 3. A picture of our apparatus. (Left) The overall setup. (Right) The ports on the Jetson board. (Down) Detailed view of the circuit.

Figure 2 shows that in the absence of positive signals in the GPIO port, the two cables of the power meter perform readings at the same logical region, which gives us a voltage of zero. Hence, energy will be zero as well. On the other hand, in face of a positive signal, the transistor lets energy flow until the relay, powering up its coil. In this way, the cables of the power meter become linked with the shunt resistor, enabling the start of the power measurement. From Eq. 2, the difference in voltage lets us probe the current at the shunt, which, in turn, gives us a way to know the current that flows into the Jetson board.

Software. The software layer of our apparatus is made of two parts. First, we provide users with a simple library that lets them send signals to the GPIO port. Additionally, this library contains routines to record which ports are in use, and to log events already performed. Figure 4 shows a program that toggles the energy measurement circuit twice.

The second part of our software layer is an interface with the data acquisition tool. We are currently using a National Instruments 6009 DAQ. During our first toils with this device, we have been using LabView[4] to read its output.

---

[4] http://www.ni.com/labview/pt/.

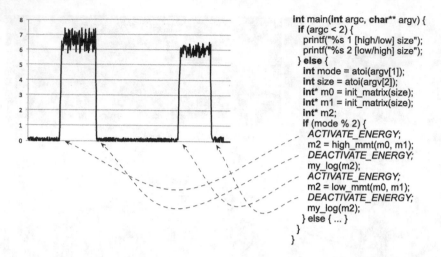

```
int main(int argc, char** argv) {
  if (argc < 2) {
    printf("%s 1 [high/low] size");
    printf("%s 2 [low/high] size");
  } else {
    int mode = atoi(argv[1]);
    int size = atoi(argv[2]);
    int* m0 = init_matrix(size);
    int* m1 = init_matrix(size);
    int* m2;
    if (mode % 2) {
      ACTIVATE_ENERGY;
      m2 = high_mmt(m0, m1);
      DEACTIVATE_ENERGY;
      my_log(m2);
      ACTIVATE_ENERGY;
      m2 = low_mmt(m0, m1);
      DEACTIVATE_ENERGY;
      my_log(m2);
    } else { ... }
  }
}
```

Fig. 4. Activation/deactivation of power data acquisition through program instrumentation. The exact behavior of the program is immaterial – it is used for illustrative purposes only.

LabView is a development environment provided by National Instruments itself, and it already comes with an interface with the DAQ. However, for the sake of flexibility, and in hopes of porting our system to different acquisition devices, we have coded a new interface ourselves. Our tool, called *CMeasure*, has been implemented in C++. It lets us (i) read data from the DAQ; (ii) integrate power, to obtain energy numbers; and (iii) produce energy reports. Concerning (ii), while on its idle state, our circuit still lets pass to the DAQ some noise, which oscillate between -0.001 and $+0.001$ watts. The expected value of this data's integral is zero. Thus, by simply integrating the entire range of power values that we obtain through CMeasure, we expect to arrive at correct energy consumption with very high confidence.

4   Experimental Evaluation

In order to validate our energy measurement system, JetsonLeap, we ran several different experiments on the NVIDIA Tegra TK1 board. The first one concerns the precision of our apparatus. We are interested in answering the following research question: what is the minimum number of instructions whose energy budget we can measure with high confidence. The second batch of experiments demonstrate the many possibilities that our platform opens up to the programming languages community. These experiments compare the energy footprint of sequential and parallel execution on the GPU, and the energy footprint of local compared with remote execution of programs. For simplicity, all the experiments using the Jetson's CPU use only one CPU, even though the board has four cores. We emphasize that these experiments, per se, are not a contribution

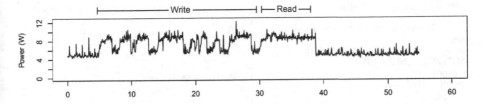

Fig. 5. Energy outline of a program that writes a sequence of records into a file, and then reads them all.

of this paper; rather, they illustrate the benefit of our framework. Nevertheless, these experiments are original: no previous work has performed them before on the Tegra board. Before we start, we provide evidence that the power dissipated by a program is not constant along its entire execution, even if it is restricted to a single core within the available hardware.

Program Phases. Figure 5 shows the energy skyline of a program that writes a large number of records into a file, and then reads this data. The different power patterns of these two phases is clearly visible in the figure. We show this example to enforce the fact that programs do not have always a uniform behavior in terms of energy consumption. It may spend more or less energy, according to the events that it produces on the hardware. This is one of the reasons that contribute to make energy modelling a very challenging endeavour.

4.1 On the Precision of the Apparatus

We have used the program in Fig. 6 (Left) to find out the minimum number of ARM instructions whose energy footprint we can measure. This program runs a loop that only increments a counter for a certain number of iterations. By varying the number of iterations, we can estimate the minimum number of instructions that gives us energy numbers with high confidence. When compiled with gcc 4.2.1, the program in Fig. 6 (Left) yields a loop with only two instructions, a comparison plus an increment.

Figure 6 (Right) gives us the result of this experiment. For each value of INTERVAL, we have tried to obtain energy numbers 10 times. Whenever we obtain a measurement, we deem it a hit; otherwise, we call it a miss. We know precisely if we get a hit or a miss on each sample because we can probe the state of the relay after we run the experiment. We started with INTERVAL equals 5,000, and then moved on to 25,000. From there, we incremented INTERVAL by 25K, until reaching 450,000. For INTERVAL equal to 5,000, we have been able to switch the relay 3 out of 10 times. After we go past 325,000, we obtain 10 hits out of each 10 tries. These numbers are in accordance with the expected switching time of our relay: less than one milisecond. Given that our ARM CPUs run at 2.3GHz, we should expect no more than 2.3 million instructions per milisecond. From this experiment, we believe that we can measure – with very high confidence – energy of events that take around 400,000 instructions to finish.

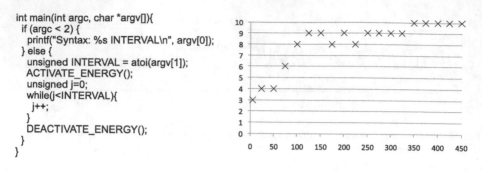

```
int main(int argc, char *argv[]){
  if (argc < 2) {
    printf("Syntax: %s INTERVAL\n", argv[0]);
  } else {
    unsigned INTERVAL = atoi(argv[1]);
    ACTIVATE_ENERGY();
    unsigned j=0;
    while(j<INTERVAL){
      j++;
    }
    DEACTIVATE_ENERGY();
  }
}
```

Fig. 6. (Left) Program used to measure precision of our apparatus. (Right) Chart relating the number of correct measurements with the value of INTERVAL in the program on the left. The Y axis gives us number of hits, out of 10 tries; the X axis gives us the value of INTERVAL (in thousands).

4.2 CPU vs GPU

We open this section by comparing the energy consumption of a program running on the CPU, versus the energy consumption of similar code running on the GPU. In this experiment, our benchmark suite is made of six programs, which we took from Etino, a tool that analyzes the asymptotic complexity of algorithms [2]. These programs are mostly related to linear algebra: Cholesky and LU decomposition, matrix multiplication and matrix sum. The other two programs are *Collinear List*, which finds collinear points among a set of samples, and *Str. Matching*, which finds patterns within strings. All these are written in standard C, without any adaptations for a Graphics Processing Unit (GPU). To compile these programs to the Tegra's GPU, we have marked their mains loops with OpenAcc directives. OpenAcc is an annotation system that lets developers indicate to the compiler which program parts are embarrassingly parallel, and can run on the graphics card. We have used accULL [13] to produce GPU binaries out of annotated programs. Therefore, in this experiment we are comparing, in essence, the product of different compilers, – targeting different processors – when given the same source code. The code that runs on the CPU has been produced with gcc 4.2.1, at the -O3 optimization level.

Figure 7 shows the amount of energy consumed by each benchmark. For each one, we have used inputs of different sizes: small, medium and large. As we can see, usually the GPU binaries spend more energy than their CPU counterparts. The only two exceptions that we have observed are Matrix Multiplication and String Matching. Figure 8 shows the runtime of each benchmark, for each input size, on each processor. The GPU version is faster – for large inputs – in four cases: Cholesky, Collinear List, Matrix Multiplication and String Matching. Notice that this runtime, as well as the energy numbers, represent the entire execution of the kernel, including the time to transfer data between CPU and GPU. However, in either case we omit the time to initialize and check results, which happen in the CPU, even for the GPU-based benchmarks. We can eliminate these phases from

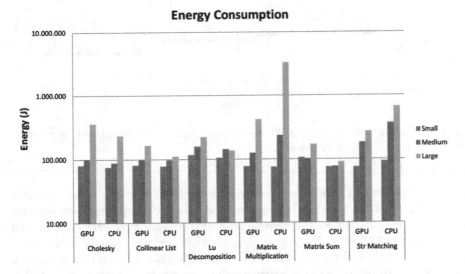

Fig. 7. Energy consumed by different programs, running either on the CPU, or on the GPU.

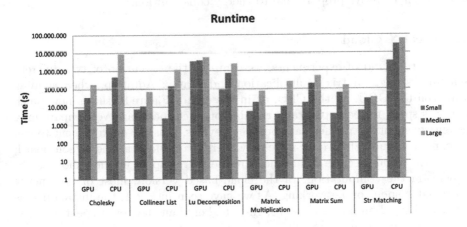

Fig. 8. Runtime for different programs, running either on the CPU, or on the GPU.

our experiment – which are the same for both CPU and GPU-based samples – because of our ability to turn off the energy measurement hardware whenever we find it necessary.

Comparing the runtime chart with the energy consumption one, we realize that, even though the GPU execution is faster for most programs, it usually consumes more energy than the CPU. In fact, only "Matrix Multiplication" and "Str Matching" give us the opposite behavior, in which the GPU consumes less energy than the CPU. This result corroborates some of the conclusions drawn by Pinto *et al.* [12], who have shown that after a certain threshold, an

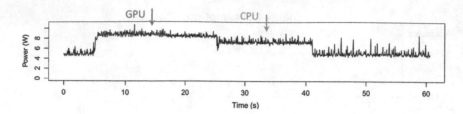

Fig. 9. A chart that illustrates the difference between power consumption by a program running on the GPU and on the CPU.

excessive number of threads may be less energy efficient, even for data-parallel applications. Notice that they have gotten their results comparing code running on a multi-core CPU with a different number of cores enabled each time. Figure 9 supports our observation. It shows a program that performs matrix summation, first on the GPU, and then on the CPU. The difference in power consumption makes it easy to tell each phase apart. During the whole execution of the GPU, its power dissipation is higher than the CPU's. We believe that these results are particularly interesting, because they show very clearly that in some scenarios, runtime is not always proportional to energy consumption.

4.3 Local X Cloud

In our third round of experiments, we compare the execution of two different benchmarks, e.g., Matrix Multiplication and Matrix Addition, when running locally on the GPU, on the CPU, or in the cloud. Figure 10 shows how much energy is spent for each program, running on each location. We compare only the energy spent to transfer data between devices, plus the energy spent to run the computation itself. We measure only energy consumed at the Jetson board; thus, in the cloud case, we do not measure the energy spent by the remote server to perform the computation. In the cloud-based version, most of the energy consumed is spent on networking. As we have seen in Fig. 1, the instantaneous power consumed on networking is slightly higher than the power spent by CPU intensive computations.

Figure 10 shows that matrix addition consumes less energy when done locally. This is a consequence of its asymptotic complexity: matrix addition involves $O(N^2)$ floating-point operations on $O(N^2)$ elements. Therefore, its computation over data ratio is $O(1)$. Thus, the time to transfer data between devices already shadows any gains from parallelism and offloading. On the other hand, when it comes to the multiplication of matrices, sending the data to a server is beneficial after a certain threshold. Matrix multiplication has higher asymptotic complexity than matrix addition, e.g., the former performs $O(N^2)$ floating-point operations. Yet, the amount of data that both algorithms manipulate is still the same: $O(N^2)$. Thus, in the case of matrix multiplication we have a linear ratio of computation over data, a fact that makes offloading much more advantageous.

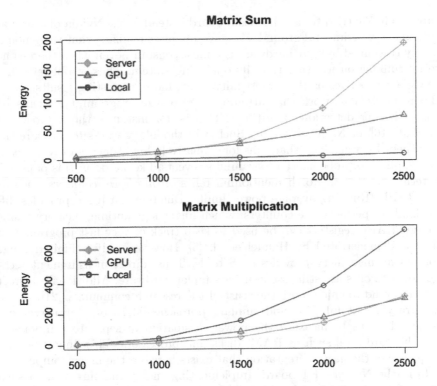

Fig. 10. Energy consumed by different versions of a matrix multiplication and a matrix addition routine.

5   Related Work

Much has been done, recently, to enable the reliable acquisition of power data from computing machinery. In this section we go over a few related work, focusing on the unique characteristics of our JetsonLeap. Before we commence our discussion, we emphasize a point: much related literature uses energy models to derive metrics [3,17]. Even though we do not contest the validity of these results, we are interested in direct energy probing. Thus, models, i.e., indirect estimation, are not part of this survey. Nevertheless, we believe that an infra-structure such as our JetsonLeap can be used to calibrate new analytical models.

The most direct inspiration of this work has been AtomLeap [11]. Like us, AtomLeap is also a system to measure energy in a System on a Chip device. However, Singh *et al.* have chosen to use the Intel Atom board as their platform of choice. Furthermore, they do not use a circuit, like we do, to toggle energy measurement. Instead, they synchronize the Atom's clock with a global watch used by the energy measurement infra-structure. By logging the time when particular events take place during the execution of a program, they are able to estimate the amount of energy consumed during a period of interest. They have not reported on the accuracy of this technique, so we cannot compare it against our approach. We tried to use the Atom board instead of the Nvidia platform as our standard experimental ground. We gave up, after realizing that the amount of energy consumed by that hardware is almost constant, even when there is no program running on it, other than its operating system. Thus, we believe that the Nvidia setup gives us the opportunity to log more interesting results.

There is previous work that attempt to recognize programming events by means of border detection algorithms. This is, for instance, the approach of Silva et al. [16], or Nazare et al. [8]. Such a methodology works to measure the energy spent by a program that runs for a relatively long time; however, it cannot be applied to probe short programming events, like we do in this paper. A final technique that is worth mentioning relies on *hardware counters*, such as Intel's RAPL (Running average power limit). Different hardware provides different kinds of performance counters, which might log runtime, memory traffic or energy. RAPL registers can be used to keep track of very fast programming events, as demonstrated by Hähnel et al. [5]. However, only a limited range of computing machinery provides such tools. Thus, direct measurement techniques such as ours are still essential for simpler hardware. Additionally, direct approaches tend to enjoy more the trust of the research community [21].

Contrary to AtomLEAP and similar approaches [4,7], our infra-structure does not allow us to measure the power dissipation of separate components within the hardware, such as RAM, disks and processors. This limitation is a consequence of the heavy integration that exists between the many components that form the Nvidia TK1 board. Implementing energy measurement in such environment, at component level is outside the scope of this work. Nevertheless, a comparison with the work of Ge et al. [4] is illustrative. They use two data acquisition devices to probe different parts of the hardware simultaneously. Synchronisation is performed through a client-server architecture, via time-stamps. Although the authors have not reported the length of programming events that they can measure, we believe that our approach enables finer measurements, as we do not experiment network delays. Besides, our infra-structure is cheaper: the fact that we control the acquisition circuitry from within the target program lets us use a simpler power meter, with only one channel.

6   Conclusion

This paper has presented JetsonLeap, an apparatus to measure energy consumption in programs running on the Nvidia Tegra board. JetsonLeap offers a number of advantages to developers and compiler writers, when compared to similar alternatives. First, it allows acquiring energy data from very brief programming events: our experiments reveal a precision of about 400,000 instructions. Such granularity enables the measurement of power-aware compiler optimizations. Second, our infra-structure is cheap: the entire framework can be constructed with less than $ 500.00. Finally, it is general: we have built it on top of a specific platform: the Nvidia Jetson TK1 board. However, the only essential feature that we require on the target hardware is the existence of a general purpose input-output port. Such port is part of the design of several different kinds of System-on-a-Chip devices, including open-source hardware, such as the Arduino.

Acknowledgement. This project is sponsored by LG Electronics Brazil. From March 2015 to February 2016, Tarsila Bessa was the recipient of a scholarship sponsored by Intel Semiconductors. Currently, Tarsila is sponsored by the Big-Sea joint cooperation between Brazil and the European Union. Fernando Pereira is supported by FAPEMIG, CNPq and CAPES.

References

1. Beloglazov, A., Abawajy, J., Buyya, R.: Energy-aware resource allocation heuristics for efficient management of data centers for cloud computing. Future Gener. Comput. Syst. **28**(5), 755–768 (2012)
2. Demontiê, F., Cezar, J., Bigonha, M., Campos, F., Magno Quintão Pereira, F.: Automatic inference of loop complexity through polynomial interpolation. In: Pardo, A., Swierstra, S.D. (eds.) SBLP 2015. LNCS, vol. 9325, pp. 1–15. Springer, Heidelberg (2015). doi:10.1007/978-3-319-24012-1_1
3. Dunkels, A., Osterlind, F., Tsiftes, N., He, Z.: Software-based on-line energy estimation for sensor nodes. In: EmNets, pp. 28–32. ACM (2007)
4. Ge, R., Feng, X., Song, S., Chang, H.-C., Li, D., Cameron, K.W.: Powerpack: energy profiling and analysis of high-performance systems and applications. IEEE Trans. Parallel Distrib. Syst. **21**(5), 658–671 (2010)
5. Hähnel, M., Döbel, B., Völp, M., Härtig, H.: Measuring energy consumption for short code paths using RAPL. SIGMETRICS Perform. Eval. Rev. **40**(3), 13–17 (2012)
6. McIntire, D., Ho, K., Yip, B., Singh, A., Wu, W., Kaiser, W.J.: The low power energy aware processing (LEAP) embedded networked sensor system. In: IPSN, pp. 449–457. ACM (2006)
7. McIntire, D., Stathopoulos, T., Reddy, S., Schmidt, T., Kaiser, W.J.: Energy-efficient sensing with the low power, energy aware processing (LEAP) architecture. ACM Trans. Embedded Comput. Syst. **11**(2), 27 (2012)
8. Nazaré, H., Maffra, I., Santos, W., Barbosa, L., Gonnord, L., Quintão Pereira, F.M.: Validation of memory accesses through symbolic analyses. In: OOPSLA, pp. 791–809. ACM (2014)
9. Domingues Neto, J.L.: User-level online offloading framework. Master's thesis, UFMG (2016)
10. Domingues Neto, J.L., Macedo, D.F., Nogueira, J.M.S.: A location aware decision engine to offload mobile computation to the cloud. In: NOMS, pp. 831–838 (2016)
11. Peterson, P.A.H., Singh, D., Kaiser, W.J., Reiher, P.L.: Investigating energy and security trade-offs in the classroom with the Atom LEAP testbed. In: CSET, pp. 1–11. USENIX (2011)
12. Pinto, G., Castor, F., Liu, Y.D.: Understanding energy behaviors of thread management constructs. In: OOPSLA, pp. 345–360. ACM (2014)
13. Reyes, R., López-Rodríguez, I., Fumero, J.J., de Sande, F.: accULL: an OpenACC implementation with CUDA and OpenCL support. In: Kaklamanis, C., Papatheodorou, T., Spirakis, P.G. (eds.) Euro-Par 2012. LNCS, vol. 7484, pp. 871–882. Springer, Heidelberg (2012)

14. Saputra, H., Kandemir, M., Vijaykrishnan, N., Irwin, M.J., Hu, J.S., Hsu, C-H., Kremer, U.: Energy-conscious compilation based on voltage scaling. In: SCOPES, pp. 2–11. ACM (2002)
15. Sartori, S., Kumar, R.: Compiling for energy efficiency on timing speculative processors. In: DAC, pp. 1301–1308. ACM (2012)
16. Silva, B.L.B., Guimarães Tavares, E.A., Martins Maciel, P.R., e Silva Nogueira, B.C., Oliveira, J., Lourenço Damaso, A.V., Rosa, N.S.: AMALGHMA -an environment for measuring execution time and energy consumption in embedded systems. In: SMC, pp. 3364–3369. IEEE (2014)
17. Steinke, S., Wehmeyer, L., Lee, B., Marwedel, P.: Assigning program and data objects to scratchpad for energy reduction. In: DATE, pp. 409–415. IEEE (2002)
18. Stokke, K.R., Stensland, H.K., Griwodz, C., Halvorsen, P.: Energy efficient video encoding using the tegra K1 mobile processor. In: MMSys, pp. 81–84. ACM (2015)
19. Valluri, M., John, L.K.: Is compiling for performance – compiling for power? In: Lee, G., Yew, P.-C. (eds.) Interaction between Compilers and Computer Architectures. The Springer International Series in Engineering and Computer Science, pp. 101–115. Springer, New York (2001)
20. Vetro, A., Ardito, L., Procaccianti, G., Morisio, M.: Definition, implementation, validation of energy code smells: an exploratory study on an embedded system. In: ENERGY, pp. 34–39 (2013)
21. Weaver, V.M., Johnson, M., Kasichayanula, K., Ralph, J., Luszczek, P., Terpstra, D., Moore, S.: Measuring energy and power with papi. In: ICPPW, pp. 262–268. IEEE (2012)
22. Yuki, T., Rajopadhye, S.: Folklore confirmed: compiling for speed = compiling for energy. In: Cascaval, C., Montesinos-Ortego, P. (eds.) LCPC 2013. LNCS, vol. 8664, pp. 169–184. Springer, Heidelberg (2014)

A Monadic Semantics for Quantum Computing in Featherweight Java

Samuel da Silva Feitosa[1]([⊠]), Juliana Kaizer Vizzotto[1],
Eduardo Kessler Piveta[1], and Andre Rauber Du Bois[2]

[1] Universidade Federal de Santa Maria, Santa Maria, Brazil
{sfeitosa,juvizzotto,piveta}@inf.ufsm.br
[2] Universidade Federal de Pelotas, Pelotas, Brazil
dubois@inf.ufpel.edu.br

Abstract. Nowadays, several languages and libraries have been proposed to program and reason about quantum programs in the imperative and functional paradigms. Although the object-oriented paradigm is one of the most used for general purpose software, there is a lack of quantum programming languages designed with this paradigm in mind. In this paper, we present the monadic semantics for *FJQuantum*, an object-oriented language based on Featherweight Java, created to reason and to develop programs handling quantum data and quantum operations, taking advantage of the characteristics of that paradigm. We also show a set of examples of quantum programs using the proposed language.

Keywords: Quantum computing · Monadic semantics · Featherweight java

1 Introduction

Quantum computing [19] is a new computational paradigm that considers devices developed at very small scales, which are governed by the quantum mechanics laws. The research field tries to find ways to handle quantum effects to enhance and sustain old computational goals in new ways. The theory of quantum computer science predicts that quantum computers will be able to perform certain computational tasks in fewer steps than any classical computer. This assertion is justified because the algorithms available to quantum computers can harness physical phenomena that are not available to classical computers [30].

One challenging research area in quantum computing is the design of high-level quantum programming languages [3,6,14,20,22,24,26,28] suitable for describing and reasoning about quantum algorithms, and also providing tools to understand how quantum computing works in general.

Although there exists different programming languages proposed to handle quantum data and operations, there is a lack of languages based on the

---

The original version of this chapter was revised: In the initially published contribution the name of the author Samuel da Silva Feitosa was incorrect. The correct name is: Samuel da Silva Feitosa. The erratum to this chapter is available at 10.1007/978-3-319-45279-1_13

© Springer International Publishing Switzerland 2016
F. Castor and Y.D. Liu (Eds.): SBLP 2016, LNCS 9889, pp. 31–45, 2016.
DOI: 10.1007/978-3-319-45279-1_3

object-oriented paradigm, which is among the most used paradigms today in software development for general purpose. In this context, this work provides the description for *FJQuantum* [10], a quantum object-oriented language, and a formal monadic semantics for it, extending Featherweight Java [13] (FJ), a small core calculus of Java, with a rigorous semantic definition of the main core aspects of Java.

The motivation for using FJ as a starting point is twofold: first it is very compact, so we can focus on the essential aspects of the quantum extension. The minimal syntax, typing rules and operational semantics is a nice tool for studying the consequences of an extension for quantum programming. Second, we are interested in the formal semantic definition of FJ, which allows modeling and proving properties of programs. In addition, we believe that the definition of an object-oriented quantum programming language could minimize the learning efforts, allowing to encapsulate quantum states and operations using classes and objects.

Technically, this paper describes a Java extension that allows the implementation of quantum computing programs. The quantum computations can be combined and used as building blocks for the design of new computations considering the concept of *monads*, implemented using *closures*. Although this Java extension is described in the context of FJ, as we give a monadic semantics for the language, it could be implemented in any object oriented language that supports closures, e.g., C#.

The remainder of this paper is organized as follows: Sect. 2 shows the basic concepts of quantum computing. Section 3 summarizes the FJ proposal [13], and presents the extensions required to implement the quantum monadic layer. Section 4 describes our quantum extensions to work with quantum states and operations. Section 5 presents some examples demonstrating how to handle quantum concepts in the proposed language. Section 6 presents some related work. Section 7 concludes the paper.

2   Quantum Computing

The basic information unit in classical computing is the traditional bit, representing a classical binary physical system, where a piece of information is encoded using two states (*true* or *false*, 0 or 1). In quantum computing, the basic information unit is represented by a *quantum bit*, or qubit, a binary *quantum* physical system. The qubit is defined by a vector usually represented as a *superposition* of basic states, using the Dirac *braket*[1] notation [19]:

$$|\psi\rangle = \alpha|0\rangle + \beta|1\rangle$$

The Dirac notation has the advantage of explicitly labeling the basis vectors. The basic states $|0\rangle$ and $|1\rangle$ can be explained by an analogy with the classical bit, i.e., they form a two-level system and are an orthonormal basis for the quantum vector space [15] (usually called the standard or computational basis).

---

[1] The *braket* name comes from the convention that a column vector is called a "ket" and is denoted by $|\ \rangle$ and a row vector is called a "bra" and is denoted by $\langle\ |$.

The coefficients α and β, also called *probability amplitudes*, are complex numbers, such that $|\alpha|^2 + |\beta|^2 = 1$. In other words, a *qubit* can be formalized as a vector in a complex vector space (Hilbert space), with norm (size) equals to one.

As an example, the classical bit 0 can be represented as the basis state $|0\rangle = 1|0\rangle + 0|1\rangle$ and the classical bit 1 as $|1\rangle = 0|0\rangle + 1|1\rangle$.

Any other state with different values for α and β is said to be in a *quantum superposition* of $|0\rangle$ and $|1\rangle$, for instance, the state $1/\sqrt{2}|0\rangle + 1/\sqrt{2}|1\rangle$.

The interpretation of the probability amplitudes α and β can be given by the following: *when we interact or measure a quantum state like $\alpha|0\rangle + \beta|1\rangle$ we will see/get the state $|0\rangle$ with probability $|\alpha|^2$ and the state $|1\rangle$ with probability $|\beta|^2$.*

The superposition of states gives to quantum computing a characteristic called quantum parallelism. Essentially, due to the superposition of states, a *qubit* can assume values of 0 and 1 at the same time. This gives an exponential power to quantum algorithms, as we can design algorithms that can verify various possibilities in parallel [19].

Table 1 shows how the *qubit* state space grows with the number of *qubits*. We can verify that the the number of possible distinguishable states doubles each time a *qubit* is added.

Table 1. State space of the qubit

# Qubits	Possibilities	Power
1	0 or 1	2
2	00,01,10,11	4
3	000,001,010,011,100,101,110,111	8
N		2^N

More formally, a composite quantum state with two or more *qubits*, as Table 1 shows, can be described using a tensor product operation $\otimes$. Again, in analogy with the classical bit, considering a state with two bits, we have four alternatives: $00, 01, 10, 11$. Then, the state of a pair of *qubits* is a linear combination of these four classical states:

$$\alpha|00\rangle + \gamma|01\rangle + \delta|10\rangle + \beta|11\rangle$$

If $q = \alpha|0\rangle + \beta|1\rangle$ and $p = \gamma|0\rangle + \delta|1\rangle$ are two independent quantum bits, then we can form a combined state using the *tensor operation* on vector spaces, $\otimes$, defined as follows:

$$q \otimes p = \alpha\gamma|00\rangle + \alpha\delta|01\rangle + \beta\gamma|10\rangle + \beta\delta|11\rangle$$

However, there are some combined quantum bits which are not in the $q \otimes p$ form. For instance, the state:

$$1/\sqrt{2}|00\rangle + 1/\sqrt{2}|11\rangle$$

is clearly not in the $q \otimes p$ form, for any q and p. This kind of *combined* state which cannot be described using the tensor product operation is called an *entangled* state.

Entanglement is another very important characteristic of quantum states. Entanglement can be understood as a strong correlation that exists between quantum particles, which states that quantum particles can be linked in a perfect union, even if separated by great distances.

3   Featherweight Java

Featherweight Java (FJ) [13] is a minimal core calculus for Java, in the sense that as many features of Java as possible are omitted, while maintaining the essential flavor of the language and its type system. However, this fragment is large enough to include many useful programs. A program in FJ consists of a declaration of a set of classes and an expression to be evaluated, that corresponds to the *public static void main* method of Java.

FJ has a similar relation with Java, like Lambda Calculus has with Haskell. It offers similar operations, providing classes, methods, attributes, inheritance and dynamic casts with semantics close to Java's. Featheweight Java project favors simplicity over expressivity and offers only five ways to create terms: object creation, method invocation, attribute access, casting and variables [13]. The following example shows how classes can be modeled in FJ. There are three classes, A, B, and Pair, with constructor and method declarations.

```
1   class A extends Object {
2       A() { super(); }
3   }
4   class B extends Object {
5       B() { super(); }
6   }
7   class Pair<X extends Object, Y extends Object>
8           extends Object {
9       X fst; Y snd;
10      Pair(X fst, Y snd) {
11          super();
12          this.fst=fst;
13          this.snd=snd;
14      }
15      Pair<X, Y> setfst(X newfst) {
16          return new Pair(newfst, this.snd);
17      }
18  }
```

FJ semantics applies a purely functional view without side effects. In other words, attributes in memory are not affected by object operations [21]. Furthermore, interfaces, overloading, call to base class methods, null pointers, base types, abstract methods, statements, access control, and exceptions are not present in the language [13].

Because the language does not allow side effects, it is possible to formalize the evaluation just using the FJ syntax, without the need of auxiliary mechanisms to model the heap [21].

Figure 1 presents the syntactic definitions originally proposed for Featherweight Java with *generic types* [13], where T refers to the type definitions, L to the classes list, K and M to constructors and methods respectively, and finally, t and v express the terms and terminal values of that language. Throughout this paper, we write $\bar{T}$ as shorthand for a possibly empty sequence $\bar{T}_1,...,\bar{T}_n$ (similarly for $\bar{C}$, $\bar{f}$, $\bar{x}$, etc.).

```
T ::= C | C<T̄>
L ::= class C<T̄> extends C { T̄ f̄; K M̄ }
K ::= C(C̄ f̄) { super(f̄); this.f̄=f̄; }
M ::= C m(C̄ x̄) { return t; }
t ::= x | t.f | t.m(t̄)
      | new C<T̄>(t̄) | (C) t
v ::= new C(v̄)
```

Fig. 1. Syntactic definitions for Featherweight Java with generic types.

Figure 2 presents the evaluation rules originally proposed for FJ, formalizing how to evaluate *attribute access* (R-Field), *method invocation* (R-Invk), and *casts* (R-Cast) [13], the only three possible terms to be used as the *main program*. The presented functions *fields* and *mbody*, are also formalized in the original paper, representing respectively a way to obtain a list of attributes of some class C, and the term inside a method m that belongs to a given class C. In the *method invocation* rule, we write $[\bar{x} \mapsto \bar{u}, this \mapsto new\ C(\bar{v})]t_0$ for the result of replacing x_1 by $u_1,...,x_n$ by u_n, and *this* by "new $C(\bar{v})$" in expression t_0. In the *cast* rule, the symbol $<:$ is used to express the sub-typing relation between C and D, stating that C is a subtype of D. These symbols are also used throughout the paper.

$$\frac{fields(C) = \bar{C}\ \bar{f}}{new\ C(\bar{v}).f_i \rightarrow v_i} \text{ [R-Field]}$$

$$\frac{mbody(m, C) = (\bar{x}, t_0)}{new\ C(\bar{v}).m(\bar{u}) \rightarrow [\bar{x} \mapsto \bar{u}, this \mapsto new\ C(\bar{v})]t_0} \text{ [R-Invk]}$$

$$\frac{C <: D}{(D)\ (new\ C(\bar{v})) \rightarrow new\ C(\bar{v})} \text{ [R-Cast]}$$

Fig. 2. Evaluation rules for Featherweight Java [13].

For short, the formalization of sub-typing relation, congruence and typing rules were omitted here, but can be found in the original FJ paper [13]. To work similarly to Java, we consider the call-by-value evaluation strategy for FJ [21].

3.1   Featherweight Java Extensions

Basically, we added primitive types, as *booleans* and *complex numbers*, and basic operations in *FJQuantum* in the standard way [21]. The *boolean* values are used to represent the basis for quantum states, and complex numbers are used to represent the probability amplitudes in quantum states. Both constructions are also possible values in the language and are not reducible. We also added a conditional (*if*) expression.

A functional version of tuples [21] was also added in our language, where for example, {false, false, true} is a 3-tuple containing three booleans, and its type is represented by {boolean, boolean, boolean}. The *tuples* can be seen as a new type in the language, which is represented by a combination of each element type. Tuples are also terminal values in the language.

As a way to work with monads in Java, we also added *closures*, the Java 8 new feature, following the extension proposed by Bellia and Occhiuto [5]. This extension models all essential features of Java related with the properties of closures. In their work, closures need to extend the FJ type system, adding *closure types*, and should be first class values which can be bound to parameters, hence applied to methods or other closures. Also, a new term was included in the language to *invoke*[2] the λ-expression. The reader should note that the current implementation of closures in Java does not have closure types, closures can be used whenever an object of an interface with a single abstract method is expected. For simplicity, we decided to use closure types instead of modeling the complete behavior of Java interfaces.

Since FJ is a functional version of Java, for syntax sugar, we also included the functional operator *let* [21].

4   Quantum Monadic Semantics

FJQuantum [10] is a quantum object-oriented language that extends Featherweight Java [13], by adding several constructions that allows for the development of programs handling quantum data and quantum operations through a monadic layer. The use of monads for quantum computing has been explored in several works [18,27–29], usually applied in functional languages. An initial informal definition of the language was defined before [11]. Here we provide the monad layer description inside FJ, including a monadic semantics formalizing the behavior of the proposed constructions.

Monad is a concept widely used in functional languages. It represents a way to structure computations in terms of values and sequences of computations. Monads allow programmers to build computations using sequential building blocks, which can themselves be computation sequences. A monad determines how combined computations form a new computation and frees the programmer from having to manually code the combination each time it is required.

---

[2] The default method `.invoke(t)`, responsible to process a *closure*, is formalized by the rules *GR-Inv-Clos* and *GRC-Inv-Clos* in the referenced paper [5].

They were first applied to Computer Science by Moggi [16,17] when he presented a category-theoretic semantics of computations. As an example of this semantic approach for computations, Moggi showed a general way to structure various computational effects in the λ-calculus, like side effects, exceptions, partial and nondeterministic computations, and many others cases.

Qubits can be seen as a computational effect, and can also be modeled as a type of monad for non-determinism [18]. The idea behind this monad is to construct the space of quantum states, which are mathematically represented as a vector of complex numbers containing the probabilities amplitudes of *qubits*. Transformations can be applied to *qubits* through *quantum gates*, which are modeled as unitary matrices, applied by the monadic operator *bind* [12].

To handle concepts of quantum computing in the *FJQuantum* language, we proposed several syntactic constructions, which allow the creation of quantum states, setting probability amplitudes and applying transformations over quantum states. The language is formalized through an operational semantics.

Figure 3 shows the *syntactic* definitions for *FJQuantum*, where we can note the addition of type *QState*, which is used to wrap the quantum states. The type QState<T_B> is a generic type, restricted to the base types T_B, which are represented by *booleans* or *tuples of booleans*. Furthermore, we defined the monadic constructors *mzero* and *mreturn*. The first represents a *zero* computation and the second is responsible for lifting the base type to a monadic value. Both of these constructors can be seen as a value in *FJQuantum*. In our proposal, the monadic operator *bind*, represented by >>=, is used to apply transformations over the quantum states. As a way to facilitate handling the probability amplitudes and also to create *superpositions*, we added the scalar product \$* and the monadic sum *mplus*.

```
T  ::= ...                    ▷ FJ Types
    | QState<T_B>
T_B ::= boolean               ▷ Base Types
    | {T_Bi^{i∈1..n}}


t  ::= ...                    ▷ FJ Expressions
    | mzero
    | mreturn t
    | t_1 >>= t_2
    | t_1 mplus t_2
    | t_1 $* t_2


v  ::= ...                    ▷ FJ Values
    | mzero
    | mreturn v
```

Fig. 3. Syntactic definitions for *FJQuantum*.

The following example shows how to create quantum states, where in the first two lines we are creating states with only one *qubit* from a *boolean* type. In the lines 3 and 4 we are creating states with two *qubits*, using a *tuple of booleans*.

```
1    mreturn false          // Creates the state |0⟩
2    mreturn true           // Creates the state |1⟩
3    mreturn {false,false}  // Creates the state |00⟩
4    mreturn {false,true}   // Creates the state |01⟩
```

The following example shows how to express a *quantum superposition* in *FJQuantum*, where a combination between the operator *mplus* and $* is required. The complex numbers $1/\sqrt{2}$ and $-1/\sqrt{2}$ are used to represent the same probability to obtain $|0\rangle$ or $|1\rangle$ when a *measurement* is applied.

$1/\sqrt{2}$ $*$ mreturn false mplus $-1/\sqrt{2}$ $*$ mreturn true

We also define *laws* for the operators *mplus* and *scalar* as we can see in Fig. 4. The *mplus* is the addition operator over quantum vectors, and should respect some laws, that are similar to the arithmetic addition. The *L-Zero* equations show the behavior when *mplus* is applied with *mzero* on the left or right side, while the *L-Comm* and *L-Assoc* equations show the commutative and associative property of that operator. The laws *L-Scalar* and *L-Scalar-Dist* show how to compute a term involving complex probability amplitudes and the addition operator.

Laws for *mplus*:

$$\text{mzero mplus } t_1 = t_1 \quad [\text{L-Zero}]$$

$$t_1 \text{ mplus mzero} = t_1 \quad [\text{L-Zero}]$$

$$t_1 \text{ mplus } t_2 = t_2 \text{ mplus } t_1 \quad [\text{L-Comm}]$$

$$t_1 \text{ mplus } (t_2 \text{ mplus } t_3) = (t_1 \text{ mplus } t_2) \text{ mplus } t_3 \quad [\text{L-Assoc}]$$

Laws for *scalar product*:

$$\alpha_1 \ \$^* \ t \text{ mplus } \alpha_2 \ \$^* \ t = (\alpha_1 + \alpha_2) \ \$^* \ t \quad [\text{L-Scalar}]$$

$$\alpha \ \$^* \ (t_1 \text{ mplus } t_2) = \alpha \ \$^* \ t_1 \text{ mplus } \alpha \ \$^* \ t_2 \quad [\text{L-Scalar-Dist}]$$

Fig. 4. Laws for *mplus* and *scalar product* operators.

Figure 5 shows the *reduction* rules which demonstrate how to compute quantum transformations over quantum states. The *R-State* rule is the most simple case, where the base value v_1 is passed as parameter to a *closure* which is inside the t_2 term. In *R-Sup* rule, a state in *superposition* (t_1 mplus t_2) of states is being applied to a *closure*, which should be inside the t_3 term. This reduction rule transforms one application of *bind* operator in two applications, one for t_1 term and one for t_2 term, joining the applications through the *mplus* operator. The last reduction rule *R-Scalar* also transforms the term $(\alpha \ \$* \ t_1)$, separating the probability amplitude α, and applying the t_1 term to the *closure*, which is inside the t_2 term. The goal of these rules is to transform the state being applied (left side) in the simple case *R-State*.

$$(\text{mreturn } v_1) \text{ >>= } t_2 \rightarrow t_2.\text{invoke}(v_1) \quad [\text{R-State}]$$

$$(t_1 \text{ mplus } t_2) \text{ >>= } t_3 \rightarrow (t_1 \text{ >>= } t_3) \text{ mplus } (t_2 \text{ >>= } t_3) \ [\text{R-Sup}]$$

$$(\alpha \ \$* \ t_1) \text{ >>= } t_2 \rightarrow \alpha \ \$* \ (t_1 \text{ >>= } t_2) \quad [\text{R-Scalar}]$$

Fig. 5. Reduction rules for quantum operators.

In addition to reduction rules, Fig. 6 presents the typing rules aiming to maintain the type safety of *FJQuantum*.

$$\frac{}{\Gamma \vdash \text{mzero} : \text{QState<T}_B\text{>}} \ [\text{T-Zero}]$$

$$\frac{\Gamma \vdash t: \text{T}_B}{\Gamma \vdash \text{mreturn } t : \text{QState<T}_B\text{>}} \quad [\text{T-Return}]$$

$$\frac{\Gamma \vdash t_1: \text{QState<T}_B\text{>} \quad \Gamma \vdash t_2: \text{T}_B \rightarrow \text{QState<T}_B\text{>}}{\Gamma \vdash t_1 \text{ >>= } t_2 : \text{QState<T}_B\text{>}} \ [\text{T-Bind}]$$

$$\frac{\Gamma \vdash t_1, t_2: \text{QState<T}_B\text{>}}{\Gamma \vdash t_1 \text{ mplus } t_2 : \text{QState<T}_B\text{>}} [\text{T-Plus}]$$

$$\frac{\Gamma \vdash t_1: \text{Complex} \quad t_2: \text{QState<T}_B\text{>}}{\Gamma \vdash t_1 \ \$* \ t_2 : \text{QState<T}_B\text{>}} \ [\text{T-Scalar}]$$

Fig. 6. Typing rules for quantum operators.

The first two rules are applied to quantum constructors, where in *T-Zero* one can see that *mzero* is of type `QState<T`$_B$`>`, and *mreturn* t is of type `QState<T`$_B$`>` if and only if t is of type T_B. As explained before, T_B ranges over the basis types. The rule *T-Bind* should concern about two constraints: (a) the term t_1 should be of type `QState<T`$_B$`>`, and the term t_2 should be a closure, which receives as parameter a base type T_B and returns a monadic type `QState<T`$_B$`>`. For the monadic operator *mplus*, the rule *T-Plus* has the responsibility to check whether the terms t_1 and t_2 are of `QState<T`$_B$`>` type. The last rule *T-Scalar* should check if t_1 is a complex number and if t_2 is of type `QState<T`$_B$`>`.

Considering these rules we can model all pure quantum states and *reversible quantum computations*. In pure quantum computing, all operations must be reversible, that is, they must avoid decoherence and loss of information [28].

As a quantum operation example coded using *FJQuantum*, consider the *hadamard* method, which is used to transform a quantum state into a superposition.

```
1  (boolean -> QState<boolean>) hadamard() {
2    return (boolean b) ->
3      if (b) {
4        1/√2 $* mreturn false mplus −1/√2 $* mreturn true
5      } else {
6        1/√2 $* mreturn false mplus 1/√2 $* mreturn true
7      };
8  }
```

We can use the equations to prove that, for example, applying *Hadamard* twice is the same as identity. Consider:

```
1    ((mreturn false) >>= obj.hadamard()) >>= obj.hadamard();
```

Figure 7 shows the sequence of reductions following the proposed semantics, considering the example above.

$\equiv$ qop.hadamard().invoke(false) >>= qop.hadamard() (1)

$\equiv$ ((1/√2 $*$ mreturn false) mplus (−1/√2 $*$ mreturn true)) >>= qop.hadamard() (2)

$\equiv$ ((1/√2 $*$ mreturn false) >>= qop.hadamard()) mplus ((−1/√2 $*$ mreturn true) >>= qop.hadamard()) (3)

$\equiv$ 1/√2 $*$ ((mreturn false) >>= qop.hadamard()) mplus −1/√2 $*$ ((mreturn true) >>= qop.hadamard()) (4)

$\equiv$ 1/√2 $*$ ((1/√2 mreturn false) mplus (1/√2 $*$ mreturn true)) mplus (1/2 $*$ mreturn false mplus -1/2 $*$ mreturn true) (5)

$\equiv$ mreturn false

Fig. 7. Proof of reversibility for *Hadamard* operator.

First of all, the *hadamard* method is evaluated using the *T-Invk*[3] rule [13] resulting in a *lambda expression*. After that, step (1) applies the reduction rule *R-State* over the initial state, passing as parameter the value *false* for that *lambda expression*, which is evaluated by *GR-Invk-Clos*[4] rule [5] to evaluate the *closure* and *E-If-False*[4] rule [21] to eval the *if statement*. Step (2) applies the *R-Sup* rule to handle the *superposition* and generates two applications of *Hadamard*.

---

[3] For short, the rules *T-Invk*, *GR-Invk-Clos* and *E-If-False* were omitted from the text, but can be found in the pointed references [5,13,21].

Step (3) uses the *R-Scalar* rule. In step (4) the *R-State* rule is applied twice for both sides of the *mplus* operator. Step (5) uses the law *L-Scalar-Dist* for *scalar product* and then uses the laws for the *mplus* operator, to simplify the term, considering the associative and commutative properties, resulting on the initial state *mreturn false*.

To have an executable version of this semantics, we implemented an interpreter[4] using the functional programming language *Haskell* and the *Happy* parser generator for *Haskell*. The next section shows some code examples demonstrating how to construct programs handling quantum concepts.

5   Examples

This first example presents a class (QOp) that implements some of the universal reversible quantum gates. The *not* method (line 3 to 10) is the quantum version of the classical *not* operator, applied to one *qubit*. The *hadamard* method (line 11 to 19) is used to put a *qubit* from a trivial state in a *superposition*, using the *scalar* and *mplus* operators, as seen previously.

```
1   class QOp extends Object {
2     // Constructor and other methods...
3     (boolean -> QState<boolean>) not() {
4       return (boolean b) ->
5         if (b) {
6           mreturn false
7         } else {
8           mreturn true
9         };
10    }
11    (boolean -> QState<boolean>) hadamard() {
12      return (boolean b) ->
13          if (b) {
14            1/√2 $* mreturn false mplus −1/√2 $* mreturn true
15          }
16          else {
17            1/√2 $* mreturn false mplus 1/√2 $* mreturn true
18          };
19    }
20  }
```

In the same class QOp, the *controlledNot* method (line 3 to 15) should be invoked with two *qubits* as parameters, representing a conditional *not*. One can note that in all these methods, we are returning a closure, to be able to work directly with the >>= operator.

---

[4] The source-code for *FJQuantum* interpreter and more examples can be found at https://github.com/fjquantum.

```
1   class QOp extends Object {
2      // Constructor and other methods...
3      ({boolean,boolean} -> QState<{boolean,boolean}>)
4         controlledNot() {
5            return ({boolean,boolean} b) ->
6               if (b.1) {
7                  if (b.2) {
8                     mreturn {true, false}
9                  } else {
10                    mreturn {true, true}
11                 }
12              } else {
13                 mreturn {b.1,b.2}
14              };
15     }
16  }
```

The last example shows a piece of code which performs complex operations over an initial state, containing several *qubits*, using the previously defined class QOp. Here we can find a way to apply partial transformations over the quantum state and how to compose operations through the *bind* operator. The program starts from line 20, creating an object of QExec and invoking the *exec* method, that receives as parameter a tuple containing three booleans. Inside the *exec* method (line 13 to 17), we build the quantum state of three *qubits* through the constructor *mreturn*, and then apply this state to *composedOperation* (line 3 to 12) using the *bind* operator.

```
1  class QExec extends Object {
2     // Constructor and other methods
3     QState<{boolean,boolean,boolean}> composedOperation() {
4        return let qop = new QOp() in
5           ({boolean,boolean,boolean} state) ->
6           ((qop.hadamard()).invoke(state.3)) >>=
7           (boolean b) ->
8           ((qop.controlledNot()).invoke({state.1,state.2})) >>=
9           ({boolean,boolean} tm) ->
10          ((qop.hadamard()).invoke(b)) >>=
11          (boolean ba) -> mreturn {tm.1,tm.2,ba};
12     }
13     QState<{boolean,boolean,boolean}>
14        exec({boolean,boolean,boolean} ini) {
15           return (mreturn ini) >>=
16              this.composedOperation();
17     }
18  }
19
20  new QExec().exec({true,true,true});
```

The method composed operation acts over a quantum state of three *qubits* applying in sequence the *Hadamard* operator to the third *qubit* (line 6), the *controlledNot* to the first and second *qubits* (line 8), and then apply the *Hadamard* operator again in the third *qubit* (line 10). After that, the modified state is rebuilt by the *mreturn* constructor (line 11).

The examples show how to handle quantum concepts using *FJQuantum*, taking advantage of the object-oriented paradigm, and demonstrate how the monadic layer fits into the original *FJ* proposal.

6   Related Work

A quantum programming language is an important tool to formally reason about quantum algorithms. For this reason, there is an effort in investigating semantic models and quantum programming languages, despite the fact that quantum hardware continues in development.

In general, quantum languages are built through the imperative or functional paradigm. The first quantum programming language was developed on the imperative paradigm, which was proposed by Knill [14]. More complete programming languages in this paradigm were proposed by Omer [20], Sanders and Zuliani [22], and Bettelli et al. [6]. In the functional paradigm, Selinger [23] is a pioneer, working together with Valiron [25]. Furthermore, we can cite the work of Altenkirch and Grattage [2], the proposal of Andre Van Tonder [26], among others [1,4,8].

Our proposed quantum extension of FJ considers other works [3,27,28], where pure quantum states were modeled as monads [16], and also in a library for quantum programming in Java using closures [7], called QJava. Another related work is a domain specific language for concurrent programming using a monadic semantics for transactional memory in Java [9].

7   Conclusions and Future Work

This paper extends the Featherweight Java language, adding features to deal with quantum concepts, adapting a monadic approach to an object-oriented context. Our contribution is a monadic semantics to reason about quantum data and quantum operations. In addition, we implement an interpreter for the proposed language, to check the semantics and the type system rules, and present some examples accepted by the interpreter.

We believe that this language can be a starting point for programmers that are not familiar with quantum computing concepts, reusing the previous knowledge about object-oriented languages. Furthermore, it is possible to perform the simulation of quantum algorithms using the developed interpreter.

As future work, it is possible to develop syntactical adjustments to facilitate visualization of quantum states in source-code, develop a *syntax-sugar* to write code similarly to imperative style (like Haskell *do-notation*), implement *closures* as in Java 8, and also add measurement operations in the proposed language. Additionally, there is the need to prove reduction and type soundness to have the all benefits of an FJ extension.

References

1. Abramsky, S.: High-level methods for quantum computation and information. In: Proceedings of the 19th Annual IEEE Symposium on Logic in Computer Science, pp. 410–414 (2004)
2. Altenkirch, T., Grattage, J.: A functional quantum programming language. In: Proceedings of the 20th Annual IEEE Symposium on Logic in Computer Science (2005)
3. Altenkirch, T., Grattage, J., Vizzotto, J.K., Sabry, A.: An algebra of pure quantum programming. Electron. Notes Theor. Comput. Sci. **170**, 23–47 (2007)
4. Arrighi, P., Dowek, G.: Linear-algebraic λ-calculus: higher-order, encodings, and confluence. In: Voronkov, A. (ed.) RTA 2008. LNCS, vol. 5117, pp. 17–31. Springer, Heidelberg (2008). eprint arXiv:quant-ph/0612199
5. Bellia, M., Occhiuto., M.: Java: proving type safety for Java simple closures. In: CSp 2010, pp. 61–72 (2010)
6. Bettelli, S., Serafini, L., Calarco, T.: Towards an architecture for quantum programming. CoRR cs.PL/0103009 (2001). http://arxiv.org/abs/cs.PL/0103009
7. Calegaro, B., Vizzotto, J.K.: Quantum monad using Java closures. In: 2nd Workshop-School on Theoretical Computer Science (WEIT), pp. 34–39, October 2013
8. Coecke, B., Duncan, R.: Interacting quantum observables. In: Aceto, L., Damgård, I., Goldberg, L.A., Halldórsson, M.M., Ingólfsdóttir, A., Walukiewicz, I. (eds.) ICALP 2008, Part II. LNCS, vol. 5126, pp. 298–310. Springer, Heidelberg (2008)
9. Du Bois, A.R., Echevarria, M.: A domain specific language for composable memory transactions in Java. In: Taha, W.M. (ed.) DSL 2009. LNCS, vol. 5658, pp. 170–186. Springer, Heidelberg (2009). doi:10.1007/978-3-642-03034-5_9
10. Feitosa, S.S.: Uma Linguagem de Programação Quântica Orientada a Objetos Baseada no Featherweight Java. Master's thesis, Universidade Federal de Santa Maria
11. Feitosa, S.S., Vizzotto, J.K., Piveta, E.K., Du Bois, A.R.: FJQuantum: uma Linguagem Quântica orientada a objetos. In: 3rd Workshop-School on Theoretical Computer Science, WEIT 2015, Porto Alegre, RS, Brazil, 14–16 October 2015, pp. 136–143 (2015)
12. Grattage, J.J., Chapman, J., Green, A., Jago, M., Swierstra, W., Jaskelioff, M.: A functional quantum programming language. In: Proceedings of the 20th Annual IEEE Symposium on Logic in Computer Science, pp. 249–258 (2005)
13. Igarashi, A., Pierce, B.C., Wadler, P.: Featherweight Java: a minimal core calculus for Java and GJ. ACM Trans. Program. Lang. Syst. (TOPLAS) **23**(3), 396–450 (2001)
14. Knill, E.: Conventions for quantum pseudocode. Technical report, Los Alamos National Laboratory (1996)
15. Mermin, N.D.: Quantum Computer Science: An Introduction. Cambridge University Press, New York (2007)
16. Moggi, E.: Computational lambda-calculus and monads. In: Proceedings of the Fourth Annual Symposium on Logic in Computer Science, pp. 14–23. IEEE Press (1989)
17. Moggi, E.: Notions of computation and monads. Inf. Comput. **93**(1), 55–92 (1991). citeseer.ist.psu.edu/moggi89notions.html
18. Mu, S.C., Bird, R.: Functional quantum programming. In: Asian Workshop on Programming Languages and Systems. KAIST, Dajeaon, Korea. http://www.cs.ox.ac.uk/people/richard.bird/online/MuBird2001Functional.pdf

19. Nielsen, M.A., Chuang, I.L.: Quantum Computation and Quantum Information, 10th edn. Cambridge University Press, New York (2011)
20. Ömer, B.: A procedural formalism for quantum computing. Technical University of Vienna, Technical report (1998)
21. Pierce, B.C.: Types and Programming Languages. MIT press, Cambridge (2002)
22. Sanders, J.W., Zuliani, P.: Quantum programming. In: Backhouse, R., Oliveira, J.N. (eds.) MPC 2000. LNCS, vol. 1837, pp. 80–99. Springer, Heidelberg (2000)
23. Selinger, P.: Towards a quantum programming language. J. Math. Struct. Comput. Sci. **14**(4), 527–586 (2004)
24. Selinger, P.: Finite dimensional hilbert spaces are complete for dagger compact closed categories. In: Proceedings of the 5th International Workshop on Quantum Physics and Logic (QPL 2008), p. 11, Reykjavik, Iceland (2008)
25. Selinger, P., Valiron, B.: A lambda calculus for quantum computation with classical control. J. Math. Struct. Comput. Sci. **16**(3), 527–552 (2006). Special Issue in Quantum Programming Languages
26. van Tonder, A.: A Lambda calculus for quantum computation. SIAM J. Comput. **33**, 1109–1135 (2004)
27. Vizzotto, J.K., Altenkirch, T., Sabry, A.: Structuring quantum effects: superoperators as arrows. J. Math. Struct. Comput. Sci. **16**, 453–468 (2006). Special Issue in Quantum Programming Languages. http://arxiv.org/abs/quant-ph/0501151
28. Vizzotto, J.K., Calegaro, B.C., Piveta, E.K.: A double effect λ-calculus for quantum computation. In: Du Bois, A.R., Trinder, P. (eds.) SBLP 2013. LNCS, vol. 8129, pp. 61–74. Springer, Heidelberg (2013). doi:10.1007/978-3-642-40922-6_5
29. Vizzotto, J.K., Du Bois, A.R., Sabry, A.: The arrow calculus as a quantum programming language. In: Ono, H., Kanazawa, M., de Queiroz, R. (eds.) WoLLIC 2009. LNCS, vol. 5514, pp. 379–393. Springer, Heidelberg (2009). http://arxiv.org/abs/0903.1489
30. Williams, C.P.: Explorations in Quantum Computing, 2nd edn. Springer Publishing Company Incorporated, New York (2008)

Memoized Zipper-Based Attribute Grammars

João Paulo Fernandes[1], Pedro Martins[2(✉)], Alberto Pardo[3], João Saraiva[4], and Marcos Viera[3]

[1] LISP/Release - Universidade da Beira Interior, Covilha, Portugal
jpf@di.ubi.pt
[2] University of California, Irvine, USA
pribeiro@uci.edu
[3] Universidad de la República, Montevideo, Uruguay
{pardo,mviera}@fing.edu.uy
[4] Universidade do Minho, Braga, Portugal
jas@di.uminho.pt

Abstract. Attribute Grammars are a powerfull, well-known formalism to implement and reason about programs which, by design, are conveniently modular.

In this work we focus on a state of the art Zipper-based embedding of Attribute Grammars and further improve its performance through controlling attribute (re)evaluation by using memoization techniques. We present the results of our optimization by comparing their impact in various implementations of different, well-studied Attribute Grammars.

Keywords: Embedded domain specific languages · Attribute Grammars · Zipper data structure · Memoization

1 Introduction

Attribute Grammars (AGs) are a declarative formalism that allows us to implement and to reason about programs in a modular and convenient way. This formalism was proposed by Knuth [12] in the late 60s, and a concrete AG relies on a context-free grammar to define the syntax of a language, while adding *attributes* to it so that it is also possible to define its semantics.

AGs have been used in practice not only to specify real programming languages, like for example Haskell [6], but also to specify powerful pretty printing algorithms [22], deforestation techniques [8] and powerful type systems [17].

When programming with AGs, modularity is achieved due the possibility of defining and using different aspects of computations as separate attributes. Attributes are distinct computation units, tipically quite simple and modular, that can be combined into elaborated solutions to complex programming problems. They can also be analyzed, debugged and maintained independently which eases program development and evolution.

AGs have proven to be particularly useful to specify computations over trees: given one tree, several AG systems such as [7,13,24] take specifications of which

© Springer International Publishing Switzerland 2016
F. Castor and Y.D. Liu (Eds.): SBLP 2016, LNCS 9889, pp. 46–61, 2016.
DOI: 10.1007/978-3-319-45279-1_4

values, or attributes, need to be computed on the tree and perform these computations. The effort put into the creation, improvement and maintenance of these AG systems, however, is tremendous, which often is an obstacle to achieving the success they deserve.

An increasingly popular alternative approach to the use of AGs relies on embedding them as first class citizens of general purpose programming languages [3,5,15,18,21,25]. This avoids the burden of implementing a totally new language and associated system by hosting it in state-of-the-art programming languages. We want to exploit the modern constructions and infrastructure that are already provided by those languages and focus on the particularities of the domain specific language that we are developing.

In this paper we focus on the embedding proposed in [15] for Haskell, which we revise in Sect. 2. This choice is motivated by the fact that this embedding ensures a notation that closely resembles AGs and even if it relies on a simple navigation engine, it has shown sufficient expressive power to incorporate state-of-the-art extensions to the AG formalism such as the possibility of defining: (i) higher-order attributes [20, 26], (ii) references [14], (iii) circular attributes [15, 21], and (iv) bidirectional transformations [16].

In spite of its elegancy and expressive power, the embedding of [15] does not ensure that attributes are computed only once on a given node. As will become clearer in the next section, the same attribute can be evaluated many times on the same node which causes unnecessary overhead on computations.

The first contribution of this paper is that we take the embedding of [15] and show how it can be extended in such a way that all attributes in an AG are evaluated only once. This extension is achieved with a memoization strategy that can systematically be applied to all embedded AGs in the setting of [15]. This contribution is introduced in Sect. 3.

A second and final main contribution of the paper is that we analyze the impact of memoization, in terms of efficiency, on several well known and well studied AG examples from the literature. This is detailed in Sect. 4. We conclude in Sect. 5.

2   Zipper-Based Attribute Grammars

In this section we describe by means of an example the embedding of AGs proposed in [15]. The example we consider, which is used as running example throughout the paper, is the *repmin* problem [4]. This is a well-known example that has been extensively used in the literature, for the same reason we have chosen it here: it is a simple, easy to understand problem which clearly illustrates the modular nature of AG and the difficulties on implementing and scheduling its computations. The goal of *repmin* is to transform a binary leaf tree of integers into a new tree with the exact same shape but where all leaves have been replaced by the minimum leaf value of the original tree. Concretely, we consider the following definition of binary leaf trees:

data *Tree* = *Leaf Int* | *Fork Tree Tree*

In order to solve *repmin*, we may define an AG with three attributes: (i) one inherited attribute, *globmin*, so that all nodes in a tree may know and use the global minimum of the tree; and two synthesized attributes: (ii) *locmin*, to compute the local minimum of each node in a tree, and (iii) *replace*, to compute at each node the *repmin* of the tree under it. These attributes should be scheduled according to the computation: we need to find the minimum value contained in the tree with *locmin*, distribute this value across all the nodes of the tree with *globmin* and analyze the structure and traverse the tree to create a new one with *replace*.

In the setting of [15] we may define the AG for *repmin* by the embedding in Haskell shown in Fig. 1. We see that, e.g., at a *Leaf* node, the global minimum of a tree is inherited from its parent node (*up t*), and that the local minimum of a *Fork* node is given by the minimum of the local minimums of the child nodes (*left t* and *right t*). Notice that the attributes are represented as functions.

Finally, *repmin* is obtained by computing the *replace* attribute on the topmost node of a tree:

$repmin :: Tree \rightarrow Tree$

$repmin\ t = replace\ (mk_{AG}\ t)$

The embedding of [15] relies on the *zipper* data structure [9] to provide the means to navigate on a tree and to define the values of attributes in terms of other attributes on neighbour nodes. An AG computation on a *Tree* is actually a function that takes a *Zipper* and returns the result of the computation:

```
-- Inherited
globmin :: AGTree Int
globmin t = case constructor t of
               C_Root   → locmin  (tree t)
               C_Leaf _ → globmin (up   t)
               C_Fork   → globmin (up   t)
   -- Synthesized
locmin :: AGTree Int
locmin t = case constructor t of
               C_Leaf l → l
               C_Fork   → min (locmin (left t)) (locmin (right t))
replace :: AGTree Tree
replace t =  case constructor t of
               C_Root   → replace (tree t)
               C_Leaf _ → Leaf (globmin t)
               C_Fork   → Fork (replace (left t)) (replace (right t))
```

Fig. 1. Repmin defined using a Zipper-based AG

type $AGTree\ a = Zipper \rightarrow a$

A zipper can be regarded as a tree together with its context:

type $Zipper = (Tree, Cxt)$

data $Cxt = Root \mid Top \mid L\ Cxt\ Tree \mid R\ Tree\ Cxt$

To construct a zipper, we mark a $Tree$ as being at the $Root$ node:

$mk_{AG} :: Tree \rightarrow Zipper$

$mk_{AG}\ t = (t, Root)$

Constructor $Root$ is artificially added as a context, since we need to distinguish the topmost tree from all the other (sub)trees. In fact, we need to bind the local minimum of the topmost tree with the global minimum of that same tree.[1]

In order to inspect the node under focus, we define a new datatype, with an associated pattern-matching function:

data $Cons = C_{Root} \mid C_{Fork} \mid C_{Leaf}\ Int$

$constructor :: Zipper \rightarrow Cons$ $constructor\ (Leaf\ l, \_)\ \ \ = C_{Leaf}\ l$

$constructor\ (\_, Root) = C_{Root}$ $constructor\ (Fork\ \_\ \_, \_) = C_{Fork}$

Now, we have defined all it takes to navigate through concrete trees. Going down on a (non topmost) tree, for example, can be implemented as follows:

$left :: Zipper \rightarrow Zipper$ $right :: Zipper \rightarrow Zipper$

$left\ (Fork\ l\ r, c) = (l, L\ c\ r)$ $right\ (Fork\ l\ r, c) = (r, R\ l\ c)$

while trying to go down the topmost tree simply creates a zipper whose (real) context is Top:

$tree :: Zipper \rightarrow Zipper$

$tree\ (t, Root) = (t, Top)$

Going up on a location on a tree may also be performed in a simple way, which actually inverts the behavior of functions $left$, $right$ and $tree$ shown above:

$up :: Zipper \rightarrow Zipper$ $up\ (t, L\ c\ r) = (Fork\ t\ r, c)$

$up\ (t, Top) = (t, Root)$ $up\ (t, R\ l\ c) = (Fork\ l\ t, c)$

Finally, we define a function that applies a transformer to the tree under focus:

$modify :: Zipper \rightarrow (Tree \rightarrow Tree) \rightarrow Zipper$

$modify\ (t, c)\ f = (f\ t, c)$

Despite its clear syntax and expressive power, the described embedding does not ensure that attributes are computed only once on a given node. We may notice that on the *repmin* solution presented earlier, the global minimum of a tree is computed as many times as the number of leaves that tree has.

As a concrete example of this, in Fig. 2 we show the function call chains that activate the computation of attributes *replace* on leaves labelled with 1 (left) and 2 (right). As defined earlier, *replace* in a leaf will call *globmin* on the same node, then *globmin* will call *globmin* at its parent, and so on, calling then *locmin* from the root to the leaves. So, while in the first computation of *replace* every attribute is computed only once, in the second case we see that some calls to

---

[1] This binding can be seen in the definition of *globmin*, in $C_{Root} \rightarrow locmin\ (tree\ t)$.

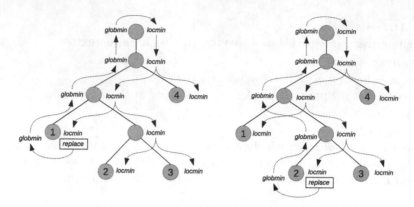

Fig. 2. Function (attribute) calls to evaluate *replace* in a leaf

globmin are new, but then we reach a point in which we start to repeat the steps that have already been taken, therefore duplicating computations and creating an unnecessary overhead, which grows proportionally with the number of leaves.

One contribution of this paper is the introduction of a strategy for solving this efficiency issue, which is presented in the next section. This is achieved by memoizing attribute computations, improving that way the performance of the solution, and allowing us to say that we provide, under a formal perspective, a real attribute grammar embedding.

Although we use *repmin* as a running example, the strategy we study has also been applied and assessed in other problems that are well know in the AG domain, some of which are presented in Sect. 4.

3 Memoized AGs

As an alternative to the solution given in Fig. 1 we present the one in Fig. 3. The structure of the new code is quite similar to the old one. Without delving into details now, it can be seen that the main differences are the use of a *memo* function, which introduces *memoization* in the evaluation of the attribute grammar, and the use of **let** to pass around a changing tree.

In order to avoid attribute recomputations, we attach a table to each node of a tree to store the value of the attributes associated to the node. We do so by transforming the original tree into a new one of same shape and with a memo table attached to each node. The new tree type is now parametric on the type m of the memo table.

data $Tree_m\ m = Fork_m\ m\ (Tree_m\ m)\ (Tree_m\ m)$
$\qquad\qquad |\ Leaf_m\ m\ Int$

A new version of the Zipper has to be defined to be able to navigate through a tree of type $Tree_m$.

type $Zipper_m\ m = (Tree_m\ m, Cxt_m\ m)$

-- Inherited

$globmin :: (Memo\ Globmin\ m\ Int, Memo\ Locmin\ m\ Int) \Rightarrow AGTree_m\ Int$

$globmin = memo\ Globmin\ \$\ \lambda z \rightarrow$ **case** $constructor_m\ z$ **of**

$$\begin{array}{ll} C_{Root} & \rightarrow locmin\ .@.\ tree_m\ z \\ C_{Leaf\ \_} & \rightarrow globmin\ `atParent`\ z \\ C_{Fork} & \rightarrow globmin\ `atParent`\ z \end{array}$$

-- Synthesized

$locmin :: (Memo\ Locmin\ m\ Int) \Rightarrow AGTree_m\ Int$

$locmin = memo\ Locmin\ \$\ \lambda z \rightarrow$ **case** $constructor_m\ z$ **of**

$$\begin{array}{ll} C_{Leaf}\ v \rightarrow (v, z) \\ C_{Fork} & \rightarrow \textbf{let}\ (left,\ z') = locmin\ .@.\ left_m\ \ z \\ & \qquad\quad (right, z'') = locmin\ .@.\ right_m\ z' \\ & \textbf{in}\ (min\ left\ right, z'') \end{array}$$

$replace :: (Memo\ Replace\ m\ Tree, Memo\ Globmin\ m\ Int, Memo\ Locmin\ m\ Int)$
$\qquad\ \Rightarrow AGTree_m\ Tree$

$replace = memo\ Replace\ \$\ \lambda z \rightarrow$ **case** $constructor_m\ z$ **of**

$$\begin{array}{ll} C_{Root} & \rightarrow replace\_m\ .@.\ tree_m\ z \\ C_{Leaf\ \_} & \rightarrow \textbf{let}\ (mini, z') = globmin\ z \\ & \qquad\quad \textbf{in}\ (Leaf\ mini, z') \\ C_{Fork} & \rightarrow \textbf{let}\ (l,\ z') = replace\ .@.\ left_m\ \ z \\ & \qquad\quad (r, z'') = replace\ .@.\ right_m\ z' \\ & \qquad\quad \textbf{in}\ (Fork\ l\ r, z'') \end{array}$$

Fig. 3. Repmin defined using memoization

data $Cxt_m\ m = Root_m \mid Top_m$
$\qquad\qquad\ \mid L_m\ m\ (Cxt_m\ m)\ (Tree_m\ m)$
$\qquad\qquad\ \mid R_m\ m\ (Tree_m\ m)\ (Cxt_m\ m)$

The combinators $mkAG_m$, $constructor_m$, $tree_m$, $left_m$, $right_m$, up_m and $modify_m$ that work on $Zipper_m$ are analogous to the ones defined in Sect. 2 for the original $Zipper$ type. For example, up_m is defined as:

$up_m :: Zipper_m\ m \rightarrow Zipper_m\ m$
$up_m\ (t, Top_m)\qquad = (t, Root_m)$
$up_m\ (t, L_m\ m\ c\ r) = (Fork_m\ m\ t\ r, c)$
$up_m\ (t, R_m\ m\ l\ c) = (Fork_m\ m\ l\ t, c)$

3.1   Memo Tables

A memo table will contain *Maybe* elements corresponding to the attribues, where *Nothing* is used to mean that the value of an attribute has not been computed yet. In our example, we store *Maybe* values for the attributes Globmin, Locmin and Replace.

We define singleton datatypes to refer to each attribute in a table:

data *Globmin* = *Globmin*
data *Locmin* = *Locmin*
data *Replace* = *Replace*

By means of a multi-parameter type class *Memo* we define functions to lookup and modify the value (of type a) of a given attribute *att* in a memo table of type m.

class *Memo att m a* **where**
   mlookup :: $att \rightarrow m \rightarrow Maybe\ a$
   mmodify :: $att \rightarrow (Maybe\ a \rightarrow Maybe\ a) \rightarrow m \rightarrow m$

The intended meaning of *mmodify att f m* is the update of the value v of attribute *att* stored in the table m by $f\ v$. The benefit of defining this class is that we can have memoized implementations of AGs that are generic in the representation of the memo tables.

There are different alternatives in how we can implement a memo table. One possibile representation is in terms of tuples. In our example, the tuple stores values corresponding to Globmin (*Int*), Locmin (*Int*) and Replace (*Tree*).

type *MemoTable* = (*Maybe Int, Maybe Int, Maybe Tree*)

The use of tuples to represent memo tables imposes an important drawback because it requires to close the universe of attributes for defining the tuple corresponding to the memo table. Consequently, the addition of a new attribute to the AG leads to the redefinition of the memo table and its associated operations. In other words, the solution with tuples is not extensible.

One way to solve this problem is by replacing tuples by some implementation of extensible records, like the heterogeneous strongly typed lists [11] defined in the HList[2] library. In our repository[3] we include an alternative version that represents the memo tables as extensible records.

Once we have decided the representation of the memo table we are in conditions to define an instance of the *Memo* class for each attribute. For example, the instance for *Globmin* for the representation in terms of tuples is as follows:

instance *Memo Globmin MemoTable Int* **where**
   mlookup _ $(g, \_, \_) = g$
   mmodify _ f (g, l, r) = $(f\ g, l, r)$

---

[2] https://hackage.haskell.org/package/HList.
[3] https://hackage.haskell.org/package/ZipperAG.

A $Tree_m$ can be generated from an input tree by attaching a given memo table to each node.

$$build_m :: Tree \rightarrow m \rightarrow Tree_m\ m$$
$$build_m\ (Fork\ l\ tr)\ mt = Fork_m\ mt\ (build_m\ l\ mt)\ (build_m\ r\ mt)$$
$$build_m\ (Leaf\ n)\quad mt = Leaf_m\ mt\ n$$

We make a final remark concerning the representation of memo tables. Our representation assumes uniformity on all nodes of the AG in the sense of all having the same attributes. However, this is not the case in every AG. Different types of nodes may have different attributes and consequently different types of memo tables. To admit this case one possible solution is to declare $MemoTable$ as a sum type with one type of memo table for each kind of node:

data $MemoTable = MTFork\ MemoTableFork \mid MTLeaf\ MemoTableLeaf$

It is then necessary to define corresponding instances of the $Memo$ class taking into account the alternative memo tables.

3.2   Attribute Computation

An attribute computation computes a value, as before, but now it may also apply modifications to memo tables contained in the tree:[4]

type $AGTree_m\ m\ a = Zipper_m\ m \rightarrow (a, Zipper_m\ m)$

The function $memo$, used in every attribute definition of Fig. 3, is who puts the memoization mechanism to work. It takes as input a reference to an attribute and an $AGTree_m$, representing the computation of that attribute, and returns as result a new $AGTree_m$ where the computation of the attribute is memoized.

$$memo :: Memo\ attr\ m\ a \Rightarrow attr \rightarrow AGTree_m\ m\ a \rightarrow AGTree_m\ m\ a$$
$$memo\ attr\ eval\ z =$$
$$\quad \textbf{case}\ mlookup\ attr\ (getMemoTable\ z)\ \textbf{of}$$
$$\quad\quad Just\ v\quad \rightarrow (v, z)$$
$$\quad\quad Nothing \rightarrow \textbf{let}\ (v, z') = eval\ z$$
$$\quad\quad\quad\quad\quad\quad \textbf{in}\ (v, modify_m\ z'\ (mmodify\ attr\ (const\ \$\ Just\ v)))$$

First of all, the memo table is obtained (by $getMemoTable$). Then the given attribute is searched in the memo table to see whether it was already computed. In the affirmative case, the stored value of the attribute is directly returned. Otherwise, we have to compute the value of the attribute at the current location

---

[4] This could also be represented in terms of a State monad, but we will not take that alternative in this paper.

of the zipper and modify the $Tree_m$ by storing the computed value in the corresponding memo table. Notice the use of $modify_m$ to update the $Zipper_m$ that will be passed to future computations.

One effect of attribute computation by memoization is a continuos movement of the computation focus. This means that the location where the computation of an attribute is taking place is continuosly changing. Changes in the computation focus correspond to location changes in the zipper. Those movements in the zipper need to be taken into account when defining the computation of an attribute because in some cases it is neccesary to return to the original location after moving. To see an example suppose we implement $locmin$ of Fig. 3 in the following way:

$$locmin = memo\ Locmin\ \$$$
$$\lambda z \rightarrow \textbf{case}\ constructor_m\ z\ \textbf{of}$$
$$C_{Leaf}\ v \rightarrow (v, z)$$
$$C_{Fork}\quad \rightarrow \textbf{let}\ (left,\quad z') = locmin\ (left_m\ z)$$
$$(right, z'') = locmin\ (right_m\ z')$$
$$\textbf{in}\quad (min\ left\ right, z'')$$

In the C_{Fork} case, the focus is first moved to the left child where $locmin$ is computed. Then, the intention is to compute $locmin$ at the right child of the original Fork. However, this is not the case, since it is actually computed at the right child of the left child of the original Fork (if that location even exists). In summary, this definition of $locmin$ is not correct. The reason of the failure is that once we move the focus to another position, using e.g. $left_m$ or $right_m$, it does not return to the original one.

To cope with this problem we define two new combinators $(.@.)$ and $atParent$ to move the focus of the $Zipper_m$ to an immediate position to compute an attribute there, returning the focus to the original location afterwards. By using $(.@.)$ an attribute is computed in the given child, and then the focus goes back to the parent using up_m:

$$(.@.) :: AGTree_m\ m\ a \rightarrow AGTree_m\ m\ a$$
$$eval\ .@.\ z = \textbf{let}\ (v, z') = eval\ z$$
$$\textbf{in}\quad (v, up_m\ z')$$

Moving the focus to the parent adds the complication of knowing the position of the child to which we have to return. This is easily solved by inspecting the context of the zipper from which we started.

$$atParent\ eval\ z = (v, (back\ z)\ z')$$
$$\textbf{where}$$
$$(v, z') = eval\ (up_m\ z)$$
$$back\ (\_, Top_m)\quad = tree_m$$

$$back\ (\_, L_m\ \_\ \_\ \_) = \mathit{left}_m$$
$$back\ (\_, R_m\ \_\ \_\ \_) = \mathit{right}_m$$

Finally, to evaluate the AG defined in Fig. 3 we compute *replace* at the initial *Tree$_m$* (with empty tables at each node), ignoring the final *Tree$_m$*.

$$repmin :: Tree \rightarrow Tree$$
$$repmin\ t = \mathit{fst}\ (replace\ (mkAG_m\ (build_m\ t\ emptyMemo)))$$

If, for example, we adopt the memo table representation in term of tuples then the empty table for this AG is given by:

$$emptyMemo = (Nothing, Nothing, Nothing)$$

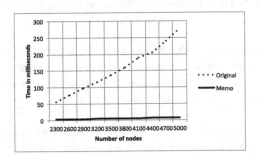

Fig. 4. Performance of the *repmin* implementations.

4   Results

In this section, we assess in terms of efficiency the memoization approach we followed in this paper against the original, non-optimized embedding of [15]. For this assessment, we test the optimized and non-optimized versions of Repmin together with three well known **AG** examples from the literature. The results are presented as running times and memory consumption.

For the benchmarks we are presenting in this section, we compiled the different approaches with the Glasgow Haskell Compiler (ghc), version 7.8.4, using the -O2 optimization flag. The computer used was a 1.3 GHz Intel Core i5 with 8 GB 1600 MHz DDR3 RAM memory (mid 2013 stock MacBook Air with RAM upgrade).

4.1   Repmin

We have started by benchmarking the running example presented throughout this paper. For this test, we used increasingly larger balanced binary leaf trees with a number of nodes ranging from 2300 to 5000, represented on Fig. 4 in the x-axis.

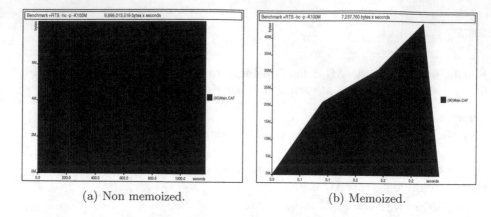

(a) Non memoized.   (b) Memoized.

Fig. 5. Heap Profile on Repmin (values in Mbytes).

The performance results of the implementations with and without memoization allow us to observe that the memoized version significantly improves the
performance of the original version. Indeed, when we reach the 5000 nodes there
is a clear gap in the time required to run *repmin* between the original and the
memoized versions.

Another interesting result is how well the memoized version scales. As we
grow from 2300 to 5000 nodes, almost 50 %, the memoized shows only a slight
increase in running time, while the original approach takes proportionally more
and more processing time.

The use of memoization strategies in programming often trades off memory
consumption to achieve better runtime performance. This is also evidenced from
the memory consumption comparison we performed on the different implementations of Repmin, which is presented in Figs. 5a and b. Both times we ran repmin
with a balanced tree with 150,000 nodes.

As expected, we observe that it is the original version that throughout its
execution has the lowest peak of memory consumption, of slightly more than 8
Mbytes. And it is the memoized version, which is the fastest in terms of runtime
performance, that reaches the highest peak of consumed memory, of around 45
Mbytes. A large difference but a burden expected by the use of the memo tables.

It is worth mentioning the time gap between the two versions. The original
took around 1500 s (around 25 min) while the memoized version took around
0.3 s. Even though these tests cannot be compared to the performance ones of
Fig. 4, because of the overhead introduced when analysing memory consumption (by the ghc profiler), among themselves there is a huge gap in run time,
confirming the exponential behavior of the non memoized version.

A final note, as mentioned earlier, the original implementation of Repmin
is an extremely heavy example of semantics requiring a large number of necessary recomputations of attributes (the minimum value of the tree is constantly

being required). So, it comes as no surprise that the memoized versions perform significantly better here. The next examples are focused on real situations.

4.2   Algol-68 Scope Rules

In this section we benchmark an implementation of the Algol 68 scope rules [8,15,19]. Algol 68 holds central characteristics of widely-used programming languages, such as a structured layout and mandatory but unique declarations of names which are used.

The semantics requirements are therefore the same as some real examples, like the ones on the Eli system [10] (to define a generic component for the name analysis task of a compiler), or the `let-in` construct of the Haskell programming language.

Algol 68 is a simple block structure language that does not require a *declare-before-use* scope rule discipline. A program consists of a block with a list containing either use or declaration of names, or a nested block. An example of a program is:

$$p = [\,use'\ y;\ decl'\ x;$$
$$[\,decl'\ y;\ use'\ y;\ use'\ w;\,]$$
$$decl'\ x;\ decl'\ y;\,]$$

In this language a definition of an identifier x is visible in the smallest enclosing block, with the exception of local blocks that also contain a definition of x. In the latter case, the definition of x in the local scope hides the definition in the global one. In a block an identifier may be declared at most once.

According to these rules, p above contains two errors: (a) at the outer level, the variable x has been declared twice, and (b) the use of the variable w, at the inner level, has no binding occurrence at all.

Implementing a validator for Algol implies not only checking each individual block for double declarations of variables, but also constantly analysing outer blocks for the declaration of variables whose definition can not be found in the current block, forcing multiple tree traversals.

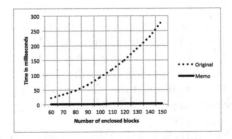

Fig. 6. Performance of the Algol implementations.

In Fig. 6, we show the results we obtained when running the different implementations on Algol programs with an increasing number of enclosing blocks. The x-axis of Fig. 6 ranges from 60 to 150 enclosing blocks, an increase of more than 50 %. Similarly to the previous examples, memoization shows better processing times.

4.3   HTML Table Formatter

We now analyze an example from [22]: we want to format HTML style tables. Namely, we want our AG to receive an abstract data type of an HTML table and to print a geometrically well defined table. Figure 7 shows an example of a possible input (left) and correspondent output (right).

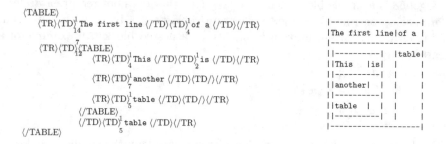

Fig. 7. HTML table formatting (Color figure online)

Notice that in the output, all the lines have the same number of columns and the columns have the same length. None of these features are required in the HTML language.

An entry in the table can be a string or a nested table, thus, the straightforward algorithm to express this table formatting requires two traversals and the definition of gluing data types to pass the width/height (blue subscripts/superscripts in Fig. 7) of nested table from the first to the second traversal. Simplifying, it is required to know the sizes of inner tables in order to resize the outer ones.

To test this AG, we computed trees representing HTML tables with the same number of rows (50) and an increasing number of columns. All the cells of the tables include the same text, excepting for the ones in the last column, which include nested tables with, recursively, the same shape but half the number of rows and columns of the containing table. The results are presented in Fig. 8a (time) and b (memory consumption), where the x-axis represents the number of columns, ranging from 10 to 100.

It can be observed from these results that, although the reduction in execution time is great, the memoized evaluator does consume much more memory. Note that, for large inputs this evaluator produces large strings. As a result, in

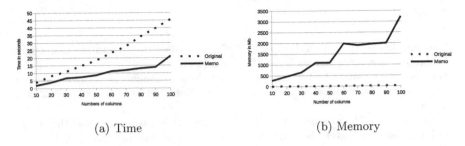

(a) Time   (b) Memory

Fig. 8. Performance of the HTML table formatters.

the memoized version, partial results are kept in the memo table: large strings in this case. As usual in memoization techniques the gain in runtime is obtained by using additional memory: the memo table. In fact, memory consumption can result in a scalability problem in certain cases. To reduce this problem several AG techniques to purge entries from a memo table have been proposed [19], which can be used in our zipper-based setting.

5   Conclusion

This paper shows how memoization is introduced in zipper-based embeddings of AGs. Regarding the programs we finally end up with, we argue that they maintain the elegance of the embedding we build upon, and in most cases show better performance, often by various different orders of magnitude.

There is a range of AG applications where this technique does not necessarily yield an advantage. For example, AGs that only have one tree traversal or heavily rely on local attributes or semantic operations on their leaves should not (greatly) benefit from the use of memoization. However, real applications of AGs do not fit into this category. In fact, we have seen through a series of standard AG examples that there is a range of problems where memoization provides real noticeable benefits modulo the memory consumption.

As a possible direction of future research, we would like to test the approach suggested here with other embeddings of AGs such as the ones of [1,2,23]. This comparison should be performed whenever possible (for example, it might be hard to perform with specific AG systems such as [7,13,24]), but other embeddings have different strategies to deal with attribute recomputation (for example, lazy evaluation). Further tests are required to see how this compares to our memoized approach.

Another line of work, could be the use of type-level programming techniques to make the AG system extensible in the sense of adding new productions to the grammars.

References

1. Badouel, E., Fotsing, B., Tchougong, R.: Yet another implementation of attribute evaluation. Research Report RR-6315, Inria (2007)
2. Badouel, E., Fotsing, B., Tchougong, R.: Attribute grammars as recursion schemes over cyclic representations of zippers. Electron. Notes Theory Comput. Sci. **229**(5), 39–56 (2011)
3. Balestrieri, F.: The productivity of polymorphic stream equations and the composition of circular traversals. PhD thesis, University of Nottingham (2015)
4. Bird, R.S.: Using circular programs to eliminate multiple traversals of data. Acta Inf. **21**, 239–250 (1984)
5. de Moor, O., Backhouse, K., Swierstra, D.: First-class attribute grammars. In: 3rd Workshop on Attribute Grammars and their Applications, Ponte de Lima, Portugal, pp. 1–20 (2000)
6. Dijkstra, A., Fokker, J., Swierstra, S.D.: The architecture of the Utrecht Haskell compiler. In: Haskell Symposium, pp. 93–104 (2009)
7. Dijkstra, A., Swierstra, D.: Typing Haskell with an attribute grammar (part I). Technical report UU-CS-2004-037, Institute of Information and Computing Sciences, Utrecht University (2004)
8. Fernandes, J.P., Saraiva, J.: Tools and libraries to model and manipulate circular programs. In: Symposium on Partial Evaluation and Program Manipulation, pp. 102–111. ACM (2007)
9. Huet, G.: The zipper. J. Funct. Program. **7**(5), 549–554 (1997)
10. Kastens, U., Pfahler, P., Jung, M.: The Eli system. In: Koskimies, K. (ed.) CC 1998. LNCS, vol. 1383, pp. 294–297. Springer, Heidelberg (1998)
11. Kiselyov, O., Lämmel, R., Schupke, K.: Strongly typed heterogeneous collections. In: Workshop on Haskell, pp. 96–107. ACM (2004)
12. Knuth, D.: Semantics of context-free languages. Math, Syst. Theory, 2(2) (1968). Correction: Math. Syst. Theory, 5(1) (1971)
13. Kuiper, M., Saraiva, J.: Lrc — a generator for incremental language-oriented tools. In: Koskimies, K. (ed.) CC 1998. LNCS, vol. 1383, pp. 298–301. Springer, Heidelberg (1998)
14. Magnusson, E., Hedin, G.: Circular reference attributed grammars - their evaluation and applications. Sci. Comput. Program. **68**(1), 21–37 (2007)
15. Martins, P., Fernandes, J.P., Saraiva, J.: Zipper-based attribute grammars and their extensions. In: Du Bois, A.R., Trinder, P. (eds.) SBLP 2013. LNCS, vol. 8129, pp. 135–149. Springer, Heidelberg (2013)
16. Martins, P., Fernandes, J.P., Saraiva, J., Van Wyk, E., Sloane, A.: Embedding attribute grammars and their extensions using functional zippers. Science of Computer Programming (2016, in Press)
17. Middelkoop, A., Dijkstra, A., Swierstra, S.D.: Iterative type inference with attribute grammars. In International Conference on Generative Programming, pp. 43–52. ACM (2010)
18. Norell, U., Gerdes, A.: Attribute grammars in Erlang. In: Workshop on Erlang, 2015, pp. 1–12. ACM (2015)
19. Saraiva, J.: Purely functional implementation of attribute grammars. PhD thesis, Utrecht University, The Netherlands, December 1999
20. Saraiva, J., Swierstra, S.D.: Generating spreadsheet-like tools from strong attribute grammars. In: Pfenning, F., Macko, M. (eds.) GPCE 2003. LNCS, vol. 2830, pp. 307–323. Springer, Heidelberg (2003)

21. Sloane, A.M., Kats, L.C.L., Visser, E.: A pure object-oriented embedding of attribute grammars. Electron. Notes Theory Comput. Sci. **253**(7), 205–219 (2010)
22. Swierstra, D., Azero, P., Saraiva, J.: Designing and implementing combinator languages. In: Swierstra, S.D., Oliveira, J.N. (eds.) AFP 1998. LNCS, vol. 1608. Springer, Heidelberg (1999)
23. Uustalu, T., Vene, V.: Comonadic functional attribute evaluation. In: Trends in Functional Programming, vol. 10, pp. 145–162. Intellect Books (2005)
24. Van Wyk, E., Bodin, D., Gao, J., Krishnan, L.: Silver: an extensible attribute grammar system. Electron. Notes Theory Comput. Sci. **203**(2), 103–116 (2008)
25. Viera, M., Swierstra, D., Swierstra, W.: First-class, attribute grammars fly: how to do aspect oriented programming in Haskell. In: International Conference on Functional Programming, pp. 245–256. ACM (2009)
26. Vogt, H., Swierstra, S.D., Kuiper, M.: Higher order attribute grammars. SIGPLAN Notices **24**(7), 131–145 (1989)

Purely Functional Incremental Computing

Denis Firsov[✉] and Wolfgang Jeltsch[✉]

Institute of Cybernetics at Tallinn University of Technology,
Akadeemia tee 21, 12618 Tallinn, Estonia
{denis,wolfgang}@cs.ioc.ee

Abstract. Many applications have to maintain evolving data sources as well as views on these sources. If sources change, the corresponding views have to be adapted. Complete recomputation of views is typically too expensive. An alternative is to convert source changes into view changes and apply these to the views. This is the key idea of incremental computing. In this paper, we use Haskell to develop an incremental computing framework. We illustrate the concepts behind this framework by implementing several example computations on sequences. Our framework allows the user to implement incremental computations using arbitrary monad families that encapsulate mutable state. This makes it possible to use highly efficient algorithms for core computations.

1 Introduction

Incremental computing is an approach to efficiently updating a view of some data source whenever the data source changes. For an explanation, let us look at the following diagram:

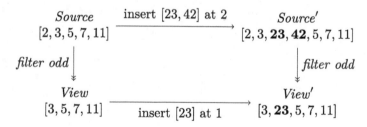

Initially, the source is the list $[2, 3, 5, 7, 11]$. We create a view of the source, defined as the list of odd numbers in the source, which is $[3, 5, 7, 11]$ initially. Next, we change the source by inserting the numbers 23 and 42 at index 2, resulting in $[2, 3, 23, 42, 5, 7, 11]$. We expect the view to adapt to the new source, that is, to become $[3, 23, 5, 7, 11]$. This can be done by fully recomputing the view from the source. However, a more efficient method is to turn the source change "insert $[23, 42]$ at 2" into a view change "insert $[23]$ at 1" and apply the latter to the view.

The most important trait of different approaches to incremental computing is the amount of automation they provide. One of the strongest achievements

© Springer International Publishing Switzerland 2016
F. Castor and Y.D. Liu (Eds.): SBLP 2016, LNCS 9889, pp. 62–77, 2016.
DOI: 10.1007/978-3-319-45279-1_5

in the field of incremental computing is the approach of self-adjusting computation developed by Acar [1]. Here, any function is incrementalized automatically using dependency tracking. However, the downside of full automation is that it provides less control over time and space complexity. For example, the trivial accumulator-based implementation of the *reverse* function requires linear time for change propagation when incrementalized automatically. One can achieve change propagation in logarithmic time by implementing *reverse* using a divide-and-conquer strategy. However, it is generally hard to come up with a function definition that results in efficient change propagation.

In this paper, we present a framework for incremental computing. This framework makes it possible to efficiently implement basic incremental computations using carefully crafted algorithms, and then build more complex computations from them by means of easy-to-use combinators. Furthermore, our framework offers composability at the type level, allowing notions of change for complex types to be derived from notions of change for simpler types. To illustrate our framework, we use sequences as our running example. We make the following contributions:

- In Sect. 2, we describe an interface to changeable values and associated changes.
- In Sect. 3, we introduce the notion of transformation. A transformation maps a source to a view. It allows for efficient updates of the view by propagating changes of the source to the view. (An example of a transformation is the *filter odd* in the above diagram.)
- In Sect. 4, we develop transformations that may use pure state to propagate changes. As a result, we can equip a wider range of operations with change propagation.
- In Sect. 5, we show that for some transformations, efficient change propagation requires mutable state, that is, state that can be updated in place. We characterize a class of monad families that can embed different kinds of mutable state into pure computations. We generalize transformations such that they can use arbitrary monad families from this class.

The remaining sections are devoted to related work, conclusions, and further work.

Our developments use the Haskell programming language and are compatible with the Glasgow Haskell Compiler (GHC), version 7.8.3. They are available as the Cabal package *incremental-computing* [6].

2 Changes and Changeables

The central notion of our framework is the change. A change describes a modification of values. Changes are typically implemented using algebraic data types.

This way, they can be inspected during change propagation. We define a type class *Change* of all types of changes:

> **class** *Change p* **where**
>   **type** *Value p* :: *
>   ($\$\$$) :: $p \to$ *Value p* $\to$ *Value p*

Each type p of changes has an associated type *Value p* of values on which the changes can act. The $\$\$$-operator denotes change application. We can see a partial application $(change \$\$)$ :: *Value p* $\to$ *Value p* as the meaning of *change*.

A change type may optionally be an instance of the *Monoid* class, in which case ε denotes the identity change, and $change_2 \bullet change_1$ denotes the change that consists of $change_1$ followed by $change_2$.

For any type of values, there is a primitive notion of change, where a change is either keeping the current value or replacing the current value by a new value:

> **data** *PrimitiveChange a* = *Keep* | *ReplaceBy a*
>
> **instance** *Monoid* (*PrimitiveChange a*) **where**
> $\varepsilon = Keep$
>   *Keep* $\bullet$ *change* = *change*
>   *ReplaceBy val* $\bullet$ _   = *ReplaceBy val*
>
> **instance** *Change* (*PrimitiveChange a*) **where**
>   **type** *Value* (*PrimitiveChange a*) = a
>   *Keep* $\$\$$ *val* = *val*
>   *ReplaceBy val* $\$\$$ _   = *val*

Each value type can have an arbitrary number of change types. However, we allow to specify a single notion of change as the default for a value type. We introduce a class *Changeable* of all value types with a default change type:

> **class** (*Monoid* (*DefaultChange a*), *Change* (*DefaultChange a*),
>   *Value* (*DefaultChange a*) $\sim a$) $\Rightarrow$ *Changeable a* **where**
>   **type** *DefaultChange a* :: *
>   **type** *DefaultChange a* = *PrimitiveChange a*

As the code specifies, default changes have to form a monoid, and each type of the form *DefaultChange a* has to be an instance of the *Change* class with a being the value type of *DefaultChange a*. If an instance declaration does not provide a declaration for *DefaultChange*, primitive changes are used as the default notion of change. Primitive changes are appropriate for primitive types, like *Bool* and *Integer*; so we can instantiate *Changeable* for primitive types easily:

> **instance** *Changeable Bool*
> **instance** *Changeable Integer*

In this paper, we want to illustrate the concepts of our framework taking lists as a running example. However, some operations on standard Haskell lists are inefficient. As a solution, the module *Data.Sequence* from the *containers* package provides a type *Seq* with operations that mostly run in $O(\log n)$ time. In particular, splitting a sequence at a given index and concatenating two sequences takes $\Theta(\log n)$ time. So we base our illustration on the *Seq* type. However, we will still use list syntax in examples to avoid notational clutter.

First, we define a type *AtomicChange* whose elements are changes of sequences:

data *AtomicChange* $a = $ *Insert Int* (*Seq a*)
  | *Delete Int Int*
  | *Shift Int Int Int*
  | *ChangeAt Int* (*DefaultChange a*)

The semantics of changes and the time complexity of change application to sequences of size n are as follows:

- *Insert ix seq* inserts *seq* at index *ix*. It takes $O(\log n + |seq|)$ time.
- *Delete ix len* deletes the part of length *len* that starts at index *ix*. It takes $O(\log n)$ time.
- *Shift src len tgt* shifts the part of length *len* that starts at index *src* to index *tgt*. It takes $O(\log n)$ time.
  Applying *Shift src len tgt* is actually equivalent to first applying *Delete src len* and then *Insert tgt seq* where *seq* is the deleted part. We provide *Shift* nevertheless, because in certain situations, change propagation for *Shift* can be done more efficiently than change propagation for the corresponding *Delete–Insert* chain.
- *ChangeAt ix elemChange* applies *elemChange* to the element at index *ix*. It takes $O(\log n + m)$ time where m is the time cost for applying *elemChange* to the element.

Note that not all changes are applicable to a given sequence. For example, a change *Insert ix seq* can only be applied to a sequence of length *len* if $0 \leqslant ix \leqslant len$. In the *incremental-computing* package, we properly deal with this issue, but in this paper, we ignore it for the sake of simplicity.

We want to use lists of atomic changes as the default changes of sequences. This way, default sequence changes form a monoid. We introduce a type *MultiChange* such that *MultiChange a* is essentially $[a]$, but differs from it in the following points:

- Concatenation takes only $O(1)$ time, which is achieved by using difference lists.
- The monoid operator • is concatenation with arguments swapped to accommodate the above-mentioned argument order of change composition.
- For every instance p of *Change*, *MultiChange p* is an instance of *Change* as well (with an obvious implementation).

We instantiate *Changeable* for sequence types as follows:

instance *Changeable a* $\Rightarrow$ *Changeable (Seq a)* **where**
  type *DefaultChange (Seq a) = MultiChange (AtomicChange a)*

For convenience, we define variants of *Insert*, *Delete*, *Shift*, and *ChangeAt*, called *insert*, *delete*, *shift*, and *changeAt*, that construct singleton multi changes instead of atomic changes.

3   Transformations Without State

Transformations are functions equipped with means for change propagation. For very simple cases, a transformation can be seen as a pair of two functions: one that maps source values to view values and one that maps source changes to view changes:

data *Trans p q = Trans (Value p $\rightarrow$ Value q) (p $\rightarrow$ q)*

For transformations that work with default changes, we provide a convenience type alias:

type *a $\twoheadrightarrow$ b = Trans (DefaultChange a) (DefaultChange b)*

As an example, we present a map combinator for sequences that works with transformations instead of functions. First, we implement a version of this combinator that only propagates atomic changes:

atomicMap :: *(Changeable a, Changeable b)*
             $\Rightarrow$ *(a $\twoheadrightarrow$ b) $\rightarrow$ Trans (AtomicChange a) (AtomicChange b)*
atomicMap (Trans elemFun elemProp) = Trans fun prop **where**
  fun = fmap elemFun

prop (Insert ix seq)	*= Insert ix (fmap elemFun seq)*
prop (Delete ix len)	*= Delete ix len*
prop (Shift src len tgt)	*= Shift src len tgt*
prop (ChangeAt ix elemChange)	*= ChangeAt ix (elemProp elemChange)*

Since the default changes of sequences are multi changes, we now develop a combinator *map* for sequences that works with multi changes. Recall that multi changes are essentially just lists of changes. We introduce a function *MultiChange.map* of type

$$Trans\ p\ q \rightarrow Trans\ (MultiChange\ p)\ (MultiChange\ q)$$

that keeps the function on values and lifts the function on changes to a function on multi changes. The definition of *map* becomes simple now:

map :: *(Changeable a, Changeable b) $\Rightarrow$ (a $\twoheadrightarrow$ b) $\rightarrow$ (Seq a $\twoheadrightarrow$ Seq b)*
map trans = MultiChange.map (atomicMap trans)

4   Transformations with Pure State

In many cases, we need additional information about the current source in order to propagate changes. An example is the *reverse* transformation. A source change *Insert ix seq*, for example, must be turned into the view change *Insert* (*len* − *ix*) (*reverse seq*) where *len* is the current length of the source. So the change propagator needs to know this length.

To remedy this problem, we extend the *Trans* type such that a transformation can use a state to track information about the source:

data *Trans p q* = ∀*s* . *Trans* (*Value p* → (*Value q, s*)) (*p* → *s* → (*q, s*))

The type *s* is the type of the state. Every value of a type *Trans p q* can use its own type *s*, which does not show up as a parameter of *Trans*. In a transformation *Trans init prop*, the function *init* turns an initial source to the corresponding view and the initial state, and the function *prop* turns a source change and a current state into the corresponding view change and the updated state. Note that *prop* is a computation in the state monad.

We can still represent transformations without state by setting the type *s* to (). However, we cannot use the previous implementation of *map* anymore, since the argument of type *a* ↠ *b* that *map* receives has the new, more complex, structure. Nevertheless, it is possible to implement *map* for transformations with pure state. The only difficulty is the propagation of *ChangeAt* changes. To propagate a change of the form *ChangeAt ix elemChange*, we have to propagate *elemChange*. This requires access to the state of the element at index *ix*. For this reason, we store the sequence of all element states as the state of the result transformation of *map*.

Another example of a transformation that requires state is *concat*, which flattens a sequence of sequences. To propagate changes, *concat* needs to translate indexes and lengths that refer to the nested source sequence into indexes and lengths that refer to the flattened view sequence. For this, it needs to know the lengths of the elements of the source. The *concat* transformation stores these as its state.

Having *concat*, we can implement a *filter* combinator with only little effort. First, we implement a helper combinator

$$gate :: Changeable\ a \Rightarrow (a \twoheadrightarrow Bool) \rightarrow (a \twoheadrightarrow Seq\ a)\ ,$$

which is also useful in other contexts. The view of a transformation *gate prd* is the empty sequence whenever *prd* yields false for the source; otherwise, it is the singleton sequence containing just the source. Figure 1 shows an example run for *gate odd*. Note that the source is of type *Integer* and thus uses changes of type *PrimitiveChange Integer*, while the view is of type *Seq Integer* and thus uses changes of type *MultiChange* (*AtomicChange Integer*). We can now implement *filter* easily by composing *map*, *concat*, and *gate* appropriately:

filter :: *Changeable a* ⇒ (*a* ↠ *Bool*) → (*Seq a* ↠ *Seq a*)
filter prd = *concat* ∘ *map* (*gate prd*)

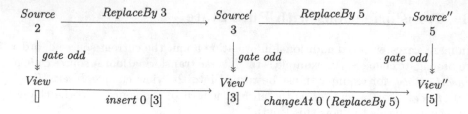

Fig. 1. Example run for *gate odd*

The given implementation uses a composition operator ∘ of type *Trans q r* → *Trans p q* → *Trans p r*, which definition is straightforward. The example from Sect. 1 illustrates the use of *filter*.

5   Transformations with Mutable State

The goal of incremental computing is to make views adapt quickly to source changes. In some cases, transformations with only pure state are not capable of propagating changes with optimal time complexity. In Subsect. 5.1, we sketch an efficient solution to incremental stable sorting that relies on mutable state, that is, state that can be updated in place. Next, in Subsect. 5.2, we develop the notion of monadic transformation, which makes it possible to use mutable state in incremental computations. Finally, in Subsect. 5.3, we discuss how transformation combinators can be implemented safely in the presence of mutable state.

5.1   Incremental Stable Sorting

A sorting algorithm is stable if it retains the relative order of elements that are considered equivalent by the comparison function. Stability is especially important in an incremental setting, as it prevents equivalent elements from changing their relative order during application of unrelated changes.

There are several solutions to incremental sorting. Acar [1] presents a randomized merge sort that he incrementalizes using self-adjusting computation. With this approach, change propagation takes logarithmic expected time for single-element insertions and deletions, and sorting is stable. Furthermore, Acar et al. [2] describe a cleverly crafted heapsort implementation, for which self-adjusting computation provides single-element change propagation in logarithmic worst-case time. Unfortunately, the use of heapsort makes sorting unstable. We overcome the tradeoff between these two approaches by implementing incremental stable sorting with logarithmic worst-case time for single-element change propagation. In this subsection, we describe the main ideas behind our implementation.

Let us first discuss incremental unstable sorting. As an example, we want to look at sequences of letters. We assume that letters are ordered according to their position in the alphabet without taking case into account. The following diagram shows an example of change propagation:

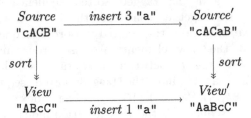

The generated view change *insert* 1 "a" is also appropriate for stable sorting. Unstable sorting, however, additionally permits the view change *insert* 0 "a", which leads to the updated view "aABcC".

The crucial part of change propagation for unstable sorting is the translation of source indexes into view indexes. To facilitate this translation, we maintain the sorted sequence as the state of the sorting transformation. We use a search tree data structure for it, so that we can find the view index of a newly inserted element or an element to be deleted in logarithmic worst-case time.

Now let us try to turn this incremental unstable approach into an approach to incremental stable sorting. It is well known how to perform non-incremental stable sorting based on an unstable sorting algorithm. First, the elements of the unsorted sequence are tagged with their indexes. Afterwards, the resulting sequence of element–index pairs is sorted lexicographically. Finally, the indexes are dropped from the sorted sequence.

We cannot adapt this approach directly to incremental sorting. When propagating an insertion, we must come up with tags for the new elements that lie between the tags of the existing elements. For an explanation, let us look at the above diagram again. We first tag the initial source "cACB" with indexes and get the sequence $[(\text{`c'}, 0), (\text{`A'}, 1), (\text{`C'}, 2), (\text{`B'}, 3)]$. Then, we sort this sequence lexicographically, obtaining $[(\text{`A'}, 1), (\text{`B'}, 3), (\text{`c'}, 0), (\text{`C'}, 2)]$. For propagating the change *insert* 3 "a", we have to create a tag that lies between the tags of 'C' and 'B'. We could use rational numbers as tags, so that the new tag could be 2.5. However with this approach, tag comparison would be linear in the worst case. Retagging the source sequence is also not an option, as it would take linear time in the worst case as well.

We solve the tagging issue by employing a solution to the order maintenance problem. In the order maintenance problem, the objective is to maintain a total order of tags subject to insertions, deletions, and tag comparison. Dietz and Sleator [5] show how to achieve constant worst-case time for all these operations. By using their solution, we are able to create tags between existing tags efficiently and still avoid linear time complexity for tag comparison. We keep the tagged sorted sequence in the form of a search tree. In addition, we maintain the tagged unsorted sequence, so that we can generate new tags based on the tags of neighboring elements.

Let us illustrate this with our running example. The initial source "cACB" leads to a tagged unsorted sequence $[(\text{'c'}, t_0), (\text{'A'}, t_1), (\text{'C'}, t_2), (\text{'B'}, t_3)]$ with $t_0 < t_1 < t_2 < t_3$ and the tagged sorted sequence $[(\text{'A'}, t_1), (\text{'B'}, t_3),$ $(\text{'c'}, t_0), (\text{'C'}, t_2)]$, which together constitute the initial state. For propagating $insert\ 3$ "a", we first use the tagged unsorted sequence to find the neighboring tags of the new element. We use order maintenance insertion to create a new tag t' between those tags, so that $t_2 < t' < t_3$. We insert the pair $(\text{'a'}, t')$ into the tagged sorted sequence, leading to $[(\text{'A'}, t_1), (\text{'a'}, t'), (\text{'B'}, t_3), (\text{'c'}, t_0), (\text{'C'}, t_2)]$. The index of this pair in the updated tagged sorted sequence is the view insertion index.

The crux is that the order maintenance solution by Dietz and Sleator relies on mutable state. So transformations with pure state are not powerful enough to implement the above incremental stable sorting strategy. Therefore, we extend our notion of transformation once more to allow for state to be mutable.

5.2   Monadic Transformations

Haskell provides the ST type to implement computations that can work with mutable variables internally, but can still be used in a pure setting [9]. ST takes a phantom type parameter s and an ordinary type parameter a, where s represents a heap of mutable variables that the computation can access, and a is the result type of the computation. There is a function $runST :: (\forall s\ .\ ST\ s\ a) \to a$ that turns an ST computation into a pure value. The use of universal quantification ensures that a computation can only work with its own, private heap, so that state mutations cannot be observed from the outside. $ST\ s$ is a monad family indexed by s in the sense that for every particular s, $ST\ s$ is a monad.

We redefine $Trans$ based on ST to enable transformations to use mutable state:

newtype $Trans\ p\ q = Trans\ (\forall s\ .\ Value\ p \to ST\ s\ (Value\ q, p \to ST\ s\ q))$

We represent a transformation by a computation that takes an initial source, sets up the initial state, and returns the initial view and a propagator. The propagator, in turn, is a computation that turns a source change into a view change. It can access the state that the initializer has set up, because it is created inside the initializer. Note that we can still express all transformations with pure state using this new definition of $Trans$, since we can store a pure state in a mutable variable.

The ST-based definition of $Trans$ allows for arbitrary transformations with mutable state. However, it restricts code reuse. For example, there is an implementation of order maintenance in the form of the $order\text{-}maintenance$ Cabal package [7], but we cannot use this package to implement a stable sorting transformation. To see why, we have to take a closer look at the interface of this package.

The $order\text{-}maintenance$ package provides a type $OrderT$ for computations that have access to a mutable totally ordered set. $OrderT$ takes type parameters

o, m, and a, where o is a phantom parameter that represents the ordered set, m is an inner monad, which provides additional effects, and a is the result type of the computation. There is a function

$$evalOrderT :: Monad\ m \Rightarrow (\forall o\ .\ OrderT\ o\ m\ a) \to m\ a$$

that turns an $OrderT$ computation into a computation in the inner monad. The use of universal quantification here is analogous to its use in $runST$. It ensures that a computation can only work with its own, private ordered set. For every monad m, $OrderT\ o\ m$ is a monad family indexed by o.

The *order-maintenance* package does not allow us to incorporate an $OrderT$ computation into an ST computation, as this would make the ordered set explicitly accessible via mutable variables and thus break the abstraction barrier. Therefore, we cannot make use of the *order-maintenance* package with the above ST-based definition of $Trans$.

If we had a variant of $Trans$ based on the monad family $OrderT\ o\ (ST\ s)$ with indexes o and s, we could use *order-maintenance* for implementing incremental stable sorting. The $OrderT$ layer would provide us with a mutable totally ordered set for holding the tags, and the ST layer would provide us with a heap for storing the remaining state. Instead of providing a $Trans$ variant for this particular monad family, we generalize $Trans$ such that we can use every monad family that has the following properties:

- It is indexed by an arbitrary number of phantom type parameters that appear at arbitrary positions in the type.
- It comes with an evaluation function, that is, a function that turns a computation in the monad family into a pure value, using universal quantification for all the index parameters to keep mutable state private. (For $ST\ s$, this function is $runST$, and for $OrderT\ o\ (ST\ s)$, it is $runST \circ evalOrderT$.)

We introduce a type alias $TransProc$ whose definition resembles the ST-based definition of $Trans$, but allows us to work in an arbitrary monad:

type $TransProc\ m\ p\ q = Value\ p \to m\ (Value\ q, p \to m\ q)$

We call a value of $TransProc$ a transformation processor. We can represent a transformation by a value of a type $\forall \overline{w}\ .\ TransProc\ \mu\ p\ q$ where μ is a monad family with indexes $\overline{w}$. As special cases, we get $\forall s\ .\ TransProc\ (ST\ s)\ p\ q$, which corresponds to the ST-based $Trans$, and $\forall o\ s\ .\ TransProc\ (OrderT\ o\ (ST\ s))\ p\ q$, which is appropriate for implementing incremental stable sorting.

It would be straightforward to define $Trans$ as a transformation processor, existentially quantifying the monad family μ. However, this would result in the following problems:

1. Since the number of indexes and the index positions depend on μ, we would have to bundle indexes as type tuples. This would require users of our framework to write considerable amounts of boilerplate code, and would require support for data type promotion, which is not a well-established language extension.

2. Since transformation processors can use different monad families, composition of transformation processors would be hard to implement.

Therefore, we represent a transformation by a pure function:

newtype *Trans p q = Trans ((Value p, [p]) → (Value q, [q]))*

The representation of a transformation captures its behavior by turning any pair of an initial source value and a list of successive source changes into a corresponding pair of an initial view value and a list of successive view changes. In practice, we typically cannot provide the initial source value and all the source changes at once, since they only become available over time. However, we can obtain parts of the output based on only parts of the input by employing laziness.

Note that there are pure functions of the above-mentioned type that are not proper representations of transformations, for example, functions where a view change depends on future source changes. Therefore, we do not export the data constructor *Trans*. Instead, we introduce a function *trans* that constructs a transformation based on a given transformation processor.

Besides the transformation processor, the *trans* function needs to know the evaluation function of the monad family of the transformation processor. So it would be best if *trans* had the type

$$\forall \mu \,.\, (\forall \overline{w} \,.\, TransProc\ \mu\ p\ q) \to (\forall r \,.\, (\forall \overline{w} \,.\, \mu\ r) \to r) \to Trans\ p\ q.$$

Unfortunately, the use of universal quantification over monad families would involve a problem similar to Problem 1 described above. Therefore, we modify the interface of *trans* step by step until *trans* has a type that does not involve universal quantification over monad families. Some of our modifications make the interface more permissive for the user, but none of them makes it less permissive. Our modification steps are as follows:

1. We switch to continuation-passing style for the transformation processor, using $\mu\ r$ with an arbitrary r as the result type of the continuation. As a consequence, the first argument of *trans* has the type

$$\forall r \,.\, \forall \overline{w} \,.\, (TransProc\ \mu\ p\ q \to \mu\ r) \to \mu\ r \;\;.$$

2. We push the quantification $\forall \overline{w}$ under the arrow, so that the type of the first argument becomes

$$\forall r \,.\, (\forall \overline{w} \,.\, TransProc\ \mu\ p\ q \to \mu\ r) \to (\forall \overline{w} \,.\, \mu\ r) \;\;.$$

3. We merge the two arguments into one that is supposed to be the composition of the former two arguments. The type of this single argument is clearly

$$\forall r \,.\, (\forall \overline{w} \,.\, TransProc\ \mu\ p\ q \to \mu\ r) \to r \;\;.$$

4. We generalize the type of the continuation such that it covers all monads. The type of the *trans* argument becomes

$$\forall r \,.\, (\forall m \,.\, Monad\ m \Rightarrow TransProc\ m\ p\ q \to m\ r) \to r \;\;.$$

5. We drop the universal quantification of μ, which is not needed anymore, as there are no more uses of μ. Now *trans* has the type

$$(\forall r \,.\, (\forall m \,.\, Monad\ m \Rightarrow TransProc\ m\ p\ q \rightarrow m\ r) \rightarrow r) \rightarrow Trans\ p\ q \ .$$

Let us look how to construct a transformation from a transformation processor *transProc* and an evaluation function *eval*. First, we turn *transProc* into continuation-passing style, which results in the function $\lambda cont \rightarrow cont\ transProc$. Then, we compose this function with the *eval* function, leading to $\lambda cont \rightarrow eval\ (cont\ transProc)$. Finally, we apply *trans* to this composed function.

By applying this technique to the monad family $ST\ s$, we can define a function *stTrans* that turns an ST-based transformation processor into a value of type *Trans*:

$stTrans :: (\forall s \,.\, TransProc\ (ST\ s)\ p\ q) \rightarrow Trans\ p\ q$
$stTrans\ transProc = trans\ (\lambda cont \rightarrow runST\ (cont\ transProc))$

We conclude this subsection with the presentation of the *trans* function implementation:

$trans :: (\forall r \,.\, (\forall m \,.\, Monad\ m \Rightarrow TransProc\ m\ p\ q \rightarrow m\ r) \rightarrow r) \rightarrow Trans\ p\ q$
$trans\ cpsProcAndEval = Trans\ conv\ \textbf{where}$

$\quad conv\ src = cpsProcAndEval\ \$\ \lambda transProc \rightarrow monadicConv\ transProc\ src$

$\quad monadicConv\ transProc \sim(val, changes) = \textbf{do}$
$\quad\quad \sim(val', prop) \leftarrow transProc\ val$
$\quad\quad changes' \leftarrow mapM\ prop\ changes$
$\quad\quad return\ (val', changes')$

Note that the interface changes to *trans* have not prevented us from generating the pure function representation, despite them making the interface more permissive.

5.3   Transformation Combinators

The use of the pure function representation for transformations becomes a challenge for the implementation of transformation combinators, that is, functions that construct new transformations from existing ones. Examples of transformation combinators are *map* and *gate*, which are described in Sects. 3 and 4, respectively. Change propagation of a combinator's result may involve change propagation of this combinator's arguments. For example, when a transformation *map elemTrans* propagates a sequence change of the form *ChangeAt ix elemChange*, it has to use *elemTrans* to propagate *elemChange*.

A transformation combinator cannot directly use the *Trans* data constructor to construct its result, since *Trans* is private; it has to invoke the *trans* function instead. Therefore, the combinator must represent its result by a transformation processor, which it can feed to *trans*. In particular, it must implement change propagation via a propagator whose type has the form $p \rightarrow \mu\ q$. Such a propagator is called with one change at a time. To propagate a given change, it

may need to propagate individual changes using the arguments of the combinator. The problem is that the arguments are represented by pure functions that
take all their source changes at once and therefore cannot propagate changes
individually.

As a solution, we develop a function *toSTProc* that turns a transformation
into an *ST*-based transformation processor. Using *toSTProc*, a transformation
combinator can obtain transformation processors for all its arguments and use
them to individually propagate changes.

A transformation processor *toSTProc* (*Trans conv*) has to apply *conv* to the
pair of the initial source and the list of all source changes in order to receive
the initial view and the view changes. So it has to provide the list of all source
changes immediately, although the source changes become known only by later
propagator calls. To resolve this conflict, we let the propagator put the source
changes into a channel and let the transformation processor construct a single lazy list of all future channel elements when it is initially invoked. For this
purpose, we implement channel support for the *ST* monad family. This support is inspired by the *Control.Concurrent.Chan* module, which works with the
IO monad.

We introduce a type *Channel* such that a value of a type *Channel s a* is
a channel that works with the monad *ST s* and contains elements of type *a*.
Furthermore, we provide a function *newChannel* :: *ST s* (*Channel s a*, [*a*]) that
creates an empty channel and returns it together with the lazy list of its future
elements, and a function *writeChannel* :: *Channel s a* → *a* → *ST s* () that puts
an element into a channel.

We are now able to convert transformations into *ST*-based transformation
processors:

```
toSTProc :: Trans p q → TransProc (ST s) p q
toSTProc (Trans conv) val = do
    (chan, changes) ← newChannel
    let (val', changes') = conv (val, changes)
    remainderRef ← newSTRef changes'
    let prop change = do
            writeChannel chan change
            next : further ← readSTRef remainderRef
            writeSTRef remainderRef further
            return next
    return (val', prop)
```

A transformation processor constructed by *toSTProc* creates a channel for the
source changes and passes its contents together with the initial source to the
pure function that represents the given transformation. This way, the transformation processor obtains the initial view and a lazy list of future view changes.
The propagator puts the given source change into the channel and fetches the
corresponding view change from the list of view changes. For this purpose, the
suffix of the view change list that contains the future view changes is kept in a
mutable variable.

6   Related Work

Approaches to incremental computing differ by the amount of automation they provide. Generally, automation of change propagation relieves the programmer from manual design of propagation algorithms and the obligation to prove that these algorithms are correct. On the other hand, automation restricts control over incrementalization strategies, which may result in suboptimal time complexity.

We have tried to find a middle ground between automation and potential for manual intervention. A user of our framework can manually define notions of change for core data types and implement core transformations by specifically crafted algorithms. On the other hand, our framework offers composability of transformations and types of changeable data, allowing the construction of complex incremental programs from the hand-crafted building blocks.

Cai et al. [3] follow a similar approach. Like us, they allow the user to define change types and change propagation algorithms for core data types. Based on these, they can incrementalize arbitrary λ-terms by means of a static transformation. In one respect, their automation goes further than ours, since it can handle higher-order programs. In another respect, however, their automation is more restrictive, because it uses only transformations with a pure state that reflects the current source value. We conjecture that this restriction necessarily results in change propagation with suboptimal time complexity for some transformations, for example, incremental stable sorting.

Substantial contributions to the field of fully automatic incremental computing are due to Acar [1]. His key approach is executing an ordinary program in an incremental fashion by maintaining a dynamic dependency graph. Based on this idea, Acar has developed the technique of self-adjusting computation. This method allows a user to write a function in the usual way and then have it incrementalized automatically by the compiler. Unfortunately, this level of automation makes it complicated to analyze the complexity of change propagation. A user who is not satisfied with the result of automatic incrementalization has little clue about how to change the implementation of his function to make it perform better when incrementalized. For example, the typical accumulator-based implementation of the *reverse* function requires linear time for change propagation. One can achieve logarithmic time by implementing *reverse* using a divide-and-conquer strategy, but this is not obvious for the lesser experienced user.

Carlsson [4] has implemented adaptive functional programming, a subset of self-adjusting computation, in Haskell. The key contribution of his work is the use of monads for integrating incremental computing into a pure language.

Self-adjusting computation does not perform well in the presence of certain reuse patterns, particularly sharing (using a computation in different contexts), swapping (changing the order of subcomputations), and switching (toggling computations back and forth). As a solution, Hammer et al. [8] have developed the λ_{ic}^{cdd}-calculus and the Adapton library, which provide automatic incremental computing based on a demand-driven semantics.

Maier et al. [10] have developed the *Scala.React* framework, which supports functional incremental reactive lists. The authors use the notions of reversible and associative folds, which are usual folds with some additional constraints on their arguments. These folds can be used for implementing new incremental functions. Obtaining incremental operations on reactive lists means translating the linear recursion of sequential folds into tree recursion of associative folds.

7 Conclusions and Further Work

We have developed a framework for incremental computing in Haskell. This framework allows the user to associate different notions of change with different data types and implement change propagation based on arbitrary monad families whose computations can be turned into pure values. Furthermore, we have implemented incremental versions of several sequence operations.

In the future, we want to develop a generic notion of change for inductive data types and use it to define generic transformations based on recursion schemes. We expect that general recursion schemes cannot be efficiently incrementalized. However, we plan to characterize recursion schemes that allow for efficient change propagation. All functions that are defined in terms of these recursion schemes can then be efficiently incrementalized automatically.

Acknowledgements. We want to thank Umut Acar, Yan Chen, Paolo Giarrusso, Magnús Halldórsson, Giuseppe Italiano, and Tarmo Uustalu for helpful discussions about the topics of this paper. This research was supported by the Estonian Research Council through the individual research grant PUT763, by the ERDF through the national ICTP project *Coinduction for Semantics, Analysis, and Verification of Communicating and Concurrent Reactive Software*, and by the Estonian Science Foundation through Grant 9398.

References

1. Acar, U.A.: Self-adjusting computation. Ph.D. thesis, Carnegie Mellon University, Pittsburgh, Pennsylvania, May 2005
2. Acar, U.A., Blelloch, G., Ley-Wild, R., Tangwongsan, K., Turkoglu, D.: Traceable data types for self-adjusting computation. In: Proceedings of the 31st ACM SIG-PLAN Conference on Programming Language Design and Implementation (PLDI 2010), pp. 483–496. ACM, New York (2010)
3. Cai, Y., Giarrusso, P.G., Rendel, T., Ostermann, K.: A theory of changes for higher-order languages: incrementalizing λ-calculi by static differentiation. In: Proceedings of the 35th ACM SIGPLAN Conference on Programming Language Design and Implementation, pp. 145–155. ACM, New York (2014)
4. Carlsson, M.: Monads for incremental computing. In: Proceedings of the Seventh ACM SIGPLAN International Conference on Functional Programming, pp. 26–35. ACM, New York (2002)
5. Dietz, P.F., Sleator, D.D.: Two algorithms for maintaining order in a list. Technical report CMU-CS-88-113, Carnegie Mellon University, Pittsburgh, Pennsylvania (1988)
6. Firsov, D., Jeltsch, W.: incremental-computing-0.0.0.0, Haskell Cabal package, Feburary 2015. http://hackage.haskell.org/package/incremental-computing-0.0.0.0

7. Firsov, D., Jeltsch, W.: order-maintenance-0.1.1.0, Haskell Cabal package, November 2015. http://hackage.haskell.org/package/order-maintenance-0.1.1.0
8. Hammer, M.A., Phang, K.Y., Hicks, M., Foster, J.S.: Adapton: composable, demand-driven incremental computation. In: Proceedings of the 35th ACM SIGPLAN Conference on Programming Language Design and Implementation (PLDI 2014), pp. 156–166. ACM, New York (2014)
9. Launchbury, J., Peyton Jones, S.: State in Haskell. LISP Symbol. Comput. **8**(4), 293–341 (1995)
10. Maier, I., Odersky, M.: Higher-order reactive programming with incremental lists. In: Castagna, G. (ed.) ECOOP 2013. LNCS, vol. 7920, pp. 707–731. Springer, Heidelberg (2013)

Automatic Annotating and Checking of Dynamic Ownership

Tingting Hu[✉], Haiyang Liu, Ke Zhang, and Zongyan Qiu

LMAM and Department of Informatics, School of Mathematical Sciences,
Peking University, Beijing, China
{hutingting.math,liuhaiyang,zksms}@pku.edu.cn,
qzy@math.pku.edu.cn

Abstract. Object ownership is an important technique in dealing with object sharing and aliasing to support verification of OO programs. *Dynamic Ownership* proposes a very flexible encapsulation discipline and has been adopted in Spec#. However, to use this technique, programmers have to keep all the ownership information in mind to decide the validation for modifying one variable. This makes the approach difficult to master and use. In this paper, we apply data-flow analysis to generate most annotations of dynamic ownership automatically, thus can potentially reduce the workload of program verification. Moreover, our technique can reveal ownership topology errors and encapsulation errors. In addition, the entire analysis of our approach is static, thus is efficient.

Keywords: Object ownership · Encapsulation · Program analysis

1   Introduction

The concept of *Object Ownership* [1,2] has been proposed in 1998 to deal with the problems caused by aliasing in heap-manipulating programs, especially OO programs. Ownership provides important benefits for verification. It allows programmers to describe the topology of data structures in a simple and natural way, at least for hierarchical structures. Moreover, ownership can be used to define and enforce encapsulation disciplines, which describe what references are valid in the execution and which operations may be performed on these references. In addition, *ownership types* support an automatic way of checking the implementations to some extent.

Various encapsulation disciplines for ownership have been proposed. The *owner-as-dominator* discipline enforces that the owner of an object is its dominator which controls every access path to the object. Another idea is *owner-as-modifier*, which enforces that all modifications to an object can only be initiated by its owner. Dietl *et al.* [3] introduced *Dynamic Ownership* based on the latter idea, and has been adopted in Spec#. Dynamic Ownership introduces the concept of ownership state for the involved objects. However, working with Dynamic

The work is supported by NSFC under grant No. 61272160 and No. 61202069.

F. Castor and Y.D. Liu (Eds.): SBLP 2016, LNCS 9889, pp. 78–94, 2016.
DOI: 10.1007/978-3-319-45279-1_6

Ownership, the developers must keep all the ownership information – ownership topology and the current ownership states – in their mind to decide whether it is valid to modify a object via a variable.

Dynamic Ownership improves the flexibility of ownership types, with the cost of more complicated annotations. The heavy annotations and unfriendliness for understanding make it difficult to master and use, thus hindered its spread in practice.

Our work address this problem. Applying data-flow analysis technique, we make the work process more automatic while keeping the flexibility. To illustrate the problem of Dynamic Ownership and our idea, we show a simple example.

Figure 1 (left) shows a class annotated with *Dynamic Ownership* notation. To modify the value of field data.f in method m, we must explicitly expose the transitive owners of f (data and this) using expose annotation. The annotations would be even more complicated for real-world programs. Our approach reduces the ownership annotations written by programmers, as in Fig. 1 (right), without losing the flexibility.

The workflow of Dynamic Ownership (especially in Spec#) is depicted in Fig. 2a. Firstly, programmers add all the ownership annotations into their program, then send the program to the model generator and the verifier. The tools check the ownership properties together with other verifications, and finally give

```
class Node {                          class Node {
  [Rep] D data;                         [Rep] D data;
  [Peer] Node next;                     [Peer] Node next;
  public m() {                          public m() {
    expose(this) {                        data.f = 0;
      expose(data) {                      next = next.next;}
        data.f = 0;}                  }
      next = next.next;}}}
```

Fig. 1. Annotations: dynamic ownership vs our approach

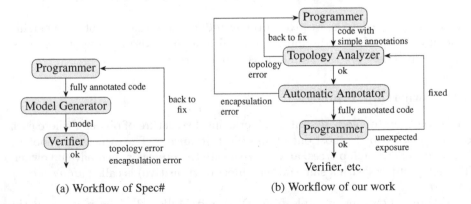

(a) Workflow of Spec#   (b) Workflow of our work

Fig. 2. Comparison of two approaches

the feedback. If any error occurs, the programmers need to modify the source code, ownership annotations, etc. to fix the error, and feed the result into the tools again.

However, the iteration in the workflow is quite long and difficult to conduct, besides the heavy annotations. Because the checking of ownership relation is combined into the general verification, programmers can only get the feedback after the time-consuming dynamic verification. In addition, the errors related to ownership relations often manifest as failure of theorem proof, which is difficult to locate and fix. This workflow is inefficient.

The workflow of our approach is shown in Fig. 2b. Now programmers write only basic ownership declarations, then feed the program into our tools. The tools work as follows: First, the *topology analyzer* checks the object topology, and reports errors immediately when it finds topological faults. Then, our *automatic annotator* tries to add necessary annotations to make all the accessing to the objects valid. It reports errors when it cannot complete the work. The programmers then check if all the annotations inserted by our tools are reasonable and conform to their intentions. This may induce another iteration. Then the program can go into the following verifications.

Our main contributions are:

1. A symbolic execution approach to extract and check the ownership topology.
2. An automatic annotation algorithm which can reduce the amount of required annotations in programs that use object ownership.
3. A prototype implementation of the algorithms.

Following our approach, we get at least three important benefits: (1) The annotation workload of the programmers is largely reduced. (2) The intellectual work to specify correct annotations now becomes a simpler work to check the satisfactory of the annotated program. (3) The tools can give feedback much earlier, and distinguish clearly the topological errors, annotation errors, etc.

2 Ownership System in Dynamic Ownership

Before going into details, we give a brief introduction to the concept of ownership topology, encapsulation discipline etc., which support verifications in Dynamic Ownership. These are the foundations of our work.

2.1 Ownership Topology

The ownership topology describes a hierarchical structure of objects, where each object is owned by at most one other object, its *owner*. The ownership topology is a forest of ownership trees, and the *roots* are the objects which have no owner. The set of objects with a same owner (direct or transitive) is called an *ownership context*.

Figure 3 shows an example from Dietl and Müller [3]. The picture on the right hand side depicts the ownership topology after the first four statements

```
class Account {              class Main {
  int value;                   [Rep] Person p1;
}                              [Rep] Person p2;
class Person {                void Demo() {
  [Rep] Account account;         p1 = new Person();
  [Peer] Person spouse;          p2 = new Person();
  Person() {                     p1.spouse = p2;
    account = new Account();      p2.spouse = p1;
    spouse = null;               ...
} }                          } }
```

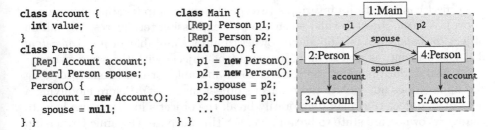

Fig. 3. Ownership topology

of method `Demo` are executed. The solid arrows denote object references, and the dashed boxes depict the borders of the ownership contexts. Here the `Main` object is the root, which owns two `Person` objects. Each `Person` object owns an `Account` object.

There are two kinds of ownership errors, which are clearly separated in [4].

- *Topology Error*: The ownership topology is not well-formed. A topology is well-formed if each object has at most one owner and the owner does not change once been assigned[1].
- *Encapsulation Error*: There are modifications which violate the encapsulation principle (see Sect. 2.4).

2.2 Ownership Qualifiers

In Dynamic Ownership, there are two qualifiers [Peer] and [Rep] for the field declarations. [Peer] f means that the object referred by f has the same owner as this object. This is equivalent to the object invariant

$$\text{invariant } f \neq null \implies f.owner = \text{this}.owner.$$

Here $o.owner$ denotes the owner of object o. In addition, [Rep] f means that this object is the owner of the object which f refers to. This is equivalent to the object invariant

$$\text{invariant } f \neq null \implies f.owner = \text{this}.$$

In Dynamic Ownership, a new created object is unowned and will acquire an owner when it is assigned to a rep or peer field of an object.

2.3 Ownership States of Objects

In Dynamic Ownership, each object has an *ownership state*, which is either *valid* or *mutable*. When *valid*, the object must satisfy its invariants, but when *mutable*,

---

[1] Some ownership systems support *ownership transfer*. For simplicity, we ignore ownership transfer in this paper.

the object can violate its invariants (except the ownership invariant mentioned above). A fresh object is valid when the new expression terminates. We call an object *consistent* if it is valid and its owner (if any) is mutable; or *peer consistent* if it is consistent, as well as all of its peers (the objects with the same owner).

A field update requires the receiver to be mutable, or consistent (providing the update does not violate the receiver's object invariant). Before modifying a field of an object that may temporarily break the object's invariant, we have to change its ownership state to be mutable. For this purpose, Dynamic Ownership introduces the expose structure, see Fig. 1. The semantics of expose(o){...} is as follows: It asserts that o is consistent, modifies the state of o to be mutable, then executes its body. Finally, expose asserts that the invariant of o holds again, and o and all objects owned by it are valid. Note that both the "asserts" above induce some state checking which may find errors.

2.4 Encapsulation Discipline

Dynamic Ownership enforces the following encapsulation rules: A valid object has to be exposed before modifications that may temporarily break its invariant. Pure methods in Dynamic Ownership require the receiver and arguments to be valid, and ensure peer validity of the result. Impure methods (and constructors) require their receiver and arguments to be peer consistent and ensure also peer consistency of their results. Then, an impure method can expose the receiver and the arguments and modify their state in its body.

The flexibility of Dynamic Ownership comes from that it does not need to restrict references as read-only, but controls their behaviors.

2.5 Object Invariants

There is some work on which object fields can be mentioned in the object invariants. If f is not a component of objects of class T, Barnett *et al.* [5] do not allow the fields of f to be mentioned in the class-T object invariant. Leino *et al.* [6] allow object invariants of T to depend on:

1. The fields of o declared in any superclass of T.
2. The fields of any object transitively owned by $[o, S]$ for any superclass S of T.
3. The fields of any specified object $o.f_1. \cdots .f_n$, $(n \geq 1)$ — that is, the objects reachable from o by a fixed sequence of field references.

Müller *et al.* [7] add constant field access to the aforementioned works. In ownership techniques, invariants of object o may depend on the mutable fields of objects that o owns.

Our work focuses on the ownership relationships. Thus, we require that the invariants $Inv(o)$ of object o depend only on the state encapsulated for o. For this purpose, $Inv(o)$ may depend only on the fields of o and objects transitively owned by o. But other settings can be easily extended into our framework.

We do not deal with inheritance in this paper, as in [3]. To support inheritance, Dynamic Ownership uses object-class pairs (o, C) to represent owners [8], that enables layered invariants and makes the operations on invariants more accurate. We can apply the same technique to extend our work without substantial difficulties.

3   Analysis and Annotations Generation

In this section, we will present our work in details. Following our approach, programmers only need to give the basic ownership annotations, [Rep] and [Peer]. The remaining annotations are generated automatically.

3.1   Overview

Our approach consists of the following steps:

1. Extract the ownership topology of the program, as well as the points-to relationships.
2. Obtain the ownership state (valid or mutable) of each object based on the ownership topology by an intra-procedure data-flow analysis.
3. Figure out all the positions to pack or unpack the objects according to the ownership state transitions of the objects between the statements.

Most of technical difficulties exist in the first step. We need to figure out reference relations between the objects, and points-to relations between variables and objects. In addition, throughout the whole program, one variable may reference to different objects. On the other hand, there may be several variables referring to one object.

There are two cases where one variable may refer to different objects. We need to deal with them in building the object ownership topology. The first case is that a variable might be reassigned to another object. We use SSA (Static Single Assignment) form to get rid of this form of reference-swing. The second is that a variable may be used in a loop to iterate over a series of objects, e.g. in a loop on a linked list,

```
while (n.next != null) {
    n.foo();
    n = n.next;
}
```

In a reasonable program with correct ownership relations, the objects iterated over by one variable must be peers, i.e. they have a common owner. This should be a loop invariant. Therefore, we take this as an assumption.

The main difficulty comes from the aliasing problem. SSA form eliminates aliasing of local variables, leaving out the aliasing of arguments and global variables, which brings inaccuracy to our analysis.

3.2   Analysis for the Ownership Topology

We perform a symbolic execution on the source code to get the ownership topology. The topological errors will be checked and reported. The result will be used in the ownership analysis algorithms. And the state transitions are recorded for the points-to analysis.

To give the symbolic execution rules, we define the program states first. A state $(\sigma, h) \in$ Store $\times$ Heap is a pair of the program store and heap, where

$$\text{Store} \triangleq \text{Name} \rightarrow \text{Ref} \quad \text{Heap} \triangleq \text{Ref} \rightarrow \text{Name} \rightarrow \text{Ref}.$$

Name and Ref are two basic sets for names and object references. A store $\sigma \in$ Store maps variable names to the corresponding object references, and a heap $h \in$ Heap is a pool for the objects, and $(r, f, r') \in h$ denotes that field f of the object denoted by reference r holds a reference r'. Then $h(\sigma x)$ gives the object of x in state (σ, h).

For briefness, we introduce the notation $\xi_{\sigma,h}(x) = h(\sigma x)(ow)$, which gives the reference to the owner of $h(\sigma x)$. Similarly, we use $\xi_{\sigma,h}(x.f) = h(h(\sigma x)(f))(ow)$ for the owner of the object denoted by x.f in state (σ, h).

Now we introduce the rules for the symbolic execution. The rule for the assignments of local variables is omitted here, as it does not affect the ownership topology.

Rules for the field assignment o.f=x are

$$\frac{\xi_{\sigma,h}(x) \in \{\xi_{\sigma,h}(o.f), \text{None}\}}{\langle o.f=x, (\sigma, h)\rangle \rightsquigarrow \langle \sigma, h \oplus \{(\sigma x, ow, \xi_{\sigma,h}(o.f)), (\sigma o, f, \sigma x)\}\rangle} \qquad \frac{\xi_{\sigma,h}(x) \notin \{\xi_{\sigma,h}(o.f), \text{None}\}}{\langle o.f=x, (\sigma, h)\rangle \rightsquigarrow \text{abort}}.$$

Before the assignment, x should be unowned, or it shares the same owner with o.f. In both cases, x will have the same owner with o.f after the assignment. Otherwise, the assignment will break the well-formedness of the ownership topology.

The if and while statements bring difficulties to the ownership analysis. In the symbolic execution, the branch/loop conditions cannot be accurately evaluated in general. In addition, it is impossible to conduct an accurate points-to analysis over branch statements statically. Therefore, we must make some reasonable abstractions.

For if statement, we require that the two branches make consistent updating to the ownership topology, otherwise an error is raised. Specially, the unowned objects should get consistent owners. The situation that two branches make inconsistent ownership topology usually indicates a programming error.

$$\frac{\sigma b = \text{true}, \quad \langle c_i, (\sigma, h)\rangle \rightsquigarrow^* \langle \sigma_i, h_i\rangle, i = 1, 2}{\langle \text{if } b \ c_1 \text{ else } c_2, (\sigma, h)\rangle \rightsquigarrow^* \langle \sigma_1, h_1\rangle} \qquad \frac{\sigma b = \text{false}, \quad \langle c_i, (\sigma, h)\rangle \rightsquigarrow^* \langle \sigma_i, h_i\rangle, i = 1, 2}{\langle \text{if } b \ c_1 \text{ else } c_2, (\sigma, h)\rangle \rightsquigarrow^* \langle \sigma_2, h_2\rangle}.$$

The loops should also keep the ownership topology consistent. Therefore, for any objects created before the loop, its owner keeps the same in the loop body.

$$\frac{\sigma b = \mathsf{true}, \quad \langle c, (\sigma, h) \rangle \rightsquigarrow \langle \sigma', h' \rangle,}{\langle \mathtt{while}\ b\ c, (\sigma', h') \rangle \rightsquigarrow^* \langle \sigma'', h'' \rangle,} \qquad \frac{\sigma b = \mathsf{false}, \quad \langle c, (\sigma, h) \rangle \rightsquigarrow^* \langle \sigma', h' \rangle,}{\forall o \in \mathsf{dom}\ h \cdot h(o)(\mathsf{ow}) = h'(o)(\mathsf{ow})}$$

$$\frac{\forall o \in \mathsf{dom}\ h \cdot h(o)(\mathsf{ow}) = h'(o)(\mathsf{ow})}{\langle \mathtt{while}\ b\ c, (\sigma, h) \rangle \rightsquigarrow^* (\sigma'', h'')} \qquad \frac{\forall o \in \mathsf{dom}\ h \cdot h(o)(\mathsf{ow}) = h'(o)(\mathsf{ow})}{\langle \mathtt{while}\ b\ c, (\sigma, h) \rangle \rightsquigarrow (\sigma, h)}.$$

We inline the invocations for non-recursive methods. And for recursive methods, we assume that each invocation returns an object with an unknown owner, and omit other effects of the invocation.

Using these rules, we can build the ownership topology for each program point.

3.3   Ownership State Analysis

Having the ownership topology, we use data-flow analysis [9] technique to track the ownership state of the objects (valid or mutable). Generally speaking, our algorithm calculates the minimum sets of mutable objects before and after each statement which maintains the encapsulation discipline (Sect. 2.4).

The algorithm works in two stages. The first stage is a forward analysis to decide the set of objects that *may* be mutable from the method entry to each of the locations. Then we make a backward analysis to decide the set of objects that *must* be mutable from the current location to the exit point of the method. The intersection of these two sets at each location is the minimum set of mutable objects to keep the encapsulation. We describe our algorithm on the control flow graph (CFG). Because the forms of the algorithms are rather standard, we leave the algorithm in our report, but give only a brief introduction here.

The forward data-flow analysis starts from the method entry, and works step by step to track which objects may be mutable. In the analysis, we propagate forward the set of mutable objects and update the set over each statement in the CFG.

For statement s, let $s.in$ and $s.out$ denote the sets of objects that may be mutable at its entry and exit points, respectively. Then for each immediate predecessor statement t of s (i.e. $t \in prec(s)$), we formulate how the *forward-mutable* set of t propagating to s:

$$s.in := \bigcup_{t \in prec(s)} t.out.$$

For each statement s, the forward-mutable set of objects at its exit, $s.out$, is the union of the set at its entry and the corresponding generated-set of s, and then subtracts the killed-set of s, that is,

$$s.out := (s.in \cup s.gen) \setminus s.kill.$$

The generated-set and killed-set will be discussed later.

The forward-mutable set at each location is initialized with an empty set. And the aforementioned process iterates until all the sets reach a fixed point.

The backward data-flow analysis works similarly, except that the branches are processed differently. Here we calculate the *backward-mutable* sets, which are the sets of objects that *must* be mutable from each of the locations to the exit point of the method. For each statement s, the backward-mutable set at its exit, $s.out$, is the intersection of the backward-mutable sets of all the immediate successor statements of s, that is,

$$s.out := \bigcap_{t \in succ(s)} t.in.$$

While the backward-mutable set at the entry point of s is obtained as before, but reversely,

$$s.in := (s.out \cup s.gen) \setminus s.kill.$$

The backward-mutable sets are also initialized with empty sets. The process iterates until it reaches a fix point.

Table 1. Terms in the transfer function

Statement	$s.gen$	$s.kill$
$\mathtt{o.f = x}$	$\{o\} \cup ACs(o)$	$\varnothing$
$\mathtt{o.m}(\overline{arg})$ (impure)	$ACs(o, \overline{arg})$	$peer^*(o, \overline{arg}) \cup Desc(peer^*(o, \overline{arg}))$
$\mathtt{o.m}(\overline{arg})$ (pure)	$\varnothing$	$\{o, \overline{arg}\} \cup Desc(o, \overline{arg})$

We use a transfer function to calculate how the current statement affects the ownership state of the objects, as defined in Table 1. For each node in the CFG, (1) if it is an assignment to a field $\mathtt{o.f}$, then o and its immediate or transitive owners should be exposed, i.e., their ownership states should be mutable; (2) if it is an invocation of some pure method, then the receiver and arguments of the invocation should be packed, i.e., their ownership states should be valid; (3) if it is an invocation for some impure method, then the ownership states of the receiver and arguments should be peer consistent. Here $ACs(\overline{obj})$ denotes the immediate and transitive owners of object sequence $\overline{obj}$, while $Desc(\overline{obj})$ denotes the objects immediately and transitively owned by $\overline{obj}$. And finally, $peer(\overline{obj})$ denotes peers of $\overline{obj}$, and $peer^*(\overline{obj})$ denotes $\{\overline{obj}\} \cup peer(\overline{obj})$.

3.4 Annotating the Program

After obtaining the exact mutable sets, we can introduce the access permission annotations into the program using Algorithm 1.

If an object is mutable in one node but valid in one of its subsequent nodes in the CFG, then a `pack` annotation for this object should be inserted between these two nodes; on the contrary, if an object is valid in one node but mutable in one of its subsequent nodes, then the object should be unpacked. More than one objects may be packed or unpacked on one edge in the CFG. And considering the hierarchical structure of the ownership topology, if o is the owner of o', then o should be unpacked before and packed after o', whenever we need to modify some field and o, o' are on the accessing path.

Algorithm 1. Add access permission annotations into the program

---

   procedure ANNOTATION(CFG, OT)   ▷ OT is the ownership tree
      $m\_fwd \leftarrow$ FORWARD(CFG, OT)   ▷ The result of forward analysis
      $m\_back \leftarrow$ BACKWARD(CFG, OT)   ▷ The result of backward analysis
      $mut \leftarrow \{\}$ ▷ The mutable object sets
      for $node \in CFG.nodes$ **do**
          $mut[node] \leftarrow m\_fwd[node] \cap m\_back[node]$
      for $edge \in CFG.edges$ **do**
          for $m \in (mut[edge.src] - mut[edge.dest])$ **do**
              Add statement pack(m) at $edge$.
          for $m \in (mut[edge.dest] - mut[edge.src])$ **do**
              Add statement unpack(m) at $edge$.

For object o, a code segment where o is mutable is named as a *mutable range* of o, if it ensures the encapsulation principle. These segments are bounded by the unpack/pack pair. Then we have the following definition.

Definition 1 (Minimal Mutable Range). *Given an object o, its mutable range R is called a* minimal mutable range *(MMR, for short), if there is not any mutable range R', such that R' is a true subsegment of R.*

We can obtain the following theorem. Its proof is given in our report.

Theorem 1. *Given a program, for each object o in the program, Algorithm 1 gives the minimal mutable ranges of o.*

3.5   An Example

Here we use an example to illustrate our approach. The class definitions are given in Fig. 3. In the upper left part of Fig. 4, we fill the rest code of the method Demo. The lower left part of Fig. 4 shows the CFG of method Demo and the mutable sets calculation during the analysis, and the right part is the annotated code.

In the lower left part, the left most two columns of the sets are the result of forward and backward analyses, where the numbers represent the objects as presented in Fig. 3. By calculating the intersection of the sets in the two columns, we get the mutable sets for each node in the CFG, and then their corresponding variables from ownership topology analysis.

```
void Demo () {
    p1 = new Person();
    p2 = new Person();
    p1.spouse = p2;
    p2.spouse = p1;
    Query();
    Account a1 = p1.account;
    Account a2 = p2.account;
    if (a1.value > 10000) {
        a1.value -= 10000; }
    a2.value += 10000;
}
```

```
void Demo () {
    unpack(this);
    p1 = new Person();
    p2 = new Person();
    unpack(p1);
    p1.spouse = p2;
    pack(p1);
    unpack(p2);
    p2.spouse = p1;
    pack(p2,this);
    Query();
    Account a1 = p1.account;
    Account a2 = p2.account;
    if (a1.value > 10000) {
        unpack(this, p1, a1);
        a1.value -= 10000;
        pack(a1, p1);
        unpack(p2, a2);
    } else {
        unpack(this, p2, a2); }
    a2.value += 10000;
    pack(a2, p2, this);
}
```

p1=...	{1}	{1,2,4}	{1}	{this}
p2=...	{1}	{1,2,4}	{1}	{this}
p1.spouse=...	{1,2}	{1,2,4}	{1,2}	{this,p1}
p2.spouse=...	{1,2,4}	{1,4}	{1,4}	{this,p2}
Query()	{}	{}	{}	{}
a1=...	{}	{1,4,5}	{}	{}
a2=...	{}	{1,4,5}	{}	{}
a1.value=...	{1,2,3}	{1,2,3,4,5}	{1,2,3}	{this,p1,a2}
a2.value=...	{1,2,3,4,5}	{1,4,5}	{1,4,5}	{this,p2,a2 }

Fig. 4. The analysis process of method Demo

With the result of the graph, we can apply Algorithm 1 to get the complete annotated program. The insertions of unpack/pack are performed according to the transitions of the objects' ownership states. For instance, object p1 is not mutable at statement p2 = new Person() but becomes mutable at statement p1.spouse = p2 according to the result mutable sets, thus it should be unpacked between these two statements.

4   Implementation and Experiments

We have implemented our algorithms as a prototype tool based on Soot [10,11], which is a framework for analyzing and transforming Java and Android applications. Due to the functionalities of Soot, our analysis and automatic annotations are performed on Shimple, an SSA-style typed 3-address representation. To deal with a Java program, we translate it to Shimple using Soot, and then run the analysis and annotations. Since Shimple is mostly a restricted subset of Java, we believe that our implementation can be also ported to original Java without substantial difficulties.

We introduce annotations into Java analogous to Spec#. We define @Rep and @Peer qualifiers as the correspondents of the [Rep] and [Peer] in Spec#. An annotated Java program is transformed automatically to the annotated Shimple code by our tool, and the result can be optionally decompiled back to Java.

To carry the analysis, we perform the symbolic execution on the Shimple code using the rules in Sect. 3.2 to extract the ownership topology and figure out the points-to relations. The symbolic execution is an intraprocedure analysis performed method by method. Since we are not interested in the actual values of the objects, we only trace the ownership and points-to relations of variables and object fields, but not the detail of values. Thanks to the SSA-style intermediate representation, reassignments of variables are eliminated, therefore we can assume that if every variable has its value (the points-to relation) unchanged in the method, then the result of the analysis is unrelated to the real control flow. This simplifies the implementation a lot.

Shimple is a low level language where the only control structure is if ... goto statement. Our tool figures out the while and if structures from the Shimple code and then applies our symbolic execution rules.

In this phase, our implementation can report some kinds of errors: When a field assignment tries to change the owner of an object, or when a variable points to objects with different owners in different branches, an ownership topology error is reported; when an uninitialized variable is used, an initialization error is reported.

To obtain the ownership states, we perform the equations in Sect. 3.3 using the data-flow analysis framework of Soot. Since Shimple is especially designed for program analysis, this phase can be represented in a neat way, and works efficiently.

The annotating phase (Sect. 3.4) gives us few difficulties, except that some control flow analysis is required to put the unpack/pack statements at proper positions. In Algorithm 1, pack and unpack statements are inserted at the edge of the CFG, therefore we should find out the proper position in the code to insert the statement, possibly changing the target of goto statement in the Shimple code.

The accuracy of the data-flow analysis annotation algorithm depends on its input, e.g., the ownership topology and points-to relationships. Since the analysis is intraprocedural, our analysis in the first phase is not completely accurate. Especially, the precise points-to analysis is not computable. Due to the inaccuracy of the analysis, our tool may treat one object as two separate objects referred by different variables. However, this does not sacrifice the safety. Contrarily, if a tool treats two objects as the same one (which is also difficult for human beings to recognize in local context), the result might be unsafe. Our tool takes a conservative way, which will not make this error.

For the performance, the analysis of ownership topology and points-to relationships can be accomplished in linear time $O(n)$, where n is the code length. The data-flow analysis runs in $O(n^2)$ time, and it runs in nearly linear time in most practical cases since the code in a block is usually short. The annotation algorithm also runs in linear time.

We evaluate our tool with the examples used in some papers of this field [3, 4,12], and some other longer example made by ourselves. In addition, we also checked JEdit, which is a cross platform programmer's text editor written in Java. Table 2 shows the experimental results. The experiments show that, our tool can precisely analyze the ownership topology of the programs, recognize the

Table 2. Experimental results

Name	LOC	Rep/Peer annot.	Generated annot.	Time(s)
PersonMain	37	5	19	0.005
LList	82	2	20	0.005
salesTaxes	722	31	81	0.010
JEdit	30 838	121	998	18.360

ownership topology violations, and automatically annotate the unpack/pack statements at proper positions.

The tool runs fast. All the experiments are completed on machine with 4 hardware threads. Specially, we used an Intel Core i5 processor with 4 cores at 3.0 GHz. The performance of our prototype is comparable with the type inference and checking tool of Universe Type [12], but supports a more flexible encapsulation discipline while fewer manual annotations are needed. In contrast, Spec# checks the ownership properties dynamically together with other verification, that makes it very slow.

As the most interesting discovery, we notice that, it is not easy to make satisfactory annotations of the expose block (or unpack/pack block) manually. During the work, our tool gets different results for some examples taken from the literature or the web site of Spec#. Carefully checking the results, we conclude that the annotation in the original examples have some inaccuracies, while our tool gives better annotations. Our automatic annotations can mark the accurate ranges, and are also easy to read and confirm by human being. One example is given in the next section.

5   Related Work and Issues

Now we give a brief overview of some related work, and discuss some issues.

5.1   Related Work on Object Ownership

Ownership technology was proposed by Clarke *et al.* [1] and Noble *et al.* [2] in 1998 to provide a strong protection to the aliasing problems. In some early work, such as [1,13], the ownership topological properties are annotated and enforced by a type system, and people emphasize static checking for the ownership properties. However, the expressiveness of those systems is limited. They do not support down-cast, and only support encapsulation disciplines stricter than *owner-as-modifier*.

Leino and Müller [6] introduce *Dynamic Ownership* to control the parts of the heap on which the class invariants may depend. In the work, the checking of ownership properties is postponed to the runtime. Dietl and Müller [3] extend the method and present it in Spec#. They emphasize that "Before a valid object can be modified by some operations that temporarily break its invariant, it has to be exposed" (or unpacked). However, this rule is too hard to follow for programmers, because it asks them to keep in mind about the ownership topology and the states of objects very clearly to avoid making annotation errors. Following our approach, most ownership annotations can be generated automatically. The work left for programmers becomes checking the reasonability of the annotations, which might be easier to carry on. Moreover, compared with their work, our framework separates the ownership-related checking from other verifications.

Huang *et al.* [12] present a unified framework for specification, type inference and type checking of some ownership type systems. The framework allows partially-annotated programs, and is able to generate the remaining ownership annotations via a kind of type inference. Their motivation is similar to ours, that is to simplify the annotations which have to be written by programmers. But their work is based on a type system, thus can only support a more restricted encapsulation discipline. Our work is based on Dynamic Ownership, program analysis, and symbolic execution, which accepts more programs which are correct in ownership properties.

In most previous work related to ownership techniques, an expose block (or unpack/pack block) denotes a code segment where the object invariant can be broken inside, and must be re-established at its end. Our work also adopts this fundamental assumption, and defines the analysis rules based on it.

5.2   Comparison Between **expose** and **unpack/pack**

During the work, we find that the annotation accuracy of unpack/pack is higher than expose, since the closing tag of expose block contains no information. For instance, the corresponding annotated program using expose enlarges the mutable range of o1 in the following situation.

```
unpack(o1);                          expose(o1){
    Access_o1;                           Access_o1;
unpack(o2);                              expose(o2){
    Access_o1_o2;                            Access_o1_o2;
pack(o1);                                    Access_o2;
    Access_o2;                           }
pack(o2);                            }
```

On the other hand, the semantics of expose, e.g., defined in Dietl and Müller [3], is not clear in considering that object and variable are two different core concepts. As a fact, an exposed variable may refer to different objects in an execution of one expose block, as shown in the below example:

```
expose(o) {    ...    o = x;    ... }
```

This problem will be more obvious with the unstructured unpack/pack pair, where the programmers must pair correctly all the unpack(s) and pack(s). This causes difficulties to the programmer in writing accessing permissions annotations, and makes their work error-prone. This is one important reason for us to consider the automatic annotations. Our tool can generate correct annotations in all above cases.

5.3   Object Invariant Assertions

The unpack/pack annotations should cooperate with other annotations for program verification. For example, in the following program,

```
unpack(o);
o.f1 = x1;
p.m();
o.f2 = x2;
pack(o);
```

The hold of the invariants of o may be useful in proving the invariants of p. The assert mechanism in Spec# and JML [14] is still useful in such situations. We can insert assert inv(o) before p.m() to declare that the object invariants of o hold. This gives a hint to the verifier and helps to improve the verification capability. Our approach does not exclude this kind of assertions.

5.4   An Example of Manual Annotations

The manual ownership annotations are easy to be inaccurate. Here we give an example from [6] (rewritten in Spec# style):

```
class Person {
  [Peer] Person spouse;
  void Marry(Person p) {
    expose (this) {
      expose (p) {
        this.spouse = p;
        p.spouse = this;
} } } }
```

The class Person has a method Marry which sets the spouse of the current person. There are two field updates in the method that require this and p to be exposed. The manual annotations provided in the paper use nested expose blocks that cover both statements, which is correct but inaccurate.

Our tool generates the annotated Marry as follows:

```
void Marry(Person p) {
  unpack(this);   this.spouse = p;   pack(this);
  unpack(p);      p.spouse = this;   pack(p);
}
```

It uses isolated unpack/pack blocks and is therefore accurate.[2]

From this example we can see that, even the experts for ownership techniques may write out annotations with some implicit inaccuracy. We also find other similar situations in the examples provided in the literature. These facts provide further supports to the automatic annotation techniques.

---

[2] Leino and Müller [6] allows invariants to mention more objects than our work. Our work will still generate more proper annotations if we extend similar rules.

6   Conclusion and Future Work

Existing ownership approaches require heavy manual annotations, which make them difficult to master and use. Based on the Dynamic Ownership, we developed a program analysis framework which can check the ownership topology and insert the necessary accessing permission annotations automatically. We use symbolic execution techniques to analyze the ownership topology and points-to relations, and introduce a two-stage data-flow analysis to figure out the ownership state for each object. Finally, we determine all the positions where some objects need to be packed or unpacked and add the annotations automatically. Our approach greatly reduces the workload of programmers and makes the approach easier to apply, as well as provides the similar expressiveness as the Dynamic Ownership technique.

To check the viability of the theory, we have built a prototype implementation of the framework for a subset of Java using Soot. Experiments on the tool show that, our approach can precisely analyze the ownership topology of the program, and automatically annotate unpack/pack properly. The performance of the tool is comparable with static type inference and checking, but supports more flexible encapsulation discipline like Dynamic Ownership.

As future work, we consider improving the accuracy of points-to analysis by extending the intraprocedural data-flow analysis to interprocedural analysis. Ownership plays an important role in program verification, for example in specification languages JML [14,15] and Spec# [16]. Our approach can be integrated into these verification frameworks, to reduce their annotations overhead and make them easier to use.

References

1. Clarke, D.G., Potter, J.M., Noble, J.: Ownership types for flexible alias protection. In: OOPSLA 1998, pp. 48–64. ACM (1998)
2. Noble, J., Vitek, J., Potter, J.: Flexible alias protection. In: Jul, E. (ed.) ECOOP 1998–Object-Oriented Programming. LNCS, vol. 1445, pp. 158–185. Springer, Heidelberg (1998)
3. Dietl, W., Müller, P.: Object ownership in program verification. In: Clarke, D., Noble, J., Wrigstad, T. (eds.) Aliasing in Object-Oriented Programming. LNCS, vol. 7850, pp. 289–318. Springer, Heidelberg (2013)
4. Cunningham, D., Dietl, W., Drossopoulou, S., Francalanza, A., Müller, P., Summers, A.J.: Universe types for topology and encapsulation. In: de Boer, F.S., Bonsangue, M.M., Graf, S., de Roever, W.-P. (eds.) FMCO 2007. LNCS, vol. 5382, pp. 72–112. Springer, Heidelberg (2008)
5. Barnett, M., DeLine, R., Fähndrich, M., Leino, K.R.M., Schulte, W.: Verification of object-oriented programs with invariants. J. Object Technol. **3**, 27 (2004)
6. Leino, K.R.M., Müller, P.: Object invariants in dynamic contexts. In: Odersky, M. (ed.) ECOOP 2004. LNCS, vol. 3086, pp. 491–515. Springer, Heidelberg (2004)
7. Müller, P., Poetzsch-Heffter, A., Leavens, G.T.: Modular invariants for layered object structures. Sci. Comput. Program. **62**(3), 253–286 (2006)

8. Leino, K.R.M., Müller, P.: Using the Spec# language, methodology, and tools to write bug-free programs. In: Müller, P. (ed.) LASER Summer School 2007/2008. LNCS, vol. 6029, pp. 91–139. Springer, Heidelberg (2010)
9. Aho, A.V., Sethi, R., Ullman, J.D.: Compilers: Principles, Techniques, and Tools. Addison-Wesley Longman Publishing Co. Inc., Redwood City (1986)
10. Einarsson, A., Nielsen, J.D.: A survivor's guide to java program analysis with soot, BRICS, Department of Computer Science, University of Aarhus, Denmark (2008)
11. Vallée-Rai, R., Co, P., Gagnon, E., Hendren, L., Lam, P., Sundaresan, V.: Soot - a java bytecode optimization framework. In: Proceedings of the 1999 Conference of the Centre for Advanced Studies on Collaborative Research, p. 13. IBM Press (1999)
12. Huang, W., Dietl, W., Milanova, A., Ernst, M.D.: Inference and checking of object ownership. In: Noble, J. (ed.) ECOOP 2012. LNCS, vol. 7313, pp. 181–206. Springer, Heidelberg (2012)
13. Müller, P., Poetzsch-Heffter, A.: Universes: a type system for controlling representation exposure. In: Programming Languages and Fundamentals of Programming, vol. 263, Fernuniversität Hagen (1999)
14. Leavens, G.T., Baker, A.L., Ruby, C.: Preliminary design of JML: a behavioral interface specification language for java. SIGSOFT Softw. Eng. Notes **31**(3), 1–38 (2006)
15. Leavens, G.T., Poll, E., Clifton, C., Cheon, Y., Ruby, C., Cok, D., Müller, P., Kiniry, J., Chalin, P., Zimmerman, D.M., et al.: JML Reference Manual (2008)
16. Barnett, M., M. Leino, K.R., Schulte, W.: The Spec# programming system: an overview. In: Barthe, G., Burdy, L., Huisman, M., Lanet, J.-L., Muntean, T. (eds.) CASSIS 2004. LNCS, vol. 3362, pp. 49–69. Springer, Heidelberg (2005)

Certified Derivative-Based Parsing
of Regular Expressions

Raul Lopes[1], Rodrigo Ribeiro[2(✉)], and Carlos Camarão[3]

[1] DECOM, Universidade Federal de Ouro Preto (UFOP), Ouro Preto, Brazil
raulfpl@gmail.com
[2] DECSI, Universidade Federal de Ouro Preto (UFOP), João Monlevade, Brazil
rodrigo@decsi.ufop.br
[3] DCC, Universidade Federal de Minas Gerais (UFMG), Belo Horizonte, Brazil
camarao@dcc.ufmg.br

Abstract. We describe the formalization of a certified algorithm for regular expression parsing based on Brzozowski derivatives, in the dependently typed language Idris. The formalized algorithm produces a proof that an input string matches a given regular expression or a proof that no matching exists. A tool for regular expression based search in the style of the well known GNU grep has been developed with the certified algorithm, and practical experiments were conducted with this tool.

1 Introduction

Parsing is the process of analysing if a string of symbols conforms to given rules, involving also, in computer science, formally specifying the rules in a grammar and also, either the construction of data that makes evident the rules that have been used to conclude that the string of symbols can be obtained from the grammar rules, or else indication of an error, representative of the fact that the string of symbols cannot be generated from the grammar rules.

In this work, we are interested in the parsing problem for regular languages (RLs) [16], i.e. languages recognized by (non-)deterministic finite automata and equivalent formalisms. Regular expressions (REs) are an algebraic and compact way of specifying RLs that are extensively used in lexical analyser generators [19] and string search utilities [15]. Since such tools are widely used and parsing is pervasive in computing, there is a growing interest on correct parsing algorithms [8,10,11]. This interest is motivated by the recent development of dependently typed languages. Such languages are powerful enough to express algorithmic properties as types, that are automatically checked by a compiler.

The use of derivatives for regular expressions were introduced by Brzozowski [7] as an alternative method to compute a finite state machine that is equivalent to a given RE and to perform RE-based parsing. According to Owens et al. [27], "derivatives have been lost in the sands of time" until his work on functional encoding of RE derivatives have renewed interest on its use for parsing [13,25]. In this work, we provide a complete formalization of an algorithm for RE parsing using derivatives,

F. Castor and Y.D. Liu (Eds.): SBLP 2016, LNCS 9889, pp. 95–109, 2016.
DOI: 10.1007/978-3-319-45279-1_7

as presented by [27], and describe a RE based search tool that has been developed by us, using the dependently typed language Idris.

More specifically, our contributions are:

- A formalization of derivative based regular expression parsing in Idris. The certified RE parsing algorithm presented produces as a result either a proof term (parse tree) that is evidence that the input string is in the language of the input RE, or a witness that such parse tree does not exist.
- A detailed explanation of the technique used to quotient derivatives with respect to ACUI axioms[1] in an implementation by Owens et al. [27], called "smart-constructors", and its proof of correctness. We give formal proofs that smart constructors indeed preserve the language recognized by REs.

The rest of this paper is organized as follows. Section 2 presents a brief introduction to Idris. Section 3 describes the encoding of REs and its parse trees. In Sect. 4 we define derivatives and smart constructors, some of their properties and describe how to build a correct parsing algorithm from them. Section 5 comments on the usage of the certified algorithm to build a tool for RE-based search and present some experiments with it. Related work is discussed on Sect. 6. Section 7 concludes.

All the source code in this article has been formalized in Idris Version 0.11, but we do not present every detail. Proofs of some properties result in functions with a long pattern matching structure, that would distract the reader from understanding the high-level structure of the formalization. In such situations we give just proof sketches and point out where all details can be found in the source code.

The complete Idris development, instructions on how to build and use it can be found at [21].

2   An Overview of Idris

Idris [5] is a dependently typed functional programming language that focus on supporting practical programs. Idris syntax is inspired by Haskell's with some minor differences. Unlike Haskell, Idris is strict by default, but lazy evaluation is supported through code annotations. Idris allows the definition of datatypes using traditional Haskell and a GADT-style syntax. The type of types is called Type, rather than $\star$[2]. Each instance of Type has an implicit level, inferred by the compiler. Levels are cumulative — everything in $Type_n$ is also in $Type_{n+1}$.

As an example of Idris code, consider the following data type of length-indexed lists, also known as vectors.

---

[1] Associativity, Commutativity and Idempotence with Unit elements axioms for REs [7].

[2] In Haskell, types are classified using kinds [28] instead of universe levels. The kind of types is denoted by $\star$ and type operators have functional kinds: $\kappa \to \kappa'$, where κ and κ' are kinds. As an example, in Haskell, type Bool has kind $\star$ and the list type constructor has kind $\star \to \star$.

```
data Nat = Z | S Nat
data Vec : Nat -> Type -> Type where
   Nil : Vec Z a
   (::) : a -> Vec n a -> Vec (S n) a
```

Constructor `Nil` builds empty vectors. The cons-operator inserts a new element in front of a vector of n elements (of type `Vec n a`) and returns a value of type `Vec (S n) a`. The `Vec` datatype is an example of a dependent type, i.e. a type that uses a value (that denotes its length). The usefulness of dependent types can be illustrated with the definition of a safe list head function: `head` can be defined to accept only non-empty vectors, i.e. values of type `Vec (S n) a`.

```
head : Vec (S n) a -> a
head (x :: xs) = x
```

In `head`'s definition, constructor `Nil` is not used. The Idris type-checker can figure out, from `head`'s parameter type, that argument `Nil` to `head` is not type-correct.

In Idris, free variables that start with a lower-case letter are considered to be implicit arguments, i.e. arguments that can be automatically infered by the compiler. It is also possible to mark arguments as implicit by surrounding them in curly braces. In function `head`, both `n : Nat` and `a : Type` are implicit arguments; they could be explicitly annotated in `head`'s type as follows:

```
head : {a : Type} -> {n : Nat} -> Vec (S n) a -> a
```

Thanks to the propositions-as-types principle[3] we can interpret types as logical formulas and terms as proofs. An example is the representation of equality as the following Idris type:

```
data (=) : a -> b -> Type where
   Refl : x = x
```

This type is called propositional equality[4]. It defines that there is a unique evidence for equality, constructor `Refl` (for reflexivity), that asserts that the only value equal to x is itself. Given a type P, type `Dec P` is used to build proofs that P is a decidable proposition, i.e. that either P or not P holds. The decidable proposition type is defined as:

```
data Dec : Type -> Type where
   Yes : p -> Dec p
   No : Not p -> Dec p
```

Constructor `Yes` stores a proof that property P holds and `No` an evidence that such proof is impossible (`Not` is an implication of falsity). Some functions used in our formalization use this type.

---

[3] Also known as Curry-Howard "isomorphism" [30].

[4] Readers who know type theory probably have noticed that this equality encoding corresponds to the so-called heterogeneous equality [23], which is used in the Idris Prelude. Detailed discussions about equality in type theory can be found in [32].

Dependently typed pattern matching is built by using the so-called `with` construct, that allows for matching intermediate values [24]. If the matched value has a dependent type, then its result can affect the form of other values. For example, consider the following code that defines a type for natural number parity. If the natural number is even, it can be represented as the sum of two equal natural numbers; if it is odd, it is equal to one plus the sum of two equal values. Pattern matching on a value of `Parity` n allows to discover if $n = j + j$ or $n = S(k + k)$, for some j and k in each branch of `with`. Note that the value of n is specialized accordingly, using information "learned" by the type-checker.

```
data Parity : Nat -> Type where
   Even : Parity (n + n)
   Odd  : Parity (S (n + n))

parity : (n : Nat) -> Parity n
parity = -- definition omitted

natToBin : Nat -> List Bool
natToBin Z = Nil
natToBin k with (parity k)
   natToBin (j + j)     | Even = False :: natToBin j
   natToBin (S (j + j)) | Odd  = True  :: natToBin j
```

A detailed discussion about the Idris language is out of the scope of this paper. A tutorial on Idris is available [17].

3   Regular Expressions

Regular expressions are defined with respect to a given alphabet. Formally, RE syntax follows the following context-free grammar

$$e ::= \emptyset \mid \epsilon \mid a \mid ee \mid e + e \mid e^\star$$

where a is a symbol from the underlying alphabet. In our formalization, we describe symbols of an alphabet as a natural number in Peano notation (type `Nat`), i.e. the symbol's numeric code. The reason for this design choice is due to the way that Idris deals with propositional equality for primitive types, like `Char`. Equalities of values of these types only reduce on concrete primitive values; this causes computation of proofs to stop under variables whose type is a primitive one. Thus, we decide to use the inductive type `Nat` to represent the codes of alphabet symbols, since computation of its equality proofs behaves as expected in other languages, like e.g. Agda [26].

Datatype `RegExp`, defined below, encodes RE syntax:

```
data RegExp : Type where
  Zero : RegExp
  Eps  : RegExp
```

```
Chr  : Nat -> RegExp
Cat  : RegExp -> RegExp -> RegExp
Alt  : RegExp -> RegExp -> RegExp
Star : RegExp -> RegExp
```

Constructors Zero and Eps denote respectively the empty language ($\emptyset$) and empty string (ϵ). Alphabet symbols are constructed using Chr constructor. Bigger REs are built using concatenation (Cat), union (Alt) and Kleene star (Star).

Using the datatype for RE syntax, we can define a relation for RL membership. Such relation can be understood as a parse tree (or a proof term) that a string, represented by a list of Nat values, belongs to the language of a given RE. Datatype InRegExp defines RE semantics inductively.

```
data InRegExp : List Nat -> RegExp -> Type where
  InEps : InRegExp [] Eps
  InChr : InRegExp [ a ] (Chr a)
  InCat : InRegExp xs l ->
          InRegExp ys r ->
          zs = xs ++ ys ->
          InRegExp zs (Cat l r)
  InAltL : InRegExp xs l ->
           InRegExp xs (Alt l r)
  InAltR : InRegExp xs r ->
           InRegExp xs (Alt l r)
  InStar : InRegExp xs (Alt Eps (Cat e (Star e))) ->
           InRegExp xs (Star e)
```

Each constructor of InRegExp datatype specifies how to build a parse tree for some string and RE. Constructor InEps states that the empty string (denoted by the empty list []) is in the language of RE Eps. Parse tree for single characters are built with InChr a, which says that the singleton string [a] is in RL for Chr a. Given parse trees for REs l and r; InRegExp xs l and InRegExp ys r, we can use constructor InCat to build a parse tree for the concatenation of these REs. Constructor InAltL (InAltR) creates a parse tree for Alt l r from a parse tree from l(r). Parse trees for Kleene star are built using the following well known equivalence of REs: $e^\star = \epsilon + e\,e^\star$.

Several inversion lemmas about RE parsing relation are necessary to formalize derivative based parsing. They consist of pattern-matching on proofs of InRegExp and are omitted for brevity.

4   Derivatives, Smart Constructors and Parsing

4.1   Preliminaries

Formally, the derivative of a formal language $L \subseteq \Sigma^\star$ with respect to a symbol $a \in \Sigma$ is the language formed by suffixes of L words without the prefix a.

An algorithm for computing the derivative of a language represented as a RE as another RE is due to Brzozowski [7] and it relies on a function (called ν) that determines if some RE accepts or not the empty string:

$$\nu(\emptyset) = \emptyset$$
$$\nu(\epsilon) = \epsilon$$
$$\nu(a) = \emptyset$$
$$\nu(e\,e') = \begin{cases} \epsilon & \text{if } \nu(e) = \nu(e') = \epsilon \\ \emptyset & \text{otherwise} \end{cases}$$
$$\nu(e + e') = \begin{cases} \epsilon & \text{if } \nu(e) = \epsilon \text{ or } \nu(e') = \epsilon \\ \emptyset & \text{otherwise} \end{cases}$$
$$\nu(e^\star) = \epsilon$$

Decidability of $\nu(e)$ is proved by function hasEmptyDec, which is defined by induction over the structure of the input RE e and returns a proof that the empty string is accepted or not, using Idris type of decidable propositions, Dec P.

```
hasEmptyDec : (e : RegExp) -> Dec (InRegExp [] e)
hasEmptyDec Zero = No (void . inZeroInv)
hasEmptyDec Eps = Yes InEps
hasEmptyDec (Chr c) = No inChrNil
hasEmptyDec (Cat e e') with (hasEmptyDec e)
  hasEmptyDec (Cat e e') | (Yes prf) with (hasEmptyDec e')
    hasEmptyDec (Cat e e') | (Yes prf) | (Yes prf')
          = Yes (InCat prf prf' Refl)
    hasEmptyDec (Cat e e') | (Yes prf) | (No contra)
          = No (contra . snd . inCatNil)
  hasEmptyDec (Cat e e') | (No contra)
          = No (contra . fst . inCatNil)
hasEmptyDec (Alt e e') with (hasEmptyDec e)
  hasEmptyDec (Alt e e') | (Yes prf)
          = Yes (InAltL prf)
  hasEmptyDec (Alt e e') | (No contra) with (hasEmptyDec e')
    hasEmptyDec (Alt e e') | (No contra) | (Yes prf)
          = Yes (InAltR prf)
    hasEmptyDec (Alt e e') | (No contra) | (No f)
          = No (void . either contra f . inAltNil)
hasEmptyDec (Star e)
          = Yes (InStar (InAltL InEps))
```

The hasEmptyDec definition uses several inversion lemmas about RE semantics. Lemma inZeroInv states that no word is in the language denoted by RE Zero and inChrNil states that the empty string (represented by an empty list) isn't in language denoted by RE Chr c, for some c : Nat. Inversion lemmas for concatenation and choice are similar.

4.2   Smart Constructors

Following Owens et al. [27], we use smart constructors to identify equivalent REs modulo identity and nullable elements, ϵ and $\emptyset$, respectively. RE equivalence is denoted by $e \approx e'$ and it's defined as usual [16]. The equivalence axioms maintained by smart constructors are:

– For union:
$$(1)\, e + \emptyset \approx e \quad (2)\, \emptyset + e \approx e$$

– For concatenation:
$$(1)\, e\,\emptyset \approx \emptyset \quad (2)\, e\,\epsilon \approx e$$
$$(3)\, \emptyset\, e \approx \emptyset \quad (4)\, \epsilon\, e \approx e$$

– For Kleene star:
$$(1)\, \emptyset^{\star} \approx \epsilon \quad (2)\, \epsilon^{\star} \approx \epsilon$$

These axioms are kept as invariants using functions that preserve them while building REs. For union, we just need to worry when one parameter denotes the empty language RE (Zero):

```
(.|.) : RegExp -> RegExp -> RegExp
Zero .|. e = e
e .|. Zero = e
e .|. e'   = Alt e e'
```

In concatenation, we need to deal with the possibility of parameters being the empty RE or the empty string RE. If one is the empty language (Zero) the result is also empty language. Since empty string RE is identity for concatenation, we return, as a result, the other parameter.

```
(.@.) : RegExp -> RegExp -> RegExp
Zero .@. e = Zero
Eps .@. e  = e
e .@. Zero = Zero
e .@. Eps  = e
e .@. e'   = Cat e e'
```

For Kleene star both Zero and Eps are replaced by Eps.

```
star : RegExp -> RegExp
star Zero = Eps
star Eps = Eps
star e = Star e
```

Since all smart constructors produce equivalent REs, they preserve the parsing relation. This property is stated as a soundness and completeness lemma, stated below, of each smart constructor with respect to InRegExp proofs.

Lemma 1 (Soundness of union). *For all REs e, e' and all strings xs, if InRegExp xs (e .|. e') holds then InRegExp xs (Alt e e') also holds.*

Proof. By case analysis on the structure of e and e'. The only interesting cases are when one of the expressions is `Zero`. If e = `Zero`, then `Zero .|. e' = e'` and the desired result follows. The same reasoning applies for e' = `Zero`.   □

Lemma 2 (Completeness of union). *For all REs e, e' and all strings xs, if InRegExp xs (Alt e e') holds then InRegExp xs (e .|. e') also holds.*

Proof. By case analysis on the structure of e, e'. The only interesting cases are when one of the REs is `Zero`. If e = `Zero`, we need to analyse the structure of `InRegExp xs (Alt e e')`. The result follows directly or by contradiction using `InRegExp xs Zero`. The same reasoning applies when e' = `Zero`.   □

Lemma 3 (Soundness of concatenation). *For all REs e, e' and all strings xs, if InRegExp xs (e .@. e') holds then InRegExp xs (Cat e e') also holds.*

Proof. By case analysis on the structure of e, e'. The interesting cases are when e or e' are equal to `Eps` or `Zero`. When some of the REs are equal to `Zero`, the result follows by contradiction. If one of the REs are equal to `Eps` the desired result is immediate, from the proof term `InRegExp xs (e .@.e')`, using list concatenation properties.   □

Lemma 4 (Completeness of concatenation). *For all REs e, e' and all strings xs, if InRegExp xs (Cat e e') holds then InRegExp xs (e .@. e') also holds.*

Proof. By case analysis on the structure of e, e'. The interesting cases are when e or e' are equal to `Eps` or `Zero`. When some of the REs are equal to `Zero`, the result follows by contradiction. If one of the REs are equal to `Eps` the desired result is immediate, using the following fact:

`InRegExp xs' e -> xs = xs' ++ [] -> InRegExp xs e`

which asserts that if a strings `xs'` is in e's language, then so is `xs' ++ []`.   □

Lemma 5 (Soundness of Kleene star). *For all REs e and string xs, if InRegExp xs (star e) then InRegExp xs (Star e).*

Proof. Straightforward case analysis on e's structure.   □

Lemma 6 (Completeness of Klenne star). *For all REs e and all strings xs, if InRegExpa xs (Star e) holds then InRegExp xs (star e) also holds.*

Proof. Straightforward case analysis on e's structure.   □

All definitions of smart constructors and their properties are contained in `SmartCons.idr`, in the project's on-line repository [21].

4.3 Derivatives and its Properties

The derivative of a RE with respect to a symbol a, denoted by $\partial_a(e)$, is defined by recursion on e's structure as follows:

$$
\begin{aligned}
\partial_a(\emptyset) &= \emptyset \\
\partial_a(\epsilon) &= \emptyset \\
\partial_a(b) &= \begin{cases} \epsilon & \text{if } b = a \\ \emptyset & \text{otherwise} \end{cases} \\
\partial_a(e\,e') &= \partial_a(e)\,e' + \nu(e)\,\partial_a(e') \\
\partial_a(e + e') &= \partial_a(e) + \partial_a(e') \\
\partial_a(e^*) &= \partial_a(e)\,e^*
\end{aligned}
$$

This function has an immediate translation to Idris. Notice that the derivative function uses smart constructors to quotient result REs with respect to the equivalence axioms presented in Sect. 4.2 and RE emptiness test. In the symbol case (constructor Chr), function decEq is used, which produces an evidence for equality of two Nat values.

```
deriv : (e : RegExp) -> Nat -> RegExp
deriv Zero c = Zero
deriv Eps c = Zero
deriv (Chr c') c with (decEq c' c)
  deriv (Chr c) c  | Yes Refl = Eps
  deriv (Chr c') c | No nprf = Zero
deriv (Alt l r) c = (deriv l c) .|. (deriv r c)
deriv (Star e) c = (deriv e c) .@. (Star e)
deriv (Cat l r) c with (hasEmptyDec l)
  deriv (Cat l r) c | Yes prf = ((deriv l c) .@. r) .|. (deriv r c)
  deriv (Cat l r) c | No nprf = (deriv l c) .@. r
```

From this definition we prove the following important properties of derivative operation. Soundness of deriv ensures that if a string xs is in deriv e x's language, then InRegExp (x ::= xs) e holds. Completeness ensures that the other direction of implication holds.

Theorem 1 (Soundness of derivative operation). *For all RE e, string xs and symbol x, if InRegExp xs (deriv x e) then InRegExp (x ::= xs) e.*

Proof. By induction on the structure of e, using the soundness lemmas for smart constructors and decidability of the emptiness test. □

Theorem 2 (Completeness of derivative operation). *For all RE e, string xs and symbol x, if InRegExp (x ::= xs) e then InRegExp xs (deriv e x).*

Proof. By induction on the structure of e using the completeness lemmas for smart constructors and decidability of the emptiness test. □

Definitions and properties of derivatives are given in Search.idr, in the project's on-line repository [21].

4.4 Parsing

RE parsing with derivatives uses the following definition that extends $\partial_a(e)$ from a single symbol to a whole word by induction on the word structure:

$$\partial_\epsilon^\star(e) \ = e$$
$$\partial_{a\,w}^\star(e) = \partial_w^\star(\partial_a(e))$$

We say that a string w is in e's language if $\partial_w^\star(e)$ is nullable, that is, if $\nu(\partial_w^\star(e)) = \epsilon$.

The Idris encoding of this function involves testing if the RE used for parsing is a prefix or a substring of the parsed string. Prefixes of a string are represented by datatype `Prefix e xs`, which expresses that a string parsed by RE `e` is a prefix of `xs`.

```
data Prefix : (e : RegExp) -> (xs : List Nat) -> Type where
   MkPrefix : (ys : List Nat)       ->
              (zs : List Nat)       ->
              (eq : xs = ys ++ zs) ->
              (re : InRegExp ys e) ->
              Prefix e xs
```

In order to state that some string `ys` is a prefix of `xs`, we need to build a proof that `ys` matches `e` and that it is indeed a prefix of `xs`, by providing an evidence that, for some `zs`, we have that `xs = ys ++ zs`.

A function for building prefixes just recurse over the structure of the input string, using derivatives. Definition of decidability of `Prefix e xs` is an immediate consequence of Theorem 1. Definitions and properties about prefixes can be found in file `Prefix.idr` in the source-code [21].

Substrings are represented by the type

```
data Substring : (e : RegExp) -> (xs : List Nat) -> Type where
   MkSubstring : (ys : List Nat)            ->
                 (ts : List Nat)            ->
                 (zs : List Nat)            ->
                 (eq : xs = ys ++ ts ++ zs) ->
                 (re : InRegExp ts e)       ->
                 Substring e xs
```

that specifies that a string `ts` is a substring of `xs` if it is parsed by `e` and if there exist strings `ys` and `zs` such that `xs = ys ++ ts ++ zs`. Deciding if a RE parses a substring of some input is straightforward by recursion over the input string using prefix decidability. Definitions about substrings can be found in `Substring.idr` [21].

5 Implementation Details and Experiments

From the algorithm formalized we built a tool for RE parsing in the style of GNU Grep [15]. We have used Lightyear [20], Idris parser combinator library, for parsing RE syntax and to deal with file I/O; we have used Idris effects library [6], which relies on dependent types to provide safe side-effect usage.

In order to validade our tool (named iGrep — for Idris Grep), we compare its performance with GNU Grep [15] (grep), Google regular expression library [29] (re2) and with Haskell RE parsing algorithms described in [13] (haskell-regexp). We run RE parsing experiments on a machine with a Intel Core I7 1.7 GHz, 8 GB RAM running Mac OS X 10.11.4; the results were collected and the median of several test runs was computed.

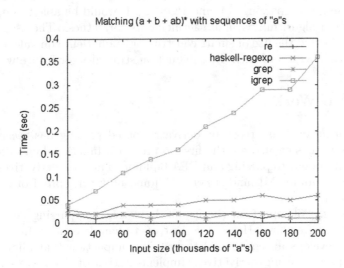

Fig. 1. Results of experiment 1.

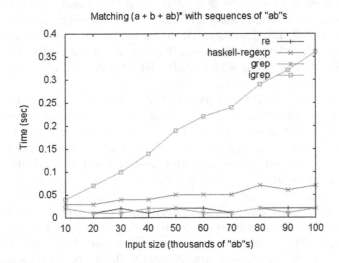

Fig. 2. Results of experiment 2.

We use the same experiments as [31] using files formed by thousands of occurrences of symbol a were parsed, using the RE $(a + b + ab)^*$; in the second, files with thousands of occurrences of ab were parsed using the same RE. Results are presented in Figs. 1 and 2, respectively.

Our tool behaves poorly when compared with all other options considered. Possible causes for this inefficiency: (1) We represent alphabet symbols as natural numbers in Peano notation which has a costly equality test (linear on the term size); (2) our algorithm relies on the Brzozowski definition of RE parsing, which needs to quotient resulting REs. We believe that the use of disambiguation strategies like greedy parsing [14] and POSIX [31] would be able to improve the efficiency of our algorithm without sacrificing its correctness. The usage of these strategies can avoid the use of smart constructor to quotient equivalent REs. We leave the formalization of such disambiguation strategies for future work.

6   Related Work

Parsing with derivatives: recently, derivative-based parsing has received a lot of attention. Owens et al. were the first to present a functional encoding of RE derivatives and use it to parsing and DFA building. They use derivatives to build scanner generators for ML and Scheme [27] and no formal proof of correctness were presented.

Might et al. [25] report on the use of derivatives for parsing not only RLs but also context-free ones. He uses derivatives to handle context-free grammars (CFG) and develops an equational theory for compaction that allows for efficient CFG parsing using derivatives. Implementation of derivatives for CFGs are described by using the Racket programming language [9]. However, Might et al. do not present formal proofs related to the use of derivatives for CFGs.

Fischer et al. describes an algorithm for RE-based parsing based on weighted automata in Haskell [13]. The paper describes the design evolution of such algorithm as a dialog between three persons. Their implementation has a competitive performance when compared with Google's RE library [29]. This work also does not consider formal proofs of RE parsing.

An algorithm for POSIX RE parsing is described in [31]. The main idea of the article is to adapt derivative parsing to construct parse trees incrementally to solve both matching and submatching for REs. In order to improve the efficiency of the proposed algorithm, Sulzmann et al. use a bit encoded representation of RE parse trees. Textual proofs of correctness of the proposed algorithm are presented in an appendix.

Certified parsing algorithms: certified algorithms for parsing also received attention recently. Firsov et al. describe a certified algorithm for RE parsing by converting an input RE to an equivalent non-deterministic finite automata (NFA) represented as a boolean matrix [10]. A matrix library based on some "block" operations [22] is developed and used Agda formalization of NFA-based parsing in Agda [26]. Compared to our work, a NFA-based formalization requires a lot more infrastructure (such as a Matrix library). No experiments with the certified algorithm were reported.

Firsov describes an Agda formalization of a parsing algorithm that deals with any CFG (CYK algorithm) [12]. Bernardy et al. describe a formalization of another CFG parsing algorithm in Agda [3]: Valiant's algorithm [33], which reduces CFG parsing to boolean matrix multiplication. In both works, no experiment with formalized parsing algorithms were reported.

A certified LR(1) CFG validator is described in [18]. The formalized checking procedure verifies if CFG and a automaton match. They proved soundness and completeness of the validator in Coq proof assistant [4]. Termination of LR(1) automaton interpreter is ensured by imposing a natural number bound.

Formalization of a parser combinator library was the subject of Danielsson's work [8]. He built a library of parser combinators using coinduction and provide correctness proofs of such combinators.

Almeida et al. [1] describes a Coq formalization of partial derivatives and its equivalence with automata. Partial derivatives were introduced by Antimirov [2] as an alternative to Brzozowski derivatives, since it avoids quotient resulting REs with respect to ACUI axioms. Almeida et al. motivation is to use such formalization as a basis for a decision procedure for RE equivalence.

7 Conclusion

We have given a complete formalization of a derivative-based parsing for REs in Idris. To the best of our knowledge, this is the first work that presents a complete certification and that uses the certified program to build a tool for RE-based search.

The developed formalization has 563 lines of code, organized in seven modules. We have proven 23 theorems and lemmas to complete the development. Most of them are immediate pattern matching functions over inductive datatypes and were omitted from this text for brevity.

As future work, we intend to work on the development of a certified program of greedy and POSIX RE parsing using Brzozowski derivatives [14,31] and investigate on ways to obtain a formalized but simple and efficient RE parsing tool.

Acknowledgements. The first author thanks Fundação de Amparo a Pesquisa de Minas Gerais (FAPEMIG) for financial support.

References

1. Almeida, J.B., Moreira, N., Pereira, D., de Sousa, S.M.: Partial derivative automata formalized in Coq. In: Domaratzki, M., Salomaa, K. (eds.) CIAA 2010. LNCS, vol. 6482, pp. 59–68. Springer, Heidelberg (2011)
2. Antimirov, V.: Partial derivatives of regular expressions and finite automaton constructions. Theor. Comput. Sci. **155**(2), 291–319 (1996)

3. Bernardy, J.-P., Jansson, P.: Certified context-free parsing: a formalisation of valiant's algorithm in agda. CoRR, abs/1601.07724 (2016)
4. Bertot, Y., Castran, P.: Interactive Theorem Proving and Program Development: Coq'Art The Calculus of Inductive Constructions, 1st edn. Springer Publishing Company, Incorporated, Heidelberg (2010)
5. Brady, E.: Idris, a general-purpose dependently typed programming language: design and implementation. J. Funct. Program. **23**, 552–593 (2013)
6. Brady, E.: Programming and reasoning with algebraic effects and dependent types. In: Proceedings of the 18th ACM SIGPLAN International Conference on Functional Programming, ICFP 2013, pp. 133–144. ACM, New York (2013)
7. Brzozowski, J.A.: Derivatives of regular expressions. J. ACM **11**(4), 481–494 (1964)
8. Danielsson, N.A.: Total parser combinators. SIGPLAN Not. **45**(9), 285–296 (2010)
9. Felleisen, M.D., Barski, C., Van Horn, D.: Realm of Racket: Learn to Program, One Game at a Time! Eight Students of Northeastern University, San Francisco (2013)
10. Firsov, D., Uustalu, T.: Certified parsing of regular languages. In: Gonthier, G., Norrish, M. (eds.) CPP 2013. LNCS, vol. 8307, pp. 98–113. Springer, Heidelberg (2013)
11. Firsov, D., Uustalu, T.: Certified CYK parsing of context-free languages. J. Log. Algebr. Meth. Program. **83**(5–6), 459–468 (2014)
12. Firsov, D., Uustalu, T.: Certified CYK parsing of context-free languages. J. Log. Algebr. Methods Program. **83**(5–6), 459–468 (2014). The 24th Nordic Workshop on Programming Theory (NWPT 2012)
13. Fischer, S., Huch, F., Wilke, T.: A play on regular expressions: Functional pearl. In: Proceedings of the 15th ACM SIGPLAN International Conference on Functional Programming, ICFP 2010, pp. 357–368. ACM, New York (2010)
14. Frisch, A., Cardelli, L.: Greedy regular expression matching. In: Díaz, J., Karhumäki, J., Lepistö, A., Sannella, D. (eds.) ICALP 2004. LNCS, vol. 3142, pp. 618–629. Springer, Heidelberg (2004)
15. GNU Grep home page. https://www.gnu.org/software/grep/
16. Hopcroft, J.E., Motwani, R., Rotwani, U., Ullman, J.D.: Introduction to Automata Theory Languages and Computability, 2nd edn. Addison-Wesley Longman Publishing Co., Inc., Boston (2000)
17. The Idris Tutorial. http://docs.idris-lang.org/en/latest/tutorial/
18. Jourdan, J.-H., Pottier, F., Leroy, X.: Validating $LR(1)$ parsers. In: Seidl, H. (ed.) Programming Languages and Systems. LNCS, vol. 7211, pp. 397–416. Springer, Heidelberg (2012)
19. Lesk, M.E., Schmidt, E.: Lex: a lexical analyzer generator. In: Unix, vol. ii. pp. 375–387. W. B. Saunders Company, Philadelphia, PA, USA (1990)
20. The Lightyear Idris Parsing Combinator Library. https://github.com/ziman/lightyear/
21. Lopes, R., Ribeiro, R., Camarão, C.: Certified derivative based parsing of regular expressions — on-linerepository (2016). https://github.com/raulfpl/idrisregexp
22. Macedo, H.D., Oliveira, J.N.: Typing linear algebra: a biproduct-oriented approach. CoRR, abs/1312.4818 (2013)
23. McBride, C.: Dependently Typed Functional Programs and their Proofs. Ph.D. thesis, Department of Informatics, University of Edinburgh (1999)
24. McBride, C., McKinna, J.: The view from the left. J. Funct. Program. **14**(1), 69–111 (2004)
25. Might, M., Darais, D., Spiewak, D.: Parsing with derivatives: a functional pearl. SIGPLAN Not. **46**(9), 189–195 (2011)

26. Norell, U.: Dependently typed programming in agda. In: Proceedings of the 4th International Workshop on Types in Language Design and Implementation, TLDI 2009, pp. 1–2. ACM, New York (2009)
27. Owens, S., Reppy, J., Turon, A.: Regular-expression derivatives re-examined. J. Funct. Program. **19**(2), 173–190 (2009)
28. Pierce, B.C.: Types and Programming Languages, 1st edn. The MIT Press, Cambridge (2002)
29. Google Regular Expression Library - re2. https://github.com/google/re2
30. Sørensen, M.H., Urzyczyn, P.: Lectures on the Curry-Howard Isomorphism. Studies in Logic and the Foundations of Mathematics, vol. 149. Elsevier Science Inc., New York (2006)
31. Sulzmann, M., Lu, K.Z.M.: POSIX regular expression parsing with derivatives. In: Codish, M., Sumii, E. (eds.) FLOPS 2014. LNCS, vol. 8475, pp. 203–220. Springer, Heidelberg (2014)
32. The Univalent Foundatiosn Program. Homotopy Type Theory: Univalent Foundations of Mathematics (2013). http://homotopytypetheory.org/book/
33. Valiant, L.G.: General context-free recognition in less than cubic time. J. Comput. Syst. Sci. **10**(2), 308–315 (1975)

Concurrent Hash Tables for Haskell

Rodrigo Medeiros Duarte[✉], André Rauber Du Bois, Mauricio L. Pilla,
Gerson G.H. Cavalheiro, and Renata H.S. Reiser

PPGC - Programa de Pós Graduação em Computação,
CDTEC - Centro de Desenvolvimento Tecnológico,
UFPel - Universidade Federal de Pelotas, Pelotas, Brazil
{rmduarte,dubois,pilla,gerson,reiser}@inf.ufpel.edu.br

Abstract. This paper presents seven hash table Haskell implementations, ranging from low-level synchronization mechanisms to high-level ones such as transactional memories. The result of the comparison between the algorithms showed that the implementation using the STM Haskell transactional memory library and fine-grain synchronization presented the best performance and good scalability.

1 Introduction

Hash table data structures are inherently concurrent, as data access may be independent for most operations. However, implementing hash tables with parallel access and good performance is not a trivial task [4]. Issues such as conflicts and increasing table capacity are difficult to implement and error prone. For example, the simplest implementation with a global lock for the entire table does not scale, as every access is done sequentially, while fine-grain locking, e.g., a lock for each entry, allows more concurrency at the cost of complexity specially while increasing the table.

Haskell is a high-level purely functional language that provides several synchronization abstractions for concurrent programming, e.g., synchronization variables (MVar [6]), transactional memory [3] and low-level instructions for synchronization, i.e., CAS (*compare and swap*). Even with all these synchronization methods, the lack of concurrent hash tables for Haskell is still a problem [9].

This work presents seven concurrent Haskell hash table implementations using different synchronization methods and four distinct hash algorithms. A performance comparison is also presented and results show that the implementation using the STM Haskell transactional memory library and fine-grain synchronization has the best performance.

This paper is organized as follows. Section 2 presents the different synchronization methods available in Haskell that were used. Section 3 introduces the concurrent hash table algorithms studied in this work and their implementations. Section 4 discusses results. Related work is presented in Sect. 5. Finally, final remarks and future work are given in Sect. 6.

ⓒ Springer International Publishing Switzerland 2016
F. Castor and Y.D. Liu (Eds.): SBLP 2016, LNCS 9889, pp. 110–124, 2016.
DOI: 10.1007/978-3-319-45279-1_8

2   Haskell Synchronization Methods

The Haskell functional programming language provides many abstractions for synchronizing threads. The models used in this work are MVar (Concurrent Haskell) [11,12], IORef + atomicModifyIORef [1,11] and STM Haskell [3]. The mechanisms are briefly described below.

2.1   Concurrent Haskell: MVars

An MVar [12] is a synchronization variable that may assume one of two states: empty or full. MVars are created with an initial value by using the newMVar :: a -> IO(MVar a) function. Two other functions manipulate MVars: takeMVar :: MVar a -> IO a and putMVar :: MVar a -> a -> IO(). The first returns a value if its argument MVar is not empty, and blocks otherwise. The latter works in the opposite way: it blocks if the MVar is not empty, or writes on it if empty [6]. MVars may be used to implement a semantics similar to critical sections protected by mutexes but, as it may contain any Haskell value, the abstraction can be used also in more interesting ways [11,12].

2.2   Low-Level Synchronization: IORef + atomicModifyIORef

This method can be used to implement non-blocking/lock free algorithms. IORefs [11] are references to memory positions providing the following operations: newIORef :: a -> IORef a (creating a new IORef), readIORef (reading an IORef), and writeIORef (writing to an IORef). These operations by themselves do not guarantee safety in the concurrent access to memory references, however, Haskell provides an atomicModifyIORefCAS which uses atomic instructions to modify a reference [1]. Hence, it provides a low-level synchronization mechanism such as using a CAS (Compare-and-Swap) instruction.

2.3   Transactional Memory: STM Haskell

STM Haskell [3] is a concurrency model for Haskell based on *Software Transactional Memories* (STM) [2]. It provides the abstraction of *transactional variables*, or TVars: memory locations that can only be accessed inside transactions. TVars can be modified using two primitives:

```
readTVar  :: TVar a -> STM a
writeTVar :: TVar a -> a -> STM a
```

The readTVar primitive takes a TVar as argument and returns an STM action that, when executed, returns the current value stored in the TVar. The writeTVar primitive is used to write a new value into a TVar. In STM Haskell,

STM actions can be composed together using the same do notation used to compose IO actions and other monads. The only way to execute a transaction is by using the `atomically` primitive:

```
atomically :: STM a -> IO a
```

`atomically` takes a transaction and executes it atomically with respect to other concurrent transactions.

3   Hash Algorithms for Concurrency

The algorithms used in this work provide three basic operations to access a hash table: *(i)* insert, *(ii)* contains, and *(iii)* delete. All algorithms use closed addressing, i.e., each table position may contain a set of items, usually implemented using a linked list. Increasing table capacity depends on the number of insertions. If they reach a limit, table capacity is doubled [5]. This is the most complex operation, and each algorithm treats it in a different way. To simplify explanation, we describe here the implementation of Hash tables of integers but we also provide a polymorphic version of the library (see Sect. 6).

3.1   Global Lock Hash

The global lock algorithm uses a single lock to protect a hash table. Each function first acquires the lock, executes its operation, and then releases the lock. Its design is simple and makes it easy to increase table capacity, at the cost of scalability: all operations are serialized. In this work we used an `MVar` as a global lock for the table:

```
type Buckets = Array Int [Int]
data HTable = TH
{
    buckets :: MVar Buckets,
    n_elements :: IORef Int,
    len_tab :: IORef Int
}
```

When a table limit is reached, `buckets` is doubled and stored into the `MVar`. The other table attributes such as number of elements and length may be stored in `IORefs`, as they are modified only by threads which acquired the `buckets` MVar.

We also implemented an alternative version of this algorithm using STM Haskell, in which a single `TVar` is used to hold the array of buckets:

```
data HTable = TH
{
    buckets :: TVar Buckets,
    n_elements :: TVar Int,
    len_tab :: TVar Int
}
```

3.2   Hash Table Using Lock Striping

This technique uses two arrays, one for buckets and another for locks. When the hash table is initialized, both arrays have the same number of elements. However, when the table's capacity is increased, only the array of buckets is doubled. Hence, each lock becomes responsible for twice as many table entries each time the table's capacity is doubled. Increasing table size is not a frequent operation, and there are two main reasons to avoid increasing the array of locks [4]:

- Associating a lock with every bucket can consume too much space, especially when tables are large and contention is low;
- Increasing the array of buckets is simple, but increasing the array of locks while in use by different threads is complicated, as discussed in the next Section.

```
type Buckets = Array Int (IORef [Int])
type Locks = Array Int (MVar Bool)
data HTable = TH
{
   buckets :: IORef Buckets,
   lock :: Locks,
   n_elemens :: IORef Int,
   len_tab :: IORef Int,
   len_lock :: Int
}
```

In this implementation, locks are represented by MVars containing Booleans. As the need for increasing a table's capacity is detected, all locks in the array of locks are acquired in ascending order to avoid deadlocks. When all locks have been acquired, the array of buckets is increased and the locks are released.

As the length attribute of a table is only modified while all locks are being held, it can be stored in an IORef. The attribute containing the number of elements is modified by a CAS operation. The length of the array of locks does not need to be protected, as it is initialized and never changed.

3.3   Fine-Grain Lock Hash Table

This algorithm also uses an array of locks and another one for buckets. However, it doubles both arrays when the table's capacity is increased. Therefore, a single array of MVars is used for both locks and buckets. A flag is used to make threads aware that the table is being increased. Implementation is as follows:

```
type Buckets = Array Int (MVar [Int])
type Locks = IORef Buckets

data ThId = ThId ThreadId | Null

data HTable = TH
{
   buckets      :: Locks,
   n_elements   :: IORef Int,
   len_tab      :: IORef Int,
   onGrow       :: IORef ThId
}
```

As the number of locks may be increased, it must be stored in a reference (IORef). Modifications of this attribute are controlled by the onGrow flag. onGrow stores the id of the thread that will increase table capacity ensuring exclusive access to the table. The function resize is as follows:

```
resize :: IORef Buckets -> Int -> IORef Int -> IORef ThId ->
   ThreadId ->IO Bool
resize buckets old_lenTab len_tab flag tId = do
   t <- readIORef flag
   if (t /= Null)
      then return False
      else do
         old_array <- readIORef buckets
         ok <- atomCAS flag t (ThId tId)
         if ok then do
            lenTab <- readIORef len_tab
            if (old_tam == lenTab)
               then do
                  (...)  -- grow operation
                  writeIORef flag Null
                  return True
               else do
                  writeIORef flag Null
                  return False
         else return False
```

Once onGrow is set, resize will acquire the MVars of all buckets, create a new array of MVars with double the size, and copy old buckets to the new array. Afterwards, the new array is stored in the buckets' IORef and the onGrow flag is reset so other threads may continue.

For this algorithm, we also implemented an alternative version using STM. Each bucket is protected by a TVar and there is no need for a flag controlling table growth as the array of buckets is stored in a TVar. Hence, if different transactions modify the array, the runtime system will detect the conflict:

```
type Buckets = Array Int (TVar [Int])
data HTable = TH
{
    buckets   :: TVar Buckets,
    n_elemens :: TVar Int,
    len_tab   :: TVar Int
}
```

3.4   Lock Free Hash

The main issue for the implementation of concurrent hash tables is growing the table's capacity. Making the array of buckets lock-free is not enough, as moving data from the old to the new table must be executed in an atomic way to avoid race conditions and CAS instructions operate on a single memory position.

Therefore, the algorithm proposed in [13] moves buckets through the items, instead of items through the buckets. All data are stored in a lock-free linked list and each bucket is a reference to a position in the list (Fig. 1).

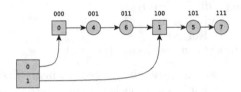

Fig. 1. Linked list for the lock-free hash.

Items are ordered by the value obtained from the reverse of its hash. This ordering allows for the division of values in the linked list between two different buckets, avoiding the need to move them [4,13]. The catch is that capacity must be a power of two. For each new bucket, a guard node that will never be removed is created to avoid situations where all data from a bucket are removed.

The implementation of the linked list is based on the lock free list described in [15]. The main difficulty here is the removal of list elements while a list is being accessed concurrently by different threads. Direct removal may break linking, and to avoid it, a lazy deletion scheme is employed. An element is never directly deleted from the list, it is marked logically as removed and waits for the next list operation for complete deletion [15]. The list structure is as follows:

```
data List = Node { val::Word, next::IORef (List)}
          | DelNode {next::IORef (List)}
          | Null
          | Guard {val::Word, next::IORef (List)}

type   ListHandle = IORef List
```

The hash table structure is as follows:

```
data Slot = PtrList {list :: ListHandle} | Nil
type Buckets = Array Int   (IORef Slot)
data HTable = TH
{
    buckets :: IORef Buckets,
    n_elemens :: IORef Int,
    len_tab :: IORef Int
}
```

The hash table is initialized with only the slot/position zero pointing to the guard zero that is also the list head:

```
newHash :: Int -> IO (HTable)
newHash size = do
    x <- replicateM size (newIORef Nil)
    let arrayHash = listArray (0, size -1) x
    let first = arrayHash ! 0
    headList <- newList
    writeIORef first (PtrList {list=headList})
    buckets <- newIORef arrayHash
    n_elemens <- newIORef 0
    len_tab <- newIORef size
    return (TH buckets n_elemens len_tab)
```

The remaining buckets are initialized when first needed using `initilizeGuards`. For each initialized bucket, a new guard is inserted in the linked list, and then the corresponding slot in the table points to it. Initialization uses the split-ordered keys method [13], where each bucket is initialized by recursive calls until an already initialized bucket is found. Then, the guard is inserted in the list and its reference is used for the next bucket's insertion:

```
initializeGuard :: Buckets -> Int -> Int -> IO ListHandle
initializeGuard slots lenTab guardVal = do
  x <- readIORef $ slots ! searchParent lenTab guardVal
  case x of
    PtrList {list = l} -> do
        inverseVal <- reverseBits guardVal
        a <- addGuardToList l inverseVal
        atomicWriteIORef (slots ! guardVal) (PtrList {list=a})
        return a
    Nil -> do
        newGuard <- initializeGuard slots lenTab $ searchParent
            lenTab guardVal
        inverseVal <- reverseBits guardVal
        a <- addGuardToList newGuard inverseVal
        atomicWriteIORef (slots ! guardVal) (PtrList {list=a})
        return a
```

The searchParent function calculates the table position were the next closer guard might be. If the table position contains a guard, the new guard is inserted in the right position of the linked list (addGuardToList). Otherwise, the position found must also be initialized, hence initilizeGuard is called again for that position. The Haskell Foreign Function Interface (FFI) [10] is used for the reverseBits function, as an efficient Haskell native library to reverse bits was not found. In the worst cases of some specific measurements we have performed, the use of Haskell native library functions were responsible for 66 % of the execution time, thus justifying the use of an external C implementation.

```
foreign import ccall safe reverseBits :: Int -> IO Word
```

We also implemented an alternative version of the Lock free algorithm using transactional memory. For this version, IORefs were substituted by TVars and we removed part of the synchronization algorithm, as the transactional system guarantees atomicity. The data structure for the List is as follows:

```
data List = Node { val::Word,  next::TVar (List)}
          | DelNode {next::TVar (List)}
          | Null
          | Guard {val::Word, next::TVar (List)}
type  ListHandle = TVar List
```

And the data types for the STM version are:

```
data Slot = List {list :: ListHandle} | Nil
type Buckets = Array Int (TVar Slot)

data HTable = TH
{
    buckets    :: TVar Buckets,
    n_elemens  :: TVar Int,
    len_tab    :: TVar Int
}
```

4   Results

Our experiments were concerned mainly with the performance of the different algorithms. Two experimental environments were used to evaluate the implemented algorithms. The first environment was a Uniform Memory Access (UMA) architecture and was comprised of an Intel Core i7 processor with 4 physical cores and hyperthreading, and 8 GB of RAM. The second environment was a Non-Uniform Memory Access (NUMA) with two Intel Xeon, each with 4 physical cores and hyperthreadding, and 12 GB of RAM. Threads in the NUMA machine incur in different memory latency times depending on the location of data in memory banks. Each set of cores is directly connected to a memory bank and, even though the address space is shared for the entire system, accesses to positions in memory banks not directly connected to a given set of cores require extra communication and, thus, increased latencies and reduced bandwidth. Both systems executed Ubuntu Linux 14.04 64 bits. The Haskell compiler used was ghc 7.6.3 with STM 2.4.2. Each experiment was executed 30 times and the average time is presented. One million operations were executed for each experiment with a mix of 10 % inserts, 10 % deletes, and 80 % reads. This experiment reflects the common use of hash tables accordingly to use statistics from [4]. An additional mix of 80 % inserts, 10 % deletes, and 10 % reads was employed to study behavior during table growth. Tests were executed for the following implementations:

- *Global lock MVar*: global lock implementation explained in Subsect. 3.1;
- *Global using STM*: also global lock, but using a `TVar` to implement the global lock;
- *Block MVar*: Lock Striping, Subsect. 3.2;
- *Fine-grain using MVar*: fine-grain lock algorithm, Subsect. 3.3;
- *Fine-grain using STM*: fine-grain lock implementation using STM, Subsect. 3.3;
- *CAS*: lock-free hash using `IORef`, Subsect. 3.4;
- *CAS using STM*: also lock-free, but substituting `IORef`s by `TVAR`s, Subsect. 3.4.

4.1 Execution Time

Figures 2 and 3 show the execution time of hash tables for the different operation mixes for the UMA machine. The horizontal axis depicts the number of threads and the vertical axis shows the execution time in seconds using a logarithm scale. Each color bar is a different implementation of the hash table algorithms explained before, and in the top of each bar the standard deviation was plotted. As expected, *Global lock MVar* showed performance loss when the number of threads is increased because of the serialization created by a single lock. *Global using STM* showed performance gains up to 4 threads as transactions that do not modify the state, such as reads, do not generate conflicts. However, when the amount of inserts was increased to 80 %, this implementation's performance was compromised as the number of conflicts increased. The worst scenario was achieved with 16 threads in the NUMA machine, where execution time exceeded 60 s (See Fig. 5). Note that *Block MVar* showed the largest standard deviation, with very different execution times in their repetitions.

With the exception of *Global lock MVar*, all implementations scaled up to 4 threads, which is also the number of physical cores. When the number of threads was increased to 8, *Block MVar*, *Fine-grain using MVar*, *Fine-grain using STM*, and *CAS* still kept low execution times even when the number of inserts was increased. *Block MVar* presented execution times lower than *Fine-grain using MVar*, as its lock acquisition and growth algorithms are simpler.

Block MVar, *Fine-grain using MVar*, and *CAS* presented similar execution times. This is due to the overhead for implementing correct synchronization using CAS which made the lock free implementation in the end similar to *Block MVar*

10% inserts, 10% deletes, 80% reads

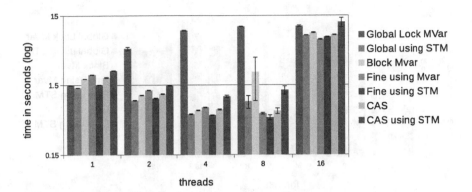

Fig. 2. Execution time, 10 % inserts, 10 % deletes, and 80 % reads, UMA machine.

80% inserts, 10% deletes, 10% reads

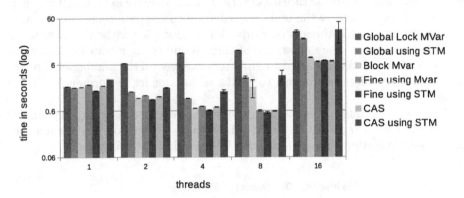

Fig. 3. Execution time, 80 % inserts, 10 % deletes, and 10 % reads, UMA machine.

and *Fine-grain using MVar*. The bad performance presented by *CAS using STM* is explained by the high number of false conflicts that happens in a linked list implemented with TVars. This issue is described in detail in Sect. 3.3 of [14]. *Fine-grain using STM* showed the lower execution time in both mixes.

Figures 4 and 5 show the execution time of hash tables for the different operation mixes for the NUMA machine. Note that the time scale is different than that used for Figs. 2 and 3. Direct comparison of execution times between the UMA and the NUMA machines is not useful as the processors are different.

For the read intensive experiment (Fig. 4), execution time shows the same trends as for the UMA machine from 1 to 4 threads. When executing 8 threads, there is a different behavior for the *Fine using STM*. From 8 threads onwards, it is possible to see the influence of the Non-Uniform Memory Architecture and

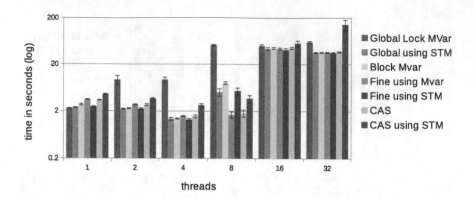

Fig. 4. Execution time, 10 % inserts, 10 % deletes, and 80 % reads, NUMA machine.

performance with 16 and 32 threads is very similar. An extra experiment was performed in order to isolate the main contribution to the performance contention when executing with 8 threads onwards. A threaded code without synchronization was executed for the same range of threads and the number of memory references and cache misses started to grow very fastly with the number of threads. Hence, memory contention seems to be the main issue for performance in these cases.

For the write intensive experiment (Fig. 5), trends were again very similar but for the *Fine using STM* and 8 threads. Memory contention was again a very important issue after 8 threads for both UMA and NUMA machines.

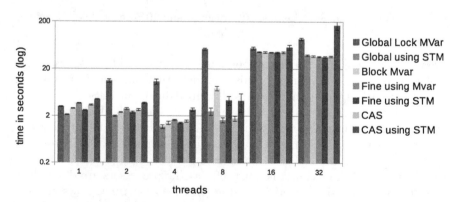

Fig. 5. Execution time, 80 % inserts, 10 % deletes, and 10 % reads, NUMA machine.

4.2 Speedup

Figures 6 and 7 show the relative speedups in the vertical axis for each implementation in the UMA machine. The relative speedup was calculated by dividing the execution time of each implementation with 1 thread by each execution time for the varying number of threads. Although this measurement does not provide a precise statement about the performance as execution time, it is useful to appreciate the scalability of each implementation as the number of threads is increased.

The behavior of relative speedups does not change significantly for each implementation in both graphs. All implementations but *Global Lock MVar* presented scalability up to 4 threads and all of them presented worse performance

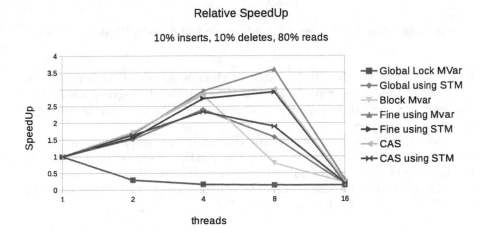

Fig. 6. Speedup, 10 % inserts, 10 % deletes, and 80 % reads, UMA machine.

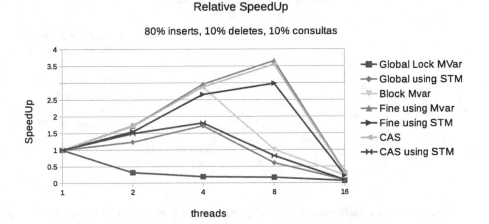

Fig. 7. Speedup, 80 % inserts, 10 % deletes, and 10 % reads, UMA machine.

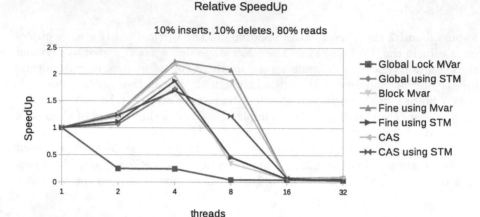

Fig. 8. Speedup, 10 % inserts, 10 % deletes, and 80 % reads, NUMA machine.

than with 1 thread when the number of threads greatly exceeded the number of cores. Among all implementations, *Block MVar*, *Fine-grain using MVar*,
Fine-grain using STM, and *CAS* presented good scalability when the number of
processors is increased.

Figures 8 and 9 show the relative speedups in the vertical axis for each implementation in the NUMA machine. *Fine using MVar* presented the best relative
speedups again, showing its potential for further scalability. *Fine using STM*
showed a different trend when compared to Figs. 6 and 7, with worse scalability
than *Global using STM* and *CAS using STM*.

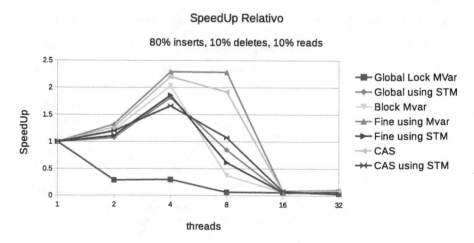

Fig. 9. Speedup, 80 % inserts, 10 % deletes, and 10 % reads, NUMA machine.

5   Related Works

Newton et al. [9] claimed the inexistence of concurrent hash tables for Haskell. Their solution employed coarse grain locks over Data.Map structures. Their results showed that the overhead of a global lock was not large, as their structure stored a small amount of data. In our work, we tried to reduce lock granularity to a minimum, even implementing a lock-free hash table.

Sulzmann, Lam, and Marlow [15] implemented linked lists using different concurrent algorithms and the same synchronization primitives explored in our work. Their implementation with `IORef` and `atomicModifyIORef` presented the best results, but the STM implementation is the most attractive by its ease of implementation and correctness guarantees, as lock free implementations using `IORefs` are complex and difficult to get right. Our implementation of a lock-free linked list described in Subsect. 3.4 used theirs as a starting point, but we implemented an ordered list with guards as references to the buckets, a substantial modification to the original algorithm.

6   Conclusions and Future Work

In this work, different concurrent implementations of hash tables for Haskell were compared. The *Block MVar*, *Fine-grain using MVar*, *Fine-grain using STM*, and *CAS* implementations showed the best performance up to 8 threads for the UMA machine. The *Block MVar* implementation compensates the performance bottleneck of a low number of locks protecting tables by its lower complexity for table duplication. On the other hand, the *Fine-grain using MVar* implementation with its higher number of locks suffered from the impact of duplicating tables, and hence its results were similar to those of *Block MVar*. The *CAS* implementation presented a high synchronization cost, with performance worse than *Block MVar*.

Performance trends for the NUMA machines are very similar to those in the UMA machine but for *Fine-gain using STM* implementation, which starts to suffer the effects of the memory hierarchy when 8 threads are executed. In general, memory contention was a very important issue as the number of threads increased in the NUMA machine. The experiments also reflect the fact that the Haskell runtime system, including its Garbage Collector, were designed mainly for UMA machines, with no optimizations for NUMA architectures [7,8].

For our execution environment, the *Fine-grain using STM* presented the best performance up to 8 threads, with the benefit of being easier to implement than the alternatives. However, the best scalability was achieved with the *CAS* implementation.

In future works, we intend to experiment with different initial table sizes and diverse conditions.

Sources of the tables presented here, and also their polymorphic versions, may be downloaded from http://lups.inf.ufpel.edu.br/~pilla/bench_hash_haskell.tgz.

Acknowledgement. This work was supported by CAPES/Brasil (Programa Nacional de Cooperação Acadêmica da Coordenação de Aperfeiçoamento de Pessoal de Nível vel Superior).

References

1. Data.CAS, July 2015. http://hackage.haskell.org/package/IORefCAS-0.1.0.1/docs/src/Data-CAS.html
2. Harris, T., Larus, J., Rajwar, R.: Transactional Memory (Synthesis Lectures on Computer Architecture). Morgan and Claypool, San Rafael (2010)
3. Harris, T., Marlow, S., Jones, S.P., Herlihy, M.: Composable memory transactions. Commun. ACM **51**, 91–100 (2008)
4. Herlihy, M., Shavit, N.: The Art of Multiprocessor Programming. Elsevier, San Francisco (2012). Revised Reprint
5. Leiserson, C.E., Rivest, R.L., Stein, C., Cormen, T.H.: Introduction to Algorithms. The MIT press, Cambridge (2001)
6. Marlow, S.: Parallel and Concurrent Programming in Haskell: Techniques for Multicore and Multithreaded Programming. O'Reilly Media, Inc., Sebastopol (2013)
7. Marlow, S., Harris, T., James, R.P., Peyton Jones, S.: Parallel generational-copying garbage collection with a block-structured heap. In: Proceedings of the 7th International Symposium on Memory Management, ISMM 2008, New York, NY, USA, pp. 11–20. ACM (2008)
8. Marlow, S., Peyton Jones, S., Singh, S.: Runtime support for multicore haskell. In: Proceedings of the 14th ACM SIGPLAN International Conference on Functional Programming, ICFP 2009, New York, NY, USA, pp. 65–78. ACM (2009)
9. Newton, R., Chen, C.-P., Marlow, S.: Intel concurrent collections for haskell. Technical report MIT-CSAIL-TR-2011-015, Massachusetts Institute of Technology, Cambridge, MA, USA (2011)
10. O'Sullivan, B., Goerzen, J., Stewart, D.B.: Real World Haskell. O'Reilly, Farnham (2008)
11. Peyton Jones, S.: Tackling the awkward squad: monadic input/output, concurrency, exceptions, and foreign-language calls in haskell. In: Hoare, T., Broy, M., Steinbruggen, R. (eds.) Engineering Theories of Software Construction, pp. 47–96. IOS Press, Amsterdam (2002)
12. Peyton Jones, S., Gordon, A., Finne, S.: Concurrent haskell. In: Proceedings of the 23rd ACM SIGPLAN-SIGACT Symposium on Principles of Programming Languages, POPL 1996, New York, NY, USA, pp. 295–308. ACM (1996)
13. Shalev, O., Shavit, N.: Split-ordered lists: lock-free extensible hash tables. J. ACM (JACM) **53**(3), 379–405 (2006)
14. Sönmez, N., Perfumo, C., Stipic, S., Cristal, A., Unsal, O.S., Valero, M.: UnreadTVar: extending haskell software transactional memory for performance. Trends Funct. Program. **8**, 89–114 (2007)
15. Sulzmann, M., Lam, E.S., Marlow, S.: Comparing the performance of concurrent linked-list implementations in haskell. In: Proceedings of the 4th Workshop on Declarative Aspects of Multicore Programming, pp. 37–46. ACM (2009)

Optional Type Classes for Haskell

Rodrigo Ribeiro[1], Carlos Camarão[2], Lucília Figueiredo[3(✉)],
and Cristiano Vasconcellos[4]

[1] DECSI, Universidade Federal de Ouro Preto (UFOP), João Monlevade, Brazil
rodrigo@decsi.ufop.br
[2] DCC, Universidade Federal de Minas Gerais (UFMG), Belo Horizonte, Brazil
camarao@dcc.ufmg.br
[3] DECOM, Universidade Federal de Ouro Preto (UFOP), Ouro Preto, Brazil
luciliacf@gmail.com
[4] DCC, Universidade do Estado de Santa Catarina (UDESC), Joinville, Brazil
cristiano.vasconcellos@udesc.br

Abstract. This paper explores an approach for allowing type classes to be optionally declared by programmers, i.e. programmers can overload symbols without declaring their types in type classes.

The type of an overloaded symbol is, if not explicitly defined in a type class, automatically determined from the anti-unification of instance types defined for the symbol in the relevant module.

This depends on a modularization of instance visibility, as well as on a redefinition of Haskell's ambiguity rule. The paper presents the modifications to Haskell's module system that are necessary for allowing instances to have a modular scope, based on previous work by the authors. The definition of the type of overloaded symbols as the anti-unification of available instance types and the redefined ambiguity rule are also based on previous works by the authors.

The added flexibility to Haskell-style of overloading is illustrated by defining a type system and by showing how overloaded record fields can be easily allowed with such a type system.

1 Introduction

This paper proposes an approach for allowing symbols to be overloaded in Haskell without explicitly declaring their types in type classes. For this, modifications to Haskell's module system are required so that instances have a modular scope, as well as a redefinition of Haskell's ambiguity rule.

The proposed approach is based on the following ideas:

1. As usual, the type of an overloaded symbol is a constrained type of the form $\forall \overline{a}.\, C \Rightarrow \tau$, where C is a set of constraints and τ is a simple type; a constraint is a class name followed by a sequence of type variables.
2. An overloaded symbol x can be defined by instance declarations of the form `instance` $x = e$, without explicitly declaring its type in a type class.

F. Castor and Y.D. Liu (Eds.): SBLP 2016, LNCS 9889, pp. 125–139, 2016.
DOI: 10.1007/978-3-319-45279-1_9

3. The type of x is automatically determined from the anti-unification of the instance types for x that are visible in the relevant module, by creating a type class with a single member (x). The algorithm used for computing the type of x is presented in Sect. 3.
4. Simple modifications to Haskell's module system are required so that instances have a modular scope. This is based on previous work by the authors which is summarized in Sect. 5.
5. Also, a redefinition of Haskell's ambiguity rule is required, as discussed in Sect. 4.

The proposed approach is formalized in Sect. 6, where a type system for a core-Haskell language where type classes can be optionally declared is presented. Modularized instance scopes with a revised ambiguity rule and optional type classes may also avoid the use of qualified imports (as used e.g. in the *classy-prelude*, used in e.g. Yesod [15]).

The added flexibility to Haskell-style of overloading is illustrated by presenting a simple implementation for overloaded record fields based on the proposed approach (cf. Sect. 7).

Related work is discussed in Sects. 8 and 9 concludes.

A prototype implementation of a type inference algorithm for Haskell supporting overloading without the need of defining a type class is available [18].

2   Preliminaries

This section introduces basic definitions and notations. Meta-variable usage and the syntax of types are given in Fig. 1.

Class Name	A
Type variable	a, b
Type constructor	T
Simple Constraint	$\pi ::= A\,\overline{\tau}$
Set of Simple Constraints	C
Constraint	$\theta ::= \forall\,\overline{a}.\,C \Rightarrow \pi$
Simple Type	$\tau, \rho ::= a \mid T \mid \tau\,\tau'$
Constrained Type	$\delta ::= C \Rightarrow \tau$
Type	$\sigma ::= \forall\,\overline{a}.\,\delta$
Substitution	ϕ

Fig. 1. Syntax of types

For simplicity and following common practice, kinds are not considered in type expressions and type expressions which are not simple types are not explicitly distinguished from simple types.

As usual, we assume the existence of type constructor $\rightarrow$, that is written as an infix operator $(\tau \rightarrow \tau')$. A type $\forall \bar{a}. C \Rightarrow \tau$ is equivalent to $C \Rightarrow \tau$ if $\bar{a}$ is empty and, similarly, $C \Rightarrow \tau$ is equivalent to τ if C is empty.

The set of type variables occurring in X is denoted by $tv(X)$, where X can be a type, a constraint, sets of types or constraints, or a typing context.

Notation $\bar{x}^n$, or simply $\bar{x}$, is used throughout this paper to denote the sequence $x_1 \cdots x_n$, or $x_1, \ldots, x_n$, or $x_1; \ldots; x_n$, depending on the context where it is used, where $n \geq 0$, and x's can be either type variables, or mappings, or bindings etc. When used in a context of a set, it denotes $\{x_1, \ldots, x_n\}$.

A substitution ϕ is a function from type variables to simple type expressions. The identity substitution is denoted by id. $\phi(\sigma)$ (or simply $\phi\sigma$) represents the capture-free operation of substituting $\phi(a)$ for each free occurrence of a in σ.

We overload the substitution application on constraints, constraint sets and sets of types. Definition of application on these elements is straightforward. The symbol $\circ$ denotes function composition and $dom(\phi) = \{\alpha \mid \phi(\alpha) \neq \alpha\}$.

The notation $\phi[\overline{a \mapsto \tau^n}]$ denotes the substitution ϕ' such that $\phi'(b) = \tau_i$ if $b = a_i$, for $i = 1, ..., n$, otherwise $\phi(b)$. Also, $[\overline{a \mapsto \tau}] = id[\overline{a \mapsto \tau^n}]$.

3   Anti-unification of Instance Types

A simple type τ is a generalization of a set of simple types $\bar{\tau}^n$ if there exist substitutions $\overline{\phi}^n$ such that $\phi_i(\tau) = \tau_i$, for $i = 1, \ldots, n$. For example, $a_0 \rightarrow a_0$, $a_1 \rightarrow a_2$, and a_3 are generalizations of $\{Int \rightarrow Int, Float \rightarrow Float\}$.[1]

We say that τ is less general than τ', written $\tau \leq \tau'$, if there exist a substitution ϕ such that $\phi(\tau') = \tau$. For example, $a_0 \rightarrow a_0 \leq a_1 \rightarrow a_2 \leq a_3$.

The *least common generalization* (lcg) of a set of types S and a type τ holds, written as $\text{lcg}_r(S, \tau)$, if, for all generalizations τ' of S we have $\tau \leq \tau'$.

The concept of least common generalization was studied by Gordon Plotkin [16,17], that defined a function constructing a generalization of two symbolic expressions. In Fig. 2, we define function *lcg*, which returns a lcg of a finite set of simple types S, by recursion on the structure of S, using function *lcg'* to compute the generalization of two simple types. For two types τ_1 and τ_2 the idea is to recursively traverse the structure of both types using a finite map to store previously generalized types. Whenever we find two different type constructors, we search on the finite map if they have been previously generalized. If this is the case, the previous generalization is returned. If these two type constructors are not in the finite map, we insert them using a fresh type variable as their generalization and return this new variable.

As an example of the use of *lcg*, consider the following types (of functions *map* on lists and trees, respectively):

$$(a \rightarrow b) \ \rightarrow \ [a] \ \rightarrow \ [b]$$
$$(a \rightarrow b) \ \rightarrow \ Tree \ a \ \rightarrow \ Tree \ b$$

---

[1] A generalization is also called a (first-order) *anti-unification* [2].

$$lcg(S) = \tau \quad \text{where } (\tau, \phi) = lcg'(S, id), \text{ for some } \phi$$

$$lcg'(\{\tau\}, \phi) = (\tau, \phi)$$

$$lcg'(\{\tau_1\} \cup S, \phi) = lcg''(\tau_1, \tau', \phi') \quad \text{where } (\tau', \phi') = lcg'(S, \phi)$$

$$lcg''(T\,\overline{\tau}^n,\, T'\,\overline{\rho}^m, \phi) =$$
$$\quad \text{if } \phi(a) = (T\,\overline{\tau}^n,\, T'\,\overline{\rho}^m) \text{ for some } a \text{ then } (a, \phi)$$
$$\quad \text{else}$$
$$\qquad \text{if } n \neq m \text{ then } (b, \phi[b \mapsto (T\,\overline{\tau}^n,\, T'\,\overline{\rho}^m)])$$
$$\qquad\quad \text{where } b \text{ is a fresh type variable}$$
$$\qquad \text{else } (\psi\,\overline{\tau'}^n, \phi_n)$$
$$\qquad\quad \text{where } (\psi, \phi_0) = \begin{cases} (T, \phi) & \text{if } T = T' \\ (a, \phi[a \mapsto (T, T')]) & \text{otherwise, } a \text{ is fresh} \end{cases}$$
$$\qquad\qquad (\tau'_i, \phi_i) = lcg''(\tau_i, \rho_i, \phi_{i-1}), \text{ for } i = 1, \dots, n$$

Fig. 2. Least common generalization

A call of *lcg* for a set with these types yields type $(a \to b) \to c\ a \to c\ b$, where c is a generalization of type constructors $[]$ and *Tree* (for c to be used in $c\ b$, mapping $c \mapsto ([], Tree)$ is saved in parameter ϕ of lcg'', to be reused).

The following theorems guarantee correctness of function *lcg*:

Theorem 1 (Soundness of *lcg*). *For all (sets of simple types) S, we have that $lcg(S)$ yields a generalization of S.*

Theorem 2 (Completeness of *lcg*). *For all (sets of simple types) S, we have that $lcg_r(S, lcg(S))$ holds (i.e. $lcg(S)$ is a generalization of S) and, for any τ that is a generalization of S, we have that $lcg(S) \leq \tau$.*

Theorem 3 (Compositionality of *lcg*). *For all non-empty (sets of simple types) S, S', we have that $lcg(lcg(S), lcg(S')) = lcg(S \cup S')$.*

Theorem 4 (Uniqueness of *lcg*). *For all (sets of simple types) S, we have that $lcg(S)$ is unique, up to variable renaming.*

The proofs use straighforward induction on the number and structural complexity of elements of S.

4   Ambiguity Rule

The versions of Haskell supported by GHC [8] — the prevailing Haskell compiler — are becoming complex, to the point of affecting the view of Haskell as the best choice for general-purpose software development. A basic issue in this regard is the need of extending the language to allow multiple parameter type classes (MPTCs). This extension is thought to require additional mechanisms, such as functional dependencies [10] or type families [3]. In another paper [1], we have shown that the introduction of MPTCs in the language can be done without the need of additional mechanisms: a simplifying change is sufficient, to Haskell's ambiguity rule. Interested readers are referred to [1]. The main ideas are summarized below.

In (GHC) Haskell, ambiguity is a property of a type: a type $\forall \overline{a}.\, C \Rightarrow \tau$ is ambiguous if there exists a type variable that occurs in the set of constraints (C) that is not uniquely determined from the set of type variables that occur in the simple type (τ). This unique determination is such that, for each type variable a that occurs in C but not in τ there must exist a functional dependency $b \mapsto a$ for some b in τ (or a similar unique determination specified via type families). Notation $b \mapsto a$ is used, instead of $b \rightarrow a$, to avoid confusion with the notation used to denote functional types.

We adopt a slightly modified definition for ambiguity, refered here as *expression ambiguity*[2], that is based on the following similar property of variable reachability, which is independent of functional dependencies and type families:

Definition 1 (Reachable Variable). *A variable* $a \in tv(C)$ *is* reachable *from a set of type variables* V *if* $a \in V$ *or if* $a \in \pi$ *for some* $\pi \in C$ *such that there exists* $b \in tv(\pi)$ *such that* b *is reachable.* $a \in tv(C)$ *is* unreachable *if it is not reachable. The set of reachable type variables of constraint set* C *from* V *is denoted by* reachableVars(C, V).

For example, in $(A_1\, a\, b, A_2\, a) \Rightarrow b$, type variable a is reachable from the set of type variables in b, because a occurs in constraint $A_1\, a\, b$, and b is reachable. Similarly, if $C = (A_1\, a\, b, A_2\, b\, c, A_3\, c)$, then c is reachable from $\{a\}$.

The presence of unreachable variables in a constraint $\pi \in C$, on a type $\sigma = C \Rightarrow \tau$, characterizes *overloading resolution*; in other words, it means that overloading for π is resolved — there is no context in which an expression with such a type (σ) could be placed that could instantiate any of the unreachable variables (occurring in π). However, the presence of unreachable variables does not necessarily imply ambiguity. Ambiguity is a property of an expression, not of a type. It depends on the context in which the expression occurs, and on *entailment* of the constraints on the expression's type. Also, because of Haskell's *open-world* style of overloading, ambiguity can be checked only when there exist unreachable variables; when there are no unreachable variables, overloading is yet unresolved.

Entailment of constraints and its algorithmic (functional) counterpart are well-known in the Haskell world (see e.g. [1,14,19]).

Informally, a set of constraints C is entailed (or satisfied) in a program P if there exists a substitution ϕ such that $\phi(C)$ is contained in the set of instance declarations of P, or is transitively implied by the set of class and instance declarations occurring in P. For a formal definition, see e.g. [1,14]. In this case we say that C is entailed by ϕ.

---

[2] In [1] it is called *delayed closure ambiguity*.

For example, *Eq* [[*Integer*]] is entailed if we have instances *Eq Integer* and *Eq a* =>*Eq* [a], visible in the context where an expression whose type has a constraint *Eq* [[*Integer*]] occurs.

If overloading is resolved for a constraint π occurring in a type $\sigma = \pi, C \Rightarrow \tau$ then exactly one of the following holds:

- π is entailed by a single instance; in this case a type simplification (also called "improvement") occurs: σ can be simplified to $C \Rightarrow \tau$;
- π is entailed by two or more instances; in this case we have a type error: ambiguity;
- π is not entailed (by any instance); in this case we have also a type error: unsatisfiability.

Note that variables in a single constraint are either all reachable or all unreachable. If they are unreachable, either the constraint can be removed, in the case of single entailment, or there is a type error (either ambiguity, in the case of two or more entailments, or unsatisfiability, in the case of no entailment).

Instead of being dependent on the specification of functional dependencies or type families, ambiguity depends on the existence of (two or more) instances in a program context when overloading is resolved for a constraint on the type of an expression.

The possibility of a modular control of the visibility of instance definitions conforms to this simplifying change. This is the subject of Sect. 5.

5 Modularization of Instances

This section presents the simple modifications to Haskell's module system that are necessary to allow instances to have a modular scope (we do not attempt to discuss any major revision to Haskell's module system). This is based on previous work presented in [13], that allows a modular control of the visibility of instance definitions.

Essentially, import and export clauses can specify, instead of just names, also **instance** $A\,\overline{\tau}$, where $\overline{\tau}$ is a (non-empty) sequence of types and A is a class name:

$$\text{module } M \text{ (instance } A\,\overline{\tau}, \ldots) \text{ where} \ldots$$

specifies that the instance of $\overline{\tau}$ for class A is exported in module M.

$$\text{import } M \text{ (instance } A\,\overline{\tau}, \ldots)$$

specifies that the instance of $\overline{\tau}$ for class A is imported from M, in the module where the import clause occurs.

The single additional rule to the work presented in [13] that enables type classes to be optionally declared by programmers is the following:

Definition 2 (Type of overloaded variable). *If the type of an overloaded variable — i.e. a variable that is introduced in an instance definition — is not* *explicitly annotated in a type class declaration, then the variable's type is the anti-unification of instance types defined for the variable in the current module; otherwise, it is the annotated type.*

5.1   Pros and Cons of Instance Modularization

Among the advantages of this simple change, we cite (following [13]):

- Programmers have better control of which entities are necessary and should be in the scope of each module in a program.
- It is possible to define and use more than one instance for the same type in a program.
- Problems with orphan instances do not occur (orphan instances are instances defined in a module where neither the definition of the data type nor the definition of the type class occur). For example, distinct instances of *Either* for class *Monad*, say one from package *mtl* and another from *transformers*, can be used in a program.
- The introduction of newtypes, as well as the use of functions that include additional (-by) parameters, such as e.g. the (first) parameter of function *sortBy* in module *Data.List* can be avoided.

With instance modularization, programmers need to be aware of which entities are exported and imported — i.e. which entities are visible in the scope of a module — *and their types*, in particular whether they are or not overloaded. A simple change like a type annotation for a variable exported from a module, can lead to a change in the semantics of using this variable in another module.

Instance modularization and the rule of expression ambiguity, that considers the context where an expression occurs to detect whether an expression is ambiguous or not, has profound consequences. Consider, for example:

```
module M where
    class Show t ...
    class Read t ...
    instance Show Int ...
    instance Read Int ...
    f = show . read

module N where
    import M
    instance Read Bool ...
    instance Show Bool ...
    g = f "123"
```

The definition of f in module M is not well-typed in Haskell, since type (*Show a, Read a*) ⇒ *String* is ambiguous. In our approach (i.e. considering ambiguity as a property of an expression, not of a type), the definition of f in module

M is well-typed, because constraints (*Show a*, *Read a*) can be removed; these can be removed because there exists a single instance, in module M, for each constraint, that entails it. As a result, f has type *String*→ *String*. Its use in module N is (then) also well-typed. That means: f's semantics is a function that receives a value of type *String* and returns a value of type *String*, according to the definition of f given in module M. The semantics of an expression involves passing a (dictionary) value that is given in the context of usage *only if* the expression has a constrained type.

6   Mini-Haskell with Optional Type Classes

In this section we present a type system for mini-Haskell, where type class declaration is optional. Programmers can overload symbols without declaring their types in type classes. The type of an overloaded symbol is, if not explicitly defined in a type class, based on the anti-unification of instance types defined for the symbol in the relevant module.

Figure 3 shows the context-free syntax of mini-Haskell: expressions, modules and programs. An instance can be specified without specifying a type class, cf. second option (after |) in Instance Declaration in Fig. 3.

For simplicity, imported and exported variables and instances must be explicitly indicated, e.g. we do not include notations for exporting and importing all variables of a module.

Multi-parameter type classes are supported. In this paper we do not consider recursivity, neither in let-bindings nor in instance declarations.

A program theory P is a set of axioms of first-order logic, generated from class and instance declarations occurring in the program, of the form $C \Rightarrow \pi$, where C is a set of simple constraints and π is a simple constraint (cf. Fig. 3).

Module Name	M, N	
Program Theory	P, Q	
Variable	x, y	
Expression	e	$::= x \mid \lambda x.\, e \mid e\, e' \mid \texttt{let } x = e \texttt{ in } e'$
Program	p	$::= \overline{m}$
Module	m	$::= \texttt{module } M\, (X) \texttt{ where } \overline{I};\, \overline{D}$
Export clause	X	$::= \overline{\iota}$
Import clause	I	$::= \texttt{import } M\, (X)$
Item	ι	$::= x \mid \texttt{instance } A\, \overline{\tau}$
Declaration	D	$::= classDecl \mid instDecl \mid \overline{B}$
Class Declaration	$classDecl$	$::= \texttt{class } C \Rightarrow A\, \overline{a} \texttt{ where } \overline{x : \delta}$
Instance Declaration	$instDecl$	$::= \texttt{instance } C \Rightarrow A\, \overline{\tau} \texttt{ where } \overline{B} \mid \texttt{instance } B$
Binding	B	$::= x = e$

Fig. 3. Context-free syntax of mini-Haskell

Entailment of a set of constraints C by a program theory P is written as $P \vdash_e C$ (see e.g. [1]).

Typing contexts are indexed by module names. $\Gamma(M)$ gives a function on variable names to types: $\Gamma(M)(x)$ gives the type of x in module M and typing context Γ. The notation $(\Gamma(M), x \mapsto \sigma)$ is used to denote the typing context Γ' that differs from Γ only by mapping x to σ in module M, i.e.: $\Gamma'(M')(x') = \sigma$ if $M' = M$ and $x' = x$, otherwise $\Gamma'(M')(x') = \Gamma(M')(x')$.

A special, empty module name, denoted by [], is used for names exported by modules, to control the scope of names that use import and export clauses. Also, a reserved name (self) is used to refer to the current module, being defined and used in the type system and relations to control import and export clauses.

It is not necessary to store multiple instance types for the same variable in a typing context, neither it is necessary to use instance types in typing contexts (they are needed only in the program theory); only the lcg of instance types is used, because of lcg compositionality (Theorem 3). When a new instance is declared, if it is an instance of a declared class the type system guarantees that each member is an instance of the type declared in the type class; otherwise (i.e. it is the single member of an undeclared class), its (new) type is given by the lcg of the existing type (an existing lcg of previous instance types) and the instance type.

We consider that a constraint set C' can be removed from a constrained type $C, C' \Rightarrow \tau$ if and only if overloading for C' has been resolved and there exists a single satisfying substitution for C' [1].

A declarative type system for core-Haskell is presented in Fig. 4, using rules of the form $P; \Gamma \vdash_0 e : \delta$, which means that e has type δ in typing context Γ and program theory P.

Rule (LET) performs constraint set simplification before type generalization. Constraint set simplification $\gg_P$ is a relation on constraints, defined as a composition of improvement and context reduction [1]. $gen(\delta, \sigma, V)$ holds if $\sigma = \forall \bar{a}. \delta$,

$$\frac{\Gamma(\mathtt{self})(x) = (\forall \bar{a}. C \Rightarrow \tau) \quad P \vdash_e \phi C \quad dom(\phi) \subseteq \bar{a}}{P; \Gamma \vdash_0 x : \phi(C \Rightarrow \tau)} \text{(VAR)}$$

$$\frac{(\Gamma(\mathtt{self}), x \mapsto \tau) \vdash_0 e : C \Rightarrow \tau'}{P; \Gamma \vdash_0 \lambda x. e : C \Rightarrow \tau \to \tau'} \text{(ABS)}$$

$$\frac{P; \Gamma \vdash_0 e : C \Rightarrow \tau' \to \tau \quad P; \Gamma \vdash_0 e' : C' \Rightarrow \tau' \quad V = tv(\tau) \cup tv(C) \quad (C \oplus_V C') \gg_P C''}{P; \Gamma \vdash_0 e e' : C'' \Rightarrow \tau} \text{(APP)}$$

$$\frac{P; \Gamma \vdash_0 e : C \Rightarrow \tau \quad C \gg_P C'' \quad gen(C'' \Rightarrow \tau, \sigma, tv(\Gamma)) \quad P; (\Gamma(\mathtt{self}), x \mapsto \sigma) \vdash_0 e' : C' \Rightarrow \tau'}{P; \Gamma \vdash_0 \mathtt{let}\ x = e\ \mathtt{in}\ e' : C' \Rightarrow \tau'} \text{(LET)}$$

Fig. 4. Core-Haskell type system

where $\bar{a} = tv(\delta) - V$; similarly, for constraints, $gen(C \Rightarrow \pi, \theta, V)$ holds if $\theta = \forall \bar{a}. C \Rightarrow \pi$, where $\bar{a} = tv(C \Rightarrow \pi) - V$.

$C \oplus_V C'$ denotes the constraint set obtained by adding to C constraints from D that have type variables reachable from V:

$$C \oplus_V C' = C \cup \{\pi \in C' \mid tv(\pi) \cap reachableVars(C', V) \neq \emptyset\}$$

In rule (APP), the constraints on the type of the result are those that occur in the function type plus not all constraints that occur in the type of the argument but only those that have variables reachable from the set of variables that occur in the simple type of the result or in the constraint set on the function type (cf. Definition 1). This allows, for example, to eliminate constraints on the type of the following expressions, where o is any expression, with a possibly non-empty set of constraints on its type: *flip const o* (where *const* has type $\forall a, b. a \rightarrow b \rightarrow a$ and *flip* has type $\forall a, b, c. (a \rightarrow b \rightarrow c) \rightarrow b \rightarrow a \rightarrow c$), which should denote an identity function, and *fst (e, o)*, which should have the same denotation as e.

The extension of core-Haskell to mini-Haskell, which allows (optional) type classes, modules and modularized instance declarations, is presented in Figs. 5, 6 and 7. Rule (MOD), in Fig. 5, uses relations ($\vdash_\Downarrow$) and ($\vdash_\Uparrow^X$), which are defined separately, for clarity, in Figs. 6 and 7.

The import relation $\Gamma \vdash_\Downarrow \bar{I} : \Gamma'$ yields a typing context (Γ') from a typing context (Γ) and a sequence of import clauses ($\bar{I}$).

Relation $P; \Gamma \vdash_\Uparrow^X \bar{D} : (E, P', \Gamma')$ is used for specifying the types of a sequence of bindings, from a typing context (Γ), a program theory (P) and a set of exported items (X); it yields the set (E) of exported variables with their types, together with both (i) a new typing context (Γ'), modified to contain elements of E, so that $\Gamma'([])$ contains the types of each $x \in E$, and (ii) a new program theory (P'), updated from class and instance declarations. Relation ($\vdash_0$) is used to check that expressions of core-Haskell that occur in declarations are well-typed.

$$\frac{\Gamma_0 \vdash_\Downarrow \bar{I} : \Gamma \quad P; \Gamma \vdash_\Uparrow^X \bar{D} : (E, P', \Gamma')}{P; \Gamma_0 \vdash \text{module } M\,(X) \text{ where } \bar{I}; \bar{D} : (E, P', \Gamma')} \;(\text{MOD})$$

Fig. 5. Mini-Haskell module rule

$$\Gamma'(M)(x) = \begin{cases} \Gamma([])(x) & \text{if } M = \text{self and, for some } 1 \leq k \leq n, \\ & \quad x = \iota_k \text{ or } (\iota_k = \text{instance } A\,\bar{\tau},\, x \text{ is a member of class } A) \\ \Gamma(M)(x) & \text{otherwise} \end{cases}$$

$$\overline{\Gamma \vdash_\Downarrow \text{import } M\,(\bar{\iota}^n) : \Gamma'}$$

$$\frac{\Gamma_0 \vdash_\Downarrow \text{import } M\,(\bar{\iota}) : \Gamma \quad \Gamma \vdash_\Downarrow \bar{I} : \Gamma'}{\Gamma_0 \vdash_\Downarrow \text{import } M\,(\bar{\iota}); \bar{I} : \Gamma'}$$

Fig. 6. Import relation

$$P; \Gamma \vdash_{\Uparrow}^{X} \overline{D} : (E, P', \Gamma')$$

$$\Gamma(M)(x) = \begin{cases} \delta_k & \text{if } x = x_k, 1 \le k \le n, M \in \{\texttt{self}, \texttt{[]}\} \\ \Gamma_0(M)(x) & \text{otherwise} \end{cases}$$

$$\rule{9cm}{0.4pt}$$

$$P; \Gamma_0 \vdash_{\Uparrow}^{X} \texttt{class } C \Rightarrow A\,\overline{a} \texttt{ where } \overline{x : \delta}^{n}; \overline{D} : (E, P', \Gamma')$$

$$P \vdash_e \phi(C) \qquad gen(\phi(C \Rightarrow \pi), \theta, tv(\Gamma)) \qquad Q = P \cup \{\theta\}$$

$$Q; \Gamma \vdash_0 e_i : \delta_i \qquad \delta_i = \phi(\Gamma([])(x_i)), \text{ for } i = 1, \ldots, n$$

$$Q; \Gamma \vdash_{\Uparrow}^{X'} \overline{D} : (E, Q', \Gamma')$$

$$(X', E') = \begin{cases} (X - \{\iota\}, E \cup \{\overline{x : \delta}^{n}\}) & \text{if } \iota \in X, \iota = \texttt{instance } \phi(C \Rightarrow \pi) \\ (X, E) & \text{otherwise} \end{cases}$$

$$\rule{9cm}{0.4pt}$$

$$P; \Gamma \vdash_{\Uparrow}^{X} \texttt{instance } \phi(C \Rightarrow \pi) \texttt{ where } \overline{x = e}^{n}; \overline{D} : (E', Q', \Gamma')$$

A is the class name generated for x

$$P; \Gamma_0 \vdash_0 e : C \Rightarrow \tau \qquad gen(C \Rightarrow A\tau, \theta, tv(\Gamma_0)) \qquad Q = P \cup \{\theta\}$$

$$Q; \Gamma \vdash_{\Uparrow}^{X'} \overline{D} : (E, Q', \Gamma') \qquad lcg_r(\{\tau\} \cup \{\Gamma_0(\texttt{self})(x)\}, \tau')$$

$$\Gamma(M)(y) = \begin{cases} A\tau' \Rightarrow \tau' & \text{if } y = x, (M = \texttt{self or } (M = \texttt{[]}, x \in X)) \\ \Gamma_0(M)(y) & \text{otherwise} \end{cases}$$

$$(X', E') = \begin{cases} (X - \{\iota\}, E \cup \{x : C \Rightarrow \tau\}) & \text{if } \iota \in X, \iota = \texttt{instance } C \Rightarrow A\tau \\ (X, E), & \text{otherwise} \end{cases}$$

$$\rule{9cm}{0.4pt}$$

$$P; \Gamma_0 \vdash_{\Uparrow}^{X} \texttt{instance } x = e; \overline{D} : (E', Q', \Gamma')$$

$$P; \Gamma_0 \vdash_0 e : C \Rightarrow \tau \qquad gen(C \Rightarrow \tau, \sigma, tv(\Gamma_0))$$

$$P; \Gamma \vdash_{\Uparrow}^{X} \overline{D} : (E, P', \Gamma')$$

$$\Gamma(M)(y) = \begin{cases} \sigma & \text{if } y = x, (M = \texttt{self or } (M = \texttt{[]}, x \in X)) \\ \Gamma_0(M)(y) & \text{otherwise} \end{cases}$$

$$(X', E') = \begin{cases} (X - \{x\}, E \cup \{x : C \Rightarrow \tau\}) & \text{if } x \in X \\ (X, E) & \text{otherwise} \end{cases}$$

$$\rule{9cm}{0.4pt}$$

$$P; \Gamma_0 \vdash_{\Uparrow}^{X} x = e; \overline{D} : (E', P', \Gamma')$$

Fig. 7. Mini-Haskell rules for declarations

There must exist a sequence of derivations for typing a sequence of modules that composes a program that starts from an empty typing context, or from a typing context that corresponds to predefined library modules. Recursive modules are not treated in this paper.

The first and second rules in Fig. 7 specify the bindigs generated by standard Haskell type classes and instance declarations, respectively. For simplicity, we omit special rules for validity of type class and instance declarations (see [8]), that are not relevant here (for example, that the class hierachy is acyclic).

The third rule accounts for instance declarations of an overloaded symbol x whose type is not explicitly specified in a type class. As stated previously, the type τ' of x is the least common generalization of the set of types $\{\tau\} \cup \{\Gamma_0(\mathtt{self})(x)\}$, where τ is the (simple) type of the expression in the current instance declaration for x and $\Gamma_0(\mathtt{self})(x)$ is the (simple) type of x in the current type environment (previously computed from other instance declarations for x that are visible in the typing context Γ_0). This is based on the compositionality of lcg (Theorem 3.) The type of x in the typing context for the current module is $A\ \tau' \Rightarrow \tau'$, where A is the class name generated for the overloaded symbol x. Also, the type of x in the current instance declaration is inserted in the export environment E, if this instance is listed in the set of items to be exported (X).

7   Records with Overloaded Fields

In this section we describe how the possibility of overloading symbols without the need of declaring type classes allows record fields to be overloaded, in an easy way. The idea is simply to transform any access to an overloaded record field into an automatically created instance of an undeclared type class, and similarly for any use of a record update of an overloaded record field.

There are certainly design decisions to be made, but below we illustrate the proposal by creating instance of *get_fieldname* and *update_fieldname* whenever there exists, respectively, an access of and an update to an overloaded record field, where *fieldname* is the name of the overloaded record field.

Consider a simple example of overloaded record fields:

$$\mathbf{data}\ Person = Person\ \{\ id\ ::\ Int,\ name\ ::\ String\ \}$$
$$\mathbf{data}\ Address = Address\ \{\ id\ ::\ Int,\ address\ ::\ String\ \}$$

The overloaded *id* fields of types *Person* and *Address* have the following types:

$$id\ ::\ Person\ \rightarrow\ Int$$
$$id\ ::\ Address\ \rightarrow\ Int$$

In our approach, we can automatically create following instance declarations without declared type classes, that are part of a record field name space that is distinct from the variable name space:

$$get\_id\ ::\ Person\ \rightarrow\ Int$$
$$\mathbf{instance}\ get\_id\ (Person\ id\ \_\ ) = id$$

$$get\_id\ ::\ Address\ \rightarrow\ Int$$
$$\mathbf{instance}\ get\_id\ (Address\ id\ \_\ ) = id$$

If record field updating is used, updating functions are created, as illustrated below. Consider for example that record field updating is used as follows:

```
update_id :: Person → Int → Person
instance update_id (Person id name) new_id = Person new_id name

update_id :: Address → Int → Address
instance update_id (Address id address) new_id = Address new_id address
```

Given any expression p of type *Person*, any use of (p {$id = new\_id$}) could then be translated to (*update_id* p *new_id*). Similarly, given any expression a of type *Address*, any use of a {$id = new\_id$} could then be translated to *update_id* a *new_id*.

8 Related Work

Haskell type system has been extended with several advanced typing features such as functional dependencies [10], type families [3] and GADTs [4], just to name a few. To the best of our knowledge, there's no previous work on optional declaration of type classes. In this section, we summarize some recent Haskell type system extensions.

Functional dependencies (FDs) were introduced by Mark Jones as a way to specify type class parameter dependencies in order to avoid ambiguity and to improve inferred types in the context of MPTCs. FDs where also used to support some form of type level programming [9] and to define heterogeneous lists and extensible records [11].

Type families [3] (TFs) where introduced as a "more functional" alternative to FDs (which is relational in nature). However, there are some issues with type family injectivity [5] that motivated so-called closed type families and type family dependencies [6]. Closed type families define all possible instances of a type family a priori and type family dependencies allows the specification of parameter dependencies, in a similar way of FDs. All type family related extensions cater to better type improvement.

Datatype promotion [5,20] lifts user defined algebraic datatypes to kinds and data constructors to types. It allows the definition of some dependently typed programs. Singleton types and promoted functions [7] have been used to automate (through Template Haskell) some constructions commonly needed in Haskell-style dependent types. Lindley and McBride [12] describe some dependently typed programs in Haskell and how to use GHC's constraint solver as a theorem prover to discharge proof obligations in an implementation of a merge-sort algorithm.

Type level literals is an extension that complements datatype promotion to numeric and string types. The Haskell prime proposal for overloaded record fields relies on this extension to overload field access and update functions. Our approach, based on optional declaration of type classes, does not demand type promotion features and does not need to create an instance for each record field (overloaded or not).

9   Conclusion

This paper has presented an approach for allowing type classes to be optionally declared by programmers, so that programmers can overload symbols without declaring their types in type classes.

An overloaded symbol is defined by means of an instance declaration that is a normal declaration with keyword `instance`. The type of an overloaded symbol is automatically determined from the anti-unification of instance types defined for the symbol in the relevant module.

The approach depends on a modularization of instance visibility, as well as on a redefinition of Haskell's ambiguity rule. The paper presents the simple modifications to Haskell's module system that are necessary for allowing instances to have a modular scope.

We have provided an illustration of the added flexibility by showing how overloaded record fields can be allowed in the presence of a presented type system that supports instance modularization and instance definitions of undeclared type classes that have a single member.

References

1. Camarão, C., Ribeiro, R., Figueiredo, L.: Ambiguity and constrained polymorphism. Sci. Comput. Program. **124**(1), 1–19 (2016)
2. Chang, C.C., Keisler, H.J.: Model Theory, 3rd edn. Dover Books on Mathematics, New York (2012)
3. Chakravarty, M.M.T., Keller, G., Jones, S.P.: Associated type synonyms. In: Proceedings of the Tenth ACM SIGPLAN International Conference on Functional Programming, ICFP 2005, pp. 241–253 (2005)
4. Chen, S., Erwig, M.: Principal type inference for GADTs. In: Proceedings of the 43rd Annual ACM SIGPLAN-SIGACT Symposium on Principles of Programming Languages, POPL 2016, pp. 416–428 (2016)
5. Eisenberg, R.A., Stolarek, J.: Promoting functions to type families in Haskell. In: Proceedings of the 2014 ACM SIGPLAN Symposium on Haskell, Haskell 2014, pp. 95–106 (2014)
6. Eisenberg, R.A., Vytiniotis, D., Jones, S.P., Weirich, S.: Closed type families with overlapping equations. In: Proceedings of the 41st ACM SIGPLAN-SIGACT Symposium on Principles of Programming Languages, POPL 2014, pp. 671–683 (2014)
7. Eisenberg, R.A., Weirich, S.: Dependently typed programming with singletons. In: Proceedings of the 2012 ACM Haskell Symposium, Haskell 2012, pp. 117–130 (2012)
8. Glasgow Haskell Compiler. http://www.haskell.org/ghc/
9. Hallgren, T.: Fun with functional dependencies. In: Proceedings of the Joint CS/CE Winter Meeting (2000)
10. Jones, M.P., Diatchki, I.S.: Language and program design for functional dependencies. In: Proceedings of the First ACM SIGPLAN Symposium on Haskell, Haskell 2008, pp. 87–98 (2008)
11. Kiselyov, O., Lämmel, R., Schupke, K.: Strongly typed heterogeneous collections. In: Nilsson, H. (ed.) Proceedings of the ACM SIGPLAN Workshop on Haskell, Haskell 2004, pp. 96–107 (2004)

12. Lindley, S., McBride, C.: Hasochism: the pleasure and pain of dependently typed Haskell programming. In: Proceedings of the 2013 ACM SIGPLAN Symposium on Haskell, Haskell 2013, pp. 81–92 (2013)
13. Silva, M., Camarão, C., Controlling the scope of instances in Haskell. In: Proceedings of SBLP 2011, pp. 29–30 (2011)
14. Jones, M.: Qualified types: theory and practice. Ph.D. thesis, Distinguished Dissertations in Computer Science. Cambridge Univ. Press (1994)
15. Snoyman, M.: Developing Web Applications with Haskell and Yesod. O'Reilly Media Inc., California (2012)
16. Plotkin, G.D.: A note on inductive generalisation. Mach. Intell. **5**(1), 153–163 (1970)
17. Plotkin, G.D.: A further note on inductive generalisation. Mach. Intell. **6**, 101 (1971)
18. Ribeiro, R., Camarão, C., Figueiredo, L., Vasconcellos, C.: Optional Type Classes for Haskell – On-line Repository (2016). https://github.com/rodrigogribeiro/mptc
19. Stuckey, P., Sulzmann, M.: A theory of overloading. ACM Trans. Program. Lang. Syst. **27**(6), 1216–1269 (2005)
20. Yorgey, B.A., Weirich, S., Cretin, J., Jones, S.P., Vytiniotis, D., Magalhães, J.P.: Giving Haskell a promotion. In: Proceedings of the 8th ACM SIGPLAN Workshop on Types in Language Design and Implementation, TLDI 2012, pp. 53–66 (2012)

An Algebraic Framework for Parallelizing Recurrence in Functional Programming

Rodrigo C.O. Rocha[1,2], Luís F.W. Góes[1], and Fernando M.Q. Pereira[2(✉)]

[1] Institute of Exact Sciences and Informatics, PUC Minas, Belo Horizonte, Brazil
lfwgoes@pucminas.br
[2] Department of Computer Science, UFMG, Belo Horizonte, Brazil
{rcor,fernando}@dcc.ufmg.br

Abstract. The main challenge faced by automatic parallelization tools in functional languages is the fact that parallelism is often hidden under the syntax of complex recursive functions. In this paper, we propose an algebraic framework for parallelizing – automatically – two special classes of recursive functions. We show that these classes are comprehensive enough to include several well-known instances. We have used our ideas to implement a source-to-source compiler in Python to parallelize Haskell code. We have applied this prototype onto six different recursive functions, achieving, on a 4-core machine, speedups of up to 2.7x.

Keywords: Recursive functions · Parallel computing · Functional programming · Algebraic framework · Abstract algebra

1 Introduction

The advent of multi-core computers has greatly spread the use of parallel programming among application developers. Yet, writing code that runs in parallel is still a difficult and error-prone task. Thus, the automatic parallelization of code has surfaced as an effective alternative to the development of high-performant programs [11,18,25]. In this sense, functional programming languages appear as a promising alternative to the development of parallel code. They provide referential transparency, reducing shared data and eliminating side effects, which makes automatic parallelization much easier. However, in spite of years of research, automatic generation of parallelism, out of functional code, is not a solved problem [12,17]. Testimony of this last statement is the fact that functional code is still manually parallelized, usually by means of parallel skeletons [4,6,17].

The main challenge faced by automatic parallelization tools in functional languages is the fact that parallelism is often hidden under the syntax of complex recursive functions. There are several techniques to discover parallelism, such as work targeting list homomorphisms [5,13,15,20], or the work of Fisher and Ghuloum [8], who parallelize imperative loops that can be translated as composition of functions. Nevertheless, the programming languages community still lacks approaches to infer parallelism on recursive functions automatically. The goal of this paper is to contribute to solve this omission by extending the family of recursive functions that can be parallelized automatically.

© Springer International Publishing Switzerland 2016
F. Castor and Y.D. Liu (Eds.): SBLP 2016, LNCS 9889, pp. 140–155, 2016.
DOI: 10.1007/978-3-319-45279-1_10

To achieve this objective, we propose an algebraic framework for parallelizing two special classes of recursive functions. These functions need to have two core properties. First: the recursive function must contain only operations that can be used to define monoids or semirings. Second: the propagation of arguments between recursive calls has to be defined by a invertible function. The proposed framework is based on the theory introduced by Fisher and Ghuloum [8]. Those authors have designed and tested an approach to parallelize imperative loops by transforming them in recurrence relations defined by the compositions of associative functions. We go beyond the work of Fisher and Ghuloum in two ways: (i) we work on recursive functions, instead of imperative loops; (ii) we provide a more general definition of parallel function composition. The key idea behind our findings is the fact that algebraic structures such as groups, monoids and semirings let us decompose recursive functions into simpler components, which are amenable to automatic parallelization.

To validate the ideas discussed in this paper, we have used them to implement a source-to-source compiler, in Python, that performs automatic parallelization of Haskell code. In Sect. 4 we show how to parallelize six different – and well-known – recursive functions. Key to efficiency is the fact that we can transform elements in the family of parallelizable functions into list homomorphisms. This transformation, which we explain in Sect. 3, to the best of our knowledge, is novel. Our experiments show that our technique is effective and useful. We have achieved speedups of up to 2.7x in a 4-core Intel processor. These results are even more meaningful if we consider that they have been obtained in a completely automatic way.

2   Overview

We will use the well-known factorial function as an example to introduce our ideas to the reader. This function can be defined as follows:

$$f(x) := \begin{cases} 1 & \text{if } x = 1 \\ x \cdot f(x-1) & \text{otherwise} \end{cases}$$

Factorial is a very simple function, and the reader familiar with the parallelization of reductions on commutative and associative operators will know immediately that this function has a very efficient parallel implementation. Key to perform this parallelization is the observation that factorial can be re-written as a sequence of multiplications, e.g.: $f(x) = x \cdot (x-1) \cdot \ldots \cdot 2 \cdot 1$.

A key property of multiplication – associativity – lets us solve them in a pairwise fashion. This possibility gives us the chance to run the above expression in $O(\ln x)$ time. The goal of this paper is to be able to apply this kind of parallelization automatically onto recursive functions. In order to achieve this objective, we shall be re-writing functions as a composition of simpler functions which are associative. In the case of factorial, this composition looks like:

$$f(x) = (f'_{x-1} \circ \ldots \circ f'_2 \circ f'_1)(1)$$

How do we find a suitable implementation of f_i'? We first provide this answer for a family of recursive functions which have the following format:

$$f(p) := \begin{cases} g_0(p) & \text{if } p = p_0 \\ g_1(p) \oplus f(h(p)) \oplus g_2(p) & \text{otherwise} \end{cases} \tag{1}$$

For any function f that can be written in the format above, we show that it is possible to decompose f into a composition of functions. We first identify h, the function used to propagate the arguments of f, which we call the *hop* function. The *hop* function must be a well-defined monotonic function, which must have an inverse. For the factorial example, we have the following *hop* function h: $h(x) = x - 1$, with inverse $h^{-1}(x) = x + 1$.

The *hop* function is fundamental for generating the next arguments of the sequence of compositions. Because it has an inverse, we use it to know $x - 1$, the number of functions which will constitute the sequence of compositions. We find out $x - 1$ after solving the following equation: $p_0 = h^{x-1}(p)$. For the factorial example, the depth is exactly the initial argument x. After identifying the *hop* function and its inverse, we re-write f in a manner suitable for the composition of functions which does not contain a recursive call, e.g.: $f_i'(s) := (i+1) \cdot s$, where s is the usually called accumulator parameter in funcional composition.

Now, we can write f such as $f(x) = (f_{x-1}' \circ f_{x-2}' \circ \cdots \circ f_2' \circ f_1')(1)$. This transformation is useful, considering that functional composition is an associative operation, which can often be parallelized if it is possible to symbolically compute and simplify intermediate compositions [8]. For instance, for $i > 1 \in \mathbb{Z}$, $(f_i' \circ f_{i-1}')(s) = (i+1) \cdot (i \cdot s)$ can be reassociated as $(f_i' \circ f_{i-1}')(s) = ((i+1) \cdot i) \cdot s$ which is essentially equivalent to the original function regarding computational complexity. Thus we can evaluate $f(x)$ by computing a reduction over a list of functions, using the functional composition operator, i.e., $f(x) = \circ / [f_{x-1}', f_{x-2}', \ldots, f_1']$.

Section 3.2 generalizes the factorial example seen in this section. In Sect. 3.3 we extend our framework a bit further, showing that we can also parallelize functions in the format below. In this case, we consider two operators $\oplus$ and $\odot$, for which we only require that $\odot$ be associative, and $\oplus$ be commutative, in addition of being associative. Again, the hop function h must have an inverse function which can be computed efficiently.

$$f(p) := \begin{cases} g_0(p) & \text{if } p = p_0 \\ g_1(p) \oplus (g_3(p) \odot f(h(p)) \odot g_4(p)) \oplus g_2(p) & \text{otherwise} \end{cases} \tag{2}$$

3   Automatic Parallelization of Recursive Functions

In this section we formalize the developments earlier seen in Sect. 2. To this end, we provide a few basic notions in Sect. 3.1. In Sect. 3.2, we show how to parallelize functions on the format given by Eq. 1. In Sect. 3.3, we move on to deal with functions defined by Eq. 2.

3.1 Technical Background

In the rest of this paper we shall use three notions borrowed from abstract algebra: *groups*, *monoids* and *semirings*. If S is a set, then we define these algebraic structures as follows:

- A group $G = (S, +)$ is a nonempty set closed under an associative binary-operation $+$, which is associative, invertible and has a zero element $\mathbf{0}$, the identity regarding $+$. For each $a \in S$, its inverse $-a$ also belongs to S. A group need not be commutative. If a group is commutative, it is usually called an abelian group [21].
- A monoid $M = (S, +)$ is a nonempty set closed under an associative binary-operation $+$ with identity $\mathbf{0}$. A monoid need not be commutative and its elements need not have inverses within the monoid.
- A semiring $R = (S, +, \cdot)$ is a nonempty set closed under two associative binary-operations $+$ and $\cdot$, called addition and multiplication, respectively [9,10]. A semiring satisfies the following conditions:
  - $(S, +)$ is a commutative monoid with identity element $\mathbf{0}$;
  - $(S, \cdot)$ is a monoid with identity element $\mathbf{1}$;
  - Multiplication distributes over addition from either side;
  - Multiplication by $\mathbf{0}$ annihilates R, i.e. $a \cdot \mathbf{0} = \mathbf{0} \cdot a = \mathbf{0}$, for all $a \in S$.

Parallelizing Functional Composition. Functional composition is an associative binary operator over functions. Previous work [8,19] has shown that, given a family of indexed functions $\mathcal{F}$ closed under functional composition $\circ$, a function $\psi : \mathbb{Z} \times \mathbb{Z} \to \mathcal{F}$ is a composition evaluator of $\mathcal{F}$ iff $i\psi j = f_i \circ f_j$, for $f_i, f_j \in \mathcal{F}$. If each function in $\mathcal{F}$ and the composition evaluator ψ are constant-time computations, then a sequence of n compositions can be efficiently computed in $O(n/p + \ln p)$, considering p processing units. A functional composition over $\mathcal{F}$ can be evaluated by using the composition evaluator ψ. Thus, given a sequence of compositions $f_n \circ f_{n-1} \circ \cdots \circ f_1$, this sequence can be efficiently computed using a reduction operator $\circ/[f_n, f_{n-1}, \ldots, f_1]$, since the following equivalence holds: $\circ/[f_n, f_{n-1}, \ldots, f_1] = \psi/[n, n-1, \ldots, 1]$.

3.2 Monoids

In this section, we generalize the solution presented in Sect. 2. We provide the formal description of the mechanism used for parallelizing the factorial recursive function, regarding general algebraic structures of groups and monoids. Let S_G and S_M be sets and $M = (S_M, +)$ a monoid. Let $f : S_G \to S_M$ be a recursive function defined as:

$$f(x) := \begin{cases} g_0(x_0) & \text{if } x = x_0 \\ g_1(x) + f(h(x)) + g_2(x) & \text{otherwise} \end{cases}$$

We assume that each $g_i : S_G \to S_M$ are pure and non-recursive functions, i.e. if $a \in S_G$ then $g_i(a) \in S_M$, for $i \in [0, 2]$. Furthermore, we assume that the *hop* function $h : S_G \to S_G$ is an invertible and monotonic function over S_G.

Proposition 1. *The recursive function $f : S_G \to S_M$ can be written as a functional composition.*

Proof. We let $f'_i : S_M \to S_M$ be the following non-recursive function:

$$f'_i(s) = g_1((h^{-1})^i(x_0)) + s + g_2((h^{-1})^i(x_0))$$

In the above definition, we let $h^{-1} : S_G \to S_G$ be the inverse function of the hop h. Function $(h^{-1})^i(x_0)$ is the i-th functional power of $h^{-1} : S_G \to S_G$. To transform the recursive function into a composition, it is important to infer the depth of the recursive stack. Let $k > 0 \in \mathbb{Z}$ such that $h^k(x) = x_0$. Thus $f(x) = (f'_k \circ f'_{k-1} \circ \cdots \circ f'_2 \circ f'_1)(g_0(x_0))$ □

From Fisher and Ghuloum [8], we know that the composition of f'_i can be computed in parallel since, for $i > 1 \in \mathbb{Z}$, we have that:

$$(f'_i \circ f'_{i-1})(s) \Leftrightarrow g_1((h^{-1})^i(x_0)) + f'_{i-1}(s) + g_2((h^{-1})^i(x_0)) \Leftrightarrow$$
$$g_1((h^{-1})^i(x_0)) + [g_1((h^{-1})^{i-1}(x_0)) + s + g_2((h^{-1})^{i-1}(x_0))] + g_2((h^{-1})^i(x_0)) \Leftrightarrow$$
$$[g_1((h^{-1})^i(x_0)) + g_1((h^{-1})^{i-1}(x_0))] + s + [g_2((h^{-1})^{i-1}(x_0)) + g_2((h^{-1})^i(x_0))]$$

Defining the Hop Function. Let $G = (S_G, +)$ be a group with identity $\mathbf{0}$. If the *hop* function h is an invertible and monotonic function, we can calculate k. Let h be generally defined as $h(x) = e_1 + x + e_2$, where $e_1, e_2 \in S_G$. Then

$$h^k(x) = x_0 \Leftrightarrow$$
$$e_1 + \cdots + e_1 + e_1 + x + e_2 + e_2 + \cdots + e_2 = x_0 \Leftrightarrow$$
$$ke_1 + x + ke_2 = x_0 \Leftrightarrow$$
$$x + ke_2 = (-ke_1) + x_0 \Leftrightarrow$$
$$x + ke_2 - x_0 = (-ke_1) \Leftrightarrow$$
$$x + (ke_2 - x_0 + ke_1) = \mathbf{0}$$

that is, $\exists k \in \mathbb{Z}$ such that $k > 0$ and $(ke_2 - x_0 + ke_1) \in S_G$ is the inverse of $x \in S_G$. Given the equality above, k can often be dynamically computed with a small overhead. If G is commutative, then $(ke_2 - x_0 + ke_1) = k(e_1 + e_2) - x_0$. From these notions, we define function h^{-1}, the inverse of the hopping function, as $h^{-1}(x) = (-e_1) + x + (-e_2)$. This equality is true, since:

$$(h^{-1} \circ h)(x) = (-e_1) + h(x) + (-e_2) \Leftrightarrow$$
$$(h^{-1} \circ h)(x) = (-e_1) + [e_1 + x + e_2] + (-e_2) \Leftrightarrow$$
$$(h^{-1} \circ h)(x) = \mathbf{0} + x + \mathbf{0} = x$$

Computing the Function Composition Using List Homomorphism. Thus far, we have seen how to re-write a function (with certain properties) as a composition of non-recursive functions. We need now a way to implement this composition efficiently. To achieve efficiency, we use list homomorphisms. We say that a function y is a list homomorphism if we have that $y(w + z) = y(w) + y(z)$, where $+$ denotes list concatenation. In this section we derive a simple implementation for such a recursive function $f : S_G \to S_M$ by means of list homomorphism.

Proposition 2. *Let $h'(i) = (h^{-1})^i(x_0)$. Then we can write the functional composition $f(x) = (f'_k \circ f'_{k-1} \circ \cdots \circ f'_2 \circ f'_1)(g_0(x_0))$ as:*

$$f(x) = (+/(g_1 \circ h') \star [k, k-1, \ldots, 1]) + g_0(x_0) + (+/(g_2 \circ h') \star [1, 2, \ldots, k]).$$

Proof. The functional composition expands as follows:

$$f(x) = g'_1(x_0) + g_0(x_0) + g'_2(x_0), \text{where:}$$
$$g'_1(x_0) = g_1((h^{-1})^k(x_0)) + g_1((h^{-1})^{k-1}(x_0)) + \cdots + g_1((h^{-1})(x_0))$$
$$g'_2(x_0) = g_2((h^{-1})(x_0)) + g_2((h^{-1})^2(x_0)) + \cdots + g_2((h^{-1})^k(x_0))$$

Since $h'(i) = (h^{-1})^i(x_0)$, then we can write:

$$g'_1(x_0) = g_1(h'(k)) + g_1(h'(k-1)) + \cdots + g_1(h'(1))$$
$$g'_2(x_0) = g_2(h'(1)) + g_2(h'(2)) + \cdots + g_2(h'(k))$$

Therefore, it is possible to compute g'_1 and g'_2 using a list homomorphism, i.e.:

$$g'_1(x_0) = +/g_1 \star (h' \star [k, k-1, \ldots, 1])$$
$$g'_2(x_0) = +/g_2 \star (h' \star [1, 2, \ldots, k])$$

where $+/\ell$ denotes the folding of the operation $+$ onto the list ℓ, and $k \star \ell$ denotes the mapping of function k onto every element of ℓ. The above expression can then be simplified as:

$$g'_1(x_0) = +/(g_1 \circ h') \star [k, k-1, \ldots, 1]$$
$$g'_2(x_0) = +/(g_2 \circ h') \star [1, 2, \ldots, k]$$

$\square$

3.3 Semirings

We now describe a second family of recursive functions that we can parallelize automatically by rethinking them under the light of algebraic structures. Let S_G and S_R be sets and $R = (S_R, +, \cdot)$ a semiring. Let $f : S_G \to S_R$ be defined as:

$$f(x) := \begin{cases} g_0(x_0) & \text{if } x = x_0 \\ g_1(x) + g_3(x)f(h(x))g_4(x) + g_2(x) & \text{otherwise} \end{cases}$$

where each $g_i : S_G \to S_R$ is a non-recursive function. Function $h : S_G \to S_G$ is the *hop*. Let $f'_i : S_R \to S_R$ be the following non-recursive function:

$$f'_i(s) = g_1((h^{-1})^i(x_0)) + g_3((h^{-1})^i(x_0))sg_4((h^{-1})^i(x_0)) + g_2((h^{-1})^i(x_0))$$

where $(h^{-1})^i(x_0)$ is the i-th functional power of h^{-1}, the inverse function of the
hop function h (see Sect. 3.2).

In order to transform the recursive function into a composition, again we
must infer the depth of the recursive stack. Let $k > 0 \in \mathbb{Z}$ such that $h^k(x) = x_0$
(see Sect. 3.2). Thus:

$$f(x) = (f_k' \circ f_{k-1}' \circ \cdots \circ f_2' \circ f_1')(g_0(x_0))$$

Computing the Function Composition Using List Homomorphism. In
this section we derive a simple implementation of a recursive function $f : S_G \to
S_R$ by means of list homomorphism. If $h'(i) = (h^{-1})^i(x_0)$, then we can write:

$$f(x) = \phi_1(k) + \phi_3(k)g_0(x_0)\phi_4(k) + \phi_2(k)$$

where $k > 0 \in \mathbb{Z}$ such that $h^k(x) = x_0$ (see Sect. 3.2). We have that:

$$\beta_1(i) = (\cdot/(g_3 \circ h') \star [k, k-1, \ldots, i+1]) \, g_1(h'(i)) \, (\cdot/(g_4 \circ h') \star [i+1, i+2, \ldots, k])$$
$$\phi_1(k) = g_1(h'(k)) + (+/\beta_1 \star [k-1, k-2, \ldots, 1])$$
$$\phi_3(k) = (\cdot/(g_3 \circ h') \star [k, k-1, \ldots, 1])$$
$$\phi_4(k) = (\cdot/(g_4 \circ h') \star [1, 2, \ldots, k])$$
$$\beta_2(i) = (\cdot/(g_3 \circ h') \star [k, k-1, \ldots, i+1]) \, g_2(h'(i)) \, (\cdot/(g_4 \circ h') \star [i+1, i+2, \ldots, k])$$
$$\phi_2(k) = (+/\beta_2 \star [1, 2, \ldots, k-1]) + g_2(h'(k))$$

There are redundant computations in the previous definition. We can opti-
mize the computation of β_1 and β_2 by pre-computing these redundant values
using a scan operation. Considering left- and right-associative scan operations
(*scanl* and *scanr*), we define lists v and w as follows:

$$[v_1, v_2, \ldots, v_{k-1}] = scanr \cdot /(g_3 \circ h') \star [k, k-1, \ldots, 2]$$
$$[w_1, w_2, \ldots, w_{k-1}] = scanl \cdot /(g_4 \circ h') \star [2, 3, \ldots, k]$$

That is, $v_i = \cdot/(g_3 \circ h') \star [k, k-1, \ldots, k-i+1]$ and $w_i = \cdot/(g_4 \circ h') \star [k -
i+1, \ldots, k-1, k]$. Once we have pre-computed v_i and w_i, we can define the
following simplified construction:

$$\beta_1(i) = v_i \cdot g_1(h'(i)) \cdot w_{k-i}$$
$$\phi_1(k) = g_1(h'(k)) + (+/\beta_1 \star [k-1, k-2, \ldots, 1])$$
$$\phi_3(k) = v_1 \cdot (g_3 \circ h')(1)$$
$$\phi_4(k) = (g_4 \circ h')(1) \cdot w_{k-1}$$
$$\beta_2(i) = v_i \cdot g_2(h'(i)) \cdot w_{k-i}$$
$$\phi_2(k) = (+/\beta_2 \star [1, 2, \ldots, k-1]) + g_2(h'(k))$$

3.4 Examples

In this section we discuss different functions that we can parallelize automatically. We shall provide examples that we can parallelize using the monoid-based

approach (Catalan Numbers and List Concatenation), and with the semiring-based approach (Financial Compound Interest, Horner's Method and Comb Filters). The actual performance of each of these example is analyzed in Sect. 4.

Catalan Numbers. Catalan numbers form a sequence of positive integers that appear in the solution of several counting problems in combinatorics, including some generating functions. Catalan numbers are defined as follows:

$$C_n = \frac{2(2n-1)}{n+1} C_{n-1} \quad \text{where } C_1 = 1$$

which can be written as $f : \mathbb{Z} \to \mathbb{Z}^*$

$$f(x) := \begin{cases} 1 & \text{if } x = 1 \\ \frac{2(2x-1)}{x+1} \cdot f(x-1) & \text{otherwise} \end{cases}$$

Similar to the factorial function seen in Sect. 2, the above function can be written as a composition of non-recursive functions: Let $h : \mathbb{Z} \to \mathbb{Z}$ be $h(x) = x - 1$, $g_1 : \mathbb{Z} \to \mathbb{Z}^*$ be $g_1(x) = \frac{2(2x-1)}{x+1}$ and $g_2 : \mathbb{Z} \to \mathbb{Z}^*$ be $g_2(x) = 1$.
Then, we can define a function $f_i' : \mathbb{Z}^* \to \mathbb{Z}^*$, such as

$$f_i'(s) = g_1((h^{-1})^i(1)) \cdot s \cdot g_2((h^{-1})^i(1)) \Leftrightarrow$$
$$f_i'(s) = g_1(i+1) \cdot s \cdot 1 \Leftrightarrow$$
$$f_i'(s) = \frac{2(2i+1)}{i+2} \cdot s$$

since $h^{-1}(x) = x + 1$. We can easily calculate that $h^k(x) = 1$ for $k = x - 1$, since $x + (0k - 1 + k(-1)) = 0 \Leftrightarrow x - k - 1 = 0$.
Therefore, $f(x) = (f_{x-1}' \circ f_{x-2}' \circ \cdots \circ f_2' \circ f_1')(1)$. Since, for every $i > 1 \in \mathbb{Z}$, the composition $(f_i' \circ f_{i-1}')(s)$ can be symbolicaly computed and simplified, i.e.

$$(f_i' \circ f_{i-1}')(s) = \frac{2(2i+1)}{i+2} \cdot f_{i-1}'(s) \Leftrightarrow$$
$$(f_i' \circ f_{i-1}')(s) = \frac{2(2i+1)}{i+2} \cdot \left(\frac{2(2i-1)}{i+1} \cdot s \right) \Leftrightarrow$$
$$(f_i' \circ f_{i-1}')(s) = \left(\frac{2(2i+1)}{i+2} \cdot \frac{2(2i-1)}{i+1} \right) \cdot s$$

Function $f(x) = (f_x' \circ f_{x-1}' \circ \cdots \circ f_1')(1)$ can be computed in parallel as a reduction.

List Concatenation. Let $L_{\mathbb{Z}}$ be the set of lists over the set of integers $\mathbb{Z}$. A list is an ordered sequence denoted by $A = [a_1, a_2, \ldots, a_n]$, where the size of A is $\#A = n$. An empty list is denoted by $[]$ and $\#[] = 0$. Concatenation is an associative binary-operation over a set of lists. Given two lists $A = [a_1, a_2, \ldots, a_n]$ and $B = [b_1, b_2, \ldots, b_m]$, the concatenation of the lists A and B is denoted by $A + B = [a_1, \ldots, a_n, b_1, \ldots, b_m]$. The identity element regarding concatenation is the empty list. Thus$(L_{\mathbb{Z}}, +\!\!+)$ is a non-commutative monoid. Let $f : \mathbb{Z} \to L_{\mathbb{Z}}$ be the following recursive function:

$$f(x) := \begin{cases} [] & \text{if } x = 0 \\ [x] +\!\!+ f(x-1) +\!\!+ [x] & \text{otherwise} \end{cases}$$

Let $h : \mathbb{Z} \to \mathbb{Z}$ be $h(x) = x - 1$, $g_1 : \mathbb{Z} \to L_{\mathbb{Z}}$ be $g_1(x) = [x]$ and $g_2 : \mathbb{Z} \to L_{\mathbb{Z}}$ be $g_2(x) = [x]$. Then, we can define a simplified function $f'_i : L_{\mathbb{Z}} \to L_{\mathbb{Z}}$, such as:

$$f'_i(s) = g_1((h^{-1})^i(0)) +\!\!+ s +\!\!+ g_2((h^{-1})^i(0)) \Leftrightarrow$$
$$f'_i(s) = g_1(i) +\!\!+ s +\!\!+ g_2(i) \Leftrightarrow$$
$$f'_i(s) = [i] +\!\!+ s +\!\!+ [i]$$

since $h^{-1}(x) = x + 1$. We have that $h^k(x) = 0$ for $k = x$, since $x + (0k - 0 + k(-1)) = 0 \Leftrightarrow x - k = 0$. Therefore, $f(x) = (f'_x \circ f'_{x-1} \circ \cdots \circ f'_2 \circ f'_1)([])$. Since, for every $i > 1 \in \mathbb{Z}$, the composition $(f'_i \circ f'_{i-1})(s)$ can be symbolicaly computed and simplified, i.e.:

$$(f'_i \circ f'_{i-1})(s) = [i] +\!\!+ f'_{i-1}(s) +\!\!+ [i] \Leftrightarrow$$
$$(f'_i \circ f'_{i-1})(s) = [i] +\!\!+ ([i-1] +\!\!+ s +\!\!+ [i-1]) +\!\!+ [i] \Leftrightarrow$$
$$(f'_i \circ f'_{i-1})(s) = ([i] +\!\!+ [i-1]) +\!\!+ s +\!\!+ ([i-1] +\!\!+ [i]) \Leftrightarrow$$
$$(f'_i \circ f'_{i-1})(s) = [i, i-1] +\!\!+ s +\!\!+ [i-1, i]$$

Thus $f(x) = (f'_x \circ f'_{x-1} \circ \cdots \circ f'_1)([])$ can be computed in parallel by a reduction.

Financial Compound Interest. We can define financial compound interest with periodic deposits recursively. Let $f : \mathbb{Z} \to \mathbb{R}$ be the following recursive function:

$$f(x) := \begin{cases} y_0 & \text{if } x = 0 \\ (1+r) \cdot f(x-1) + y_x & \text{otherwise} \end{cases}$$

where y_0 is the initial deposit, r is the compounded rate, and y_x is the deposit on the x-th period. Let $h : \mathbb{Z} \to \mathbb{Z}$ is $h(x) = x - 1$, $g_1 : \mathbb{Z} \to \mathbb{R}$ is $g_1(x) = 0$, $g_3 : \mathbb{Z} \to \mathbb{R}$ is $g_3(x) = (1+r)$, $g_4 : \mathbb{Z} \to \mathbb{R}$ is $g_4(x) = 1$, $g_2 : \mathbb{Z} \to \mathbb{R}$ is $g_2(x) = y_x$. From these notions, we define a simplified function $f'_i : \mathbb{R} \to \mathbb{R}$ as follows:

$$f'_i(s) = g_1((h^{-1})^i(0)) + g_3((h^{-1})^i(0))sg_4((h^{-1})^i(0)) + g_2((h^{-1})^i(0)) \Leftrightarrow$$
$$f'_i(s) = g_1(i) + g_3(i)sg_4(i) + g_2(i) \Leftrightarrow$$
$$f'_i(s) = (1+r)s + y_i \Leftrightarrow$$

since $h^{-1}(x) = x + 1$. We have that $h^k(x) = 0$ for $k = x$, since $x + (0k - 0 + k(-1)) = 0 \Leftrightarrow x - k = 0$. Hence, $f(x) = (f'_x \circ f'_{x-1} \circ \cdots \circ f'_2 \circ f'_1)(y_0)$. Since, for every $i > 1 \in \mathbb{Z}$, the composition $(f'_i \circ f'_{i-1})(s)$ can be symbolicaly computed and simplified, i.e.:

$$(f'_i \circ f'_{i-1})(s) = (1+r)f'_{i-1}(s) + y_i \Leftrightarrow$$
$$(f'_i \circ f'_{i-1})(s) = (1+r)((1+r)s + y_{i-1}) + y_i \Leftrightarrow$$
$$(f'_i \circ f'_{i-1})(s) = (1+r)(1+r)s + (1+r)y_{i-1} + y_i \Leftrightarrow$$
$$(f'_i \circ f'_{i-1})(s) = (1+r)^2 s + [(1+r)y_{i-1} + y_i]$$

Thus $f(x) = (f'_x \circ f'_{x-1} \circ \cdots \circ f'_2 \circ f'_1)(y_0)$ can be computed in parallel.

Horner's Method. Horner's method is useful to solve polynomials defined recursively. Its implementation can be parallelized as done in the previous example of financial compound interest. Let c_i be the coefficients, for $0 \leq i \leq n$. Thus a polynomial of degree n can be evaluated, for a given value of x, by the following recursive formula, as described by the Horner's method:

$$f(n) := \begin{cases} c_0 & \text{if } n = 0 \\ f(n-1) \cdot x + c_n & \text{otherwise} \end{cases}$$

Comb Filter in Signal Processing. Comb filters have several applications in signal processing [23]. The following equation represents the feedback form used by comb filters: $y_t = \alpha y_{t-T} + (1-\alpha)x_t$, where x_t is the input signal at a given time t and α controls the intensity that the delayed signal is fed back into the output y_t given a delay time T. Let $f : \mathbb{Z} \to \mathbb{R}$ be the following recursive function:

$$f(t) := \begin{cases} y_0 & \text{if } t = 0 \\ \alpha f(t-T) + (1-\alpha)x_t & \text{otherwise} \end{cases}$$

3.5   Implementation

We have used the ideas discussed in this paper to implement a prototype of our automatic parallelizer that performs source-to-source transformations. This prototype is written in Python, and it performs symbolic computations using Python's sympy package. Symbolic computing allows us to find the inverse of the hop function and also to infer the depth of the recursive stack (as discussed in Sects. 3.2 and 3.3). Below we show the source-to-source transformation that we produce for the list concatenation example:

```
# Sequential version:
f :: Integer -> [Integer]
f 0 = []
f n = [n] ++ f(n-1) ++ [n]


# Parallel version:
f_g_1 :: Integer -> [Integer]
f_g_1 _HOP_i = [(_HOP_i)]
f_g_2 :: Integer -> [Integer]
f_g_2 _HOP_i = [(_HOP_i)]
f :: Integer -> [Integer]
f n = (parFoldr (++) (map f_g_1 (reverse [1..(n)]))) ++ [] ++
      (parFoldr (++) (map f_g_2 [1..(n)]))
```

In general, for the monoid-based case, we receive inputs in the format below:

```
f :: Integer -> IMGSET
f e_0 = y_0
f n = g_1(n) * f(n-e_1) * g_2(n)
```

The prototype's output consists of three new functions: f_g_1, f_g_2 and f, which have the following general format:

```
f_g_1 :: Integer -> IMGSET
f_g_1 _HOP_i = g_1((_HOP_i*e_1 + e_0))
f_g_2 :: Integer -> IMGSET
f_g_2 _HOP_i = g_2((_HOP_i*e_1 + e_0))
f :: Integer -> IMGSET
f n = (parFoldr (*) (map f_g_1 (reverse [1..((-e_0 + n)/e_1)]))) * y_0 *
      (parFoldr (*) (map f_g_2 [1..((-e_0 + n)/e_1)]))
```

4   Evaluation

To validate the ideas discussed in this paper, we have implemented our source-to-source compiler that generates parallel Haskell, using the parallel library provided by the **Strategies** package, available in the Glasgow Haskell Compiler (GHC) [1,16]. The experiments were performed in four physical cores of an Ivy Bridge-based Intel processor technology, with 2 GHz of clock and 15 GB of RAM. In this section, we show results for six benchmarks – three illustrating monoid-based parallelization (factorial, catalan and concatenation), and three illustrating semiring-based parallelization (compound interest, Horner's method and Comb Filter). For the experiments with all six applications we evaluated the speedup varying the number of threads from 1 to 4, while fixing the input argument of each function in 50,000. We consider a 95 % confidence interval for a total of five executions.

Monoids. Figure 1 presents the results for the parallelization of recursive functions based on monoids. Vertical bars show confidence interval. For the parallelization of the three monoid-based applications we implemented the construction using the list homomorphism presented in Sect. 3.2. Parallelization was achieved by means of a right-associative fold operator, which is part of the Parallel Haskell library. We achieved a maximum speedup of 1.78× in the implementation of Catalan Numbers.

Semirings. Figure 2 shows the results for the parallelization of recursive functions based on semirings. Our largest speedup was 2.71 in the Horner's Method example. For the other two examples, we got more modest speedups. For the parallelization of the three semiring-based applications we implemented the construction using the list homomorphism discussed in Sect. 3.3. We have used the same parallel implementation of the right-associative fold operator which we applied on the monoid-based examples.

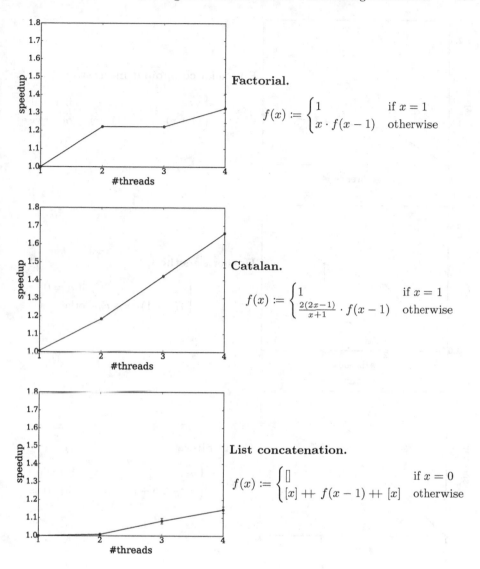

Factorial.

$$f(x) := \begin{cases} 1 & \text{if } x = 1 \\ x \cdot f(x-1) & \text{otherwise} \end{cases}$$

Catalan.

$$f(x) := \begin{cases} 1 & \text{if } x = 1 \\ \frac{2(2x-1)}{x+1} \cdot f(x-1) & \text{otherwise} \end{cases}$$

List concatenation.

$$f(x) := \begin{cases} [] & \text{if } x = 0 \\ [x] \mathbin{+\!\!+} f(x-1) \mathbin{+\!\!+} [x] & \text{otherwise} \end{cases}$$

Fig. 1. Speedup analysis of monoid-based examples.

Discussion. We have been able to observe actual speedups on the six examples that we have played with. These speedups were usually sublinear, e.g., we could not observe a four-fold speedup in any of the cases. We believe that this sublinearity is due to the overhead imposed by the reduction operator required by the proposed parallel construction. Nevertheless, we would like to emphasize that all these results have been obtained by means of automatic transformations. In other words, the use of our techniques does not require any intervention from the programmer who has implemented the original version of each function that we parallelize.

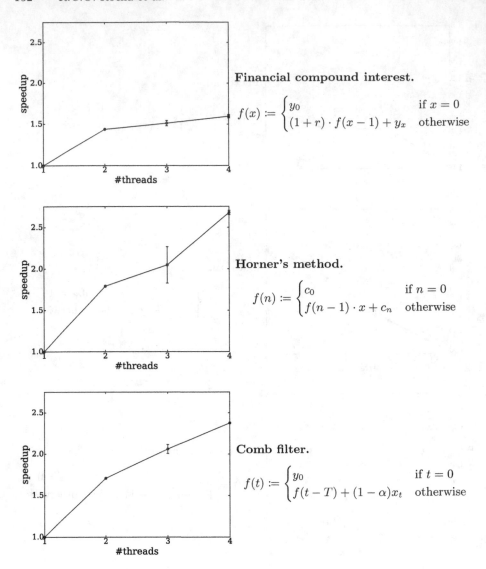

Financial compound interest.

$$f(x) := \begin{cases} y_0 & \text{if } x = 0 \\ (1+r) \cdot f(x-1) + y_x & \text{otherwise} \end{cases}$$

Horner's method.

$$f(n) := \begin{cases} c_0 & \text{if } n = 0 \\ f(n-1) \cdot x + c_n & \text{otherwise} \end{cases}$$

Comb filter.

$$f(t) := \begin{cases} y_0 & \text{if } t = 0 \\ f(t-T) + (1-\alpha)x_t & \text{otherwise} \end{cases}$$

Fig. 2. Speedup analysis of semiring-based examples.

5   Related Work

There are several automatic parallelization techniques that, similarly to ours, seek common patterns in code. Strategies based on matrix-multiplication are a well-known example. Kogge and Stone [14] have shown how to parallelize a recurrence equation by rewriting it in a form of matrix multiplication, also called *state-vector update* form. An expression e in a loop is a recurring expression if, and only if, e is computed from some loop-carried value. Sato and Iwasaki [22] have described a framework based on matrix multiplication for automatically parallelizing affine loops that consist of reduce or scan operations. They have also provided algorithms for recognizing the normal form and max-operators automatically. They have been able to report considerable speedups and high scalability by applying their framework onto simple benchmarks. Also along this line, Zou and Rajopadhye [26] have proposed a way to parallelize scan operations using the matrix multiplication framework with the polyhedral model [2,3,24]. They can handle arbitrary nested affine loops; the polyhedron model itself has already been used to parallelize different types of loops in imperative programming languages [7]. Contrary to our work, these previous approaches search for a way to deconstruct a loop as multiplication of matrices, we search for a way to deconstruct a function as a composition of monoid/semiring operations. The programs that can be parallelized by these two approaches are different.

Fisher and Ghuloum [8] provide a generalized formalization for automatic parallelization of loops by extracting function composition as the main associative operator. If a function is closed under composition, its compositions can be computed efficiently. They describe loops that compute reduction or scan as the composition of its *modeling function*. For loops that fit the allowed format, they can be implemented in a manner that computes the composition of the modelling function in parallel. Our work improves on theirs, because we extend their approach to recursive functions. In fact, this is our main contribution: a general way to extract parallelism buried under the syntax of potentially convoluted recursive functions. In addition, we also provide a more general definition of parallel code by means of algebraic structures such as monoids and semirings.

There exists vast literature about list homomorphisms [5,13,15,20]. List homomorphism is a special class of natural recursive functions on lists, which has algebraic properties suitable for parallelism. We rely on list homomorphisms to build efficient parallel computations of recursive functions. However, our approach does not target exclusively functions that work on lists. As many of our examples illustrate, we are able to generate parallel code for functions involving just numbers, or even for more complex data-structures that can be processed by monoid-based operators.

6   Conclusion

This paper has presented a theoretical approach to parallelize recursive functions. This contribution is important because previous work has reported difficulties to infer parallel behavior out of recursive function. In this case, parallelism is usually buried under heavy and convoluted syntax. We have delineated two classes of recursive functions which we can parallelize automatically. These functions have the following property: they can be re-written as the combination of themselves (through a recursive call) with non-recursive functions by means of monoid or semiring operators. There are several examples of functions that fit this framework, including typical functional implementations of algorithms to compute factorials, sum up elements of lists, concatenate lists, etc.

As future work, we intend to broaden the classes of recursive functions that our algebraic framework can automatically parallelize. We also intend to perform optimizations on the parallel code generated by our source-to-source compiler.

References

1. Berthold, J., Marlow, S., Hammond, K., Al Zain, A.: Comparing and optimising parallel Haskell implementations for multicore machines. In: ADPNA. IEEE (2009)
2. Bondhugula, U., Baskaran, M., Krishnamoorthy, S., Ramanujam, J., Rountev, A., Sadayappan, P.: Automatic transformations for communication-minimized parallelization and locality optimization in the polyhedral model. In: Hendren, L. (ed.) CC 2008. LNCS, vol. 4959, pp. 132–146. Springer, Heidelberg (2008)
3. Bondhugula, U., Hartono, A., Ramanujam, J., Sadayappan, P.: A practical automatic polyhedral parallelizer and locality optimizer. In: PLDI. ACM (2008)
4. Brown, C., Danelutto, M., Hammond, K., Kilpatrick, P., Elliott, A.: Cost-directed refactoring for parallel erlang programs. Int. J. Parallel Programm. **42**(4), 564–582 (2013)
5. Cole, M.: Parallel programming with list homomorphisms. Parallel Process. Lett. **5**(02), 191–203 (1995)
6. Collins, A., Grewe, D., Grover, V., Lee, S., Susnea, A.: NOVA: a functional language for data parallelism. In: ARRAY. ACM (2014)
7. Feautrier, P.: Automatic parallelization in the polytope model. In: Perrin, G.-R., Darte, A. (eds.) The Data Parallel Programming Model. LNCS, vol. 1132, pp. 79–103. Springer, Heidelberg (1996)
8. Fisher, A.L., Ghuloum, A.M.: Parallelizing complex scans and reductions. In: PLDI. ACM (1994)
9. Golan, J.S.: Power Algebras over Semirings: With Applications in Mathematics and Computer Science. Mathematics and Its Applications, vol. 488, 1st edn. Springer, Basel (1999)
10. Golan, J.S.: Semirings and their Applications, 1st edn. Springer, Heidelberg (1999)
11. Govindarajan, R., Anantpur, J.: Runtime dependence computation and execution of loops on heterogeneous systems. In: CGO. IEEE/ACM (2013)
12. Hammond, K., Berthold, J., Loogen, R.: Automatic skeletons in template haskell. Parallel Process. Lett. **13**(03), 413–424 (2003)
13. Hu, Z., Iwasaki, H., Takechi, M.: Formal derivation of efficient parallel programs by construction of list homomorphisms. Trans. Program. Lang. Syst. **19**(3), 444–461 (1997)
14. Kogge, P.M., Stone, H.S.: A parallel algorithm for the efficient solution of a general class of recurrence equations. Trans. Comput. **22**(8), 786–793 (1973)
15. Liu, Y., Hu, Z., Matsuzaki, K.: Towards systematic parallel programming over MapReduce. In: Namyst, R., Roman, J., Jeannot, E. (eds.) Euro-Par 2011, Part II. LNCS, vol. 6853, pp. 39–50. Springer, Heidelberg (2011)
16. Marlow, S., Maier, P., Loidl, H.W., Aswad, M.K., Trinder, P.W.: Seq no more: Better strategies for parallel Haskell. In: Haskell Symposium. ACM Press (2010)
17. Marlow, S., Peyton Jones, S., Singh, S.: Runtime support for multicore haskell. In: ICFP, pp. 65–78. ACM (2009)
18. Misailovic, S., Kim, D., Rinard, M.: Parallelizing sequential programs with statistical accuracy tests. Trans. Embed. Comput. Syst. **12**(2), 88 (2013)

19. Morihata, A., Matsuzaki, K.: Automatic parallelization of recursive functions using quantifier elimination. In: Blume, M., Kobayashi, N., Vidal, G. (eds.) FLOPS 2010. LNCS, vol. 6009, pp. 321–336. Springer, Heidelberg (2010)
20. Morita, K., Morihata, A., Matsuzaki, K., Hu, Z., Takeichi, M.: Automatic inversion generates divide-and-conquer parallel programs. In: PLDI. ACM (2007)
21. Rotman, J.J.: Advanced Modern Algebra, 2nd edn. Prentice Hall, Upper Saddle River (2003)
22. Sato, S., Iwasaki, H.: Automatic parallelization via matrix multiplication. In: PLDI. ACM (2011)
23. Schlecht, S.J., Habets, E.A.P.: Connections between parallel and serial combinations of comb filters and feedback delay networks. In: IWAENC (2012)
24. Trifunovic, K., Nuzman, D., Cohen, A., Zaks, A., Rosen, I.: Polyhedral-model guided loop-nest auto-vectorization. In: PACT. IEEE (2009)
25. Wang, Z., Tournavitis, G., Franke, B., O'Boyle, M.F.P.: Integrating profile-driven parallelism detection and machine-learning-based mapping. Trans. Archit. Code Optim. 11(1), 2 (2014)
26. Zou, Y., Rajopadhye, S.: Scan detection and parallelization in "inherently sequential" nested loop programs. In: CGO. ACM (2012)

A Platform of Scientific Workflows for Orchestration of Parallel Components in a Cloud of High Performance Computing Applications

Jefferson de Carvalho Silva$^{(\boxtimes)}$ and Francisco Heron de Carvalho Junior

Mestrado e Doutorado em Ciência da Computação, Universidade Federal do Ceará,
Fortaleza, Brazil
{jeffersoncarvalho,heron}@lia.ufc.br

Abstract. HPC Shelf is a proposal of a cloud computing platform for development, deployment and execution of component-based HPC applications with large-scale parallel processing requirements. Through components, it addresses the challenge of dealing with heterogeneous resources in high-end parallel computing systems, including both software and hardware. This paper introduces SAFe, a framework for deriving HPC Shelf applications, and SAFeSWL, a scientific workflow language for describing the architectural and orchestration parts of parallel computing systems deployed by HPC Shelf applications through SAFe.

1 Introduction

In discussions about emerging High Performance Computing (HPC) applications, "large-scale" and "heterogeneous" became recurrent keywords associated to data processing, software architecture and parallel computer architectures.

Large-scale data processing applications demand for a huge amount of processing power that is beyond the capacity even of high-end parallel computing platforms. A number of these applications recently emerged, with the exponential growth of data produced in sciences, social networks and sensors [5], making the so-called Big Data applications important driving forces of HPC technologies.

In turn, the scale and complexity of software in HPC have increased significantly since the 1990s, with advent of web technologies and the need of integrating software contributions from different sources, including legacy software written some decades ago, for solving more challenging problems [22].

Finally, the complexity of parallel computer architectures has also increased, with the advent of multi-core processors [16], deep memory hierarchies under the explicit programmer control, and computational accelerators, such as FPGAs [12], GPUs [14] and MICs [13], forcing HPC application development to be concerned with requirements of *heterogeneous computing* [21].

The increase in complexity both in software and hardware have motivated a number of research initiatives aimed at proposing and validating new techniques for large-scale software development for attending the requirements of

© Springer International Publishing Switzerland 2016
F. Castor and Y.D. Liu (Eds.): SBLP 2016, LNCS 9889, pp. 156–170, 2016.
DOI: 10.1007/978-3-319-45279-1_11

HPC applications [22,25,27]. Among these initiatives, we are particularly interested in component-based HPC platforms [3,4,6,9]. We are also interested in *Scientific Workflow Management Systems* (SWfMS) [1,11,18,23,29], which have introduced techniques and component-based abstractions for specification and execution of complex data processing procedures by scientists and engineers.

Cloud computing [2,20] has also been consolidated as a suitable abstraction for on-demand provisioning of HPC Services [7,24,28,30]. Almost all the HPC cloud services fits the SaaS (software-as-a-service) and IaaS (infrastructure-as-a-service) models. The former ones implement problem-solving environments targeting domain-specialist users. In turn, the later ones provide the ability of instantiating parallel computing platforms (virtual computer nodes, network and programming libraries) according to the requirements of users' programs.

HPC Shelf is a proposal of platform for cloud-based HPC services, providing a substratum for development, deployment and execution of HPC applications, where users may describe problems that will be solved by automatically generated parallel computing systems built of components. It may be viewed as a SaaS cloud from the perspective of *application users*, a PaaS (platform-as-a-service) cloud from the perspective of *application providers* and *component developers*, and a IaaS cloud from the perspective of *infrastructure maintainers*.

This paper introduces SAFe (*Shelf Application Framework*), the application framework of HPC Shelf. It is a CBHPC platform for large-scale and heterogeneous parallel computing that uses the workflow language SAFeSWL (*SAFe Scientific Workflow Language*) for orchestrating parallel components engaged in long running computations and deployed across a set of parallel computing platforms. These components and parallel computing platforms form parallel computing systems. SAFeSWL is integrated with the contextual contract system of HPC Shelf for the selection of component implementations according to application requirements and characteristics of the parallel computing platforms.

For accomplishing the objectives of this paper, Sect. 2 gives an overview about HPC Shelf, whereas SAFe and SAFeSWL are detailed in Sect. 3, by using workflows from the MapReduce and Montage applications as examples. Then, Sect. 4 presents the contributions of SAFe and SAFeSWL in the context of SWfMS, where they are more prominent. Finally, Sect. 5 concludes this paper and outlines further works.

2   HPC Shelf: A Cloud of HPC Services

HPC Shelf is a component-based platform for clouds that provide services for development, deployment and execution of HPC applications whose computational requirements for solving problems that specialists of a given domain could be interested justifies the employment of a set of parallel computing platforms.

In HPC Shelf, *parallel computing systems* are built of components that represent their hardware and software elements, including parallel computing platforms, algorithms, data structures, communication/synchronization patterns, and so on. For that, components comply to Hash, a model of parallel components where *component kinds* may represent these different composition elements [8].

2.1   The Component Kinds of HPC Shelf

The component kinds of HPC Shelf are: **platforms**, representing distributed-memory parallel computing platforms (*virtual platforms*); **computations**, representing implementations of parallel algorithms that exploit the features of a class of virtual platforms; **data sources**, representing data sources that may interest to computations; **connectors**, which couple a set of computations and data sources placed in distinct virtual platforms, for either orchestrating them or making the role of a substratum for their choreography; and **bindings**, for connecting *service* and *action ports* exported by components for synchronization.

A *service binding* connects a *user* to a *provider* port, allowing a component to consume a service offered by another component. A user and a provider port are compatible if a service binding exists for connecting them. In turn, action bindings connect a set of *action ports* that export the same set of action names. Components react to the synchronous activation of these actions.

An application is represented by two components in a parallel computing system, so-called *Application* and *Workflow*. Through service ports, Application exchanges data with *solution components* during execution. In turn, through task ports, Workflow orchestrates actions of solution components through a specification written in the orchestration subset of SAFeSWL (Sect. 3.1).

2.2   Stakeholders

The following stakeholders orbit around HPC Shelf. The **specialists** use applications for specification of problems and execution of solutions offered by the application. They do not manipulate components directly, which are hidden behind the domain-specific application abstractions. In turn, the **providers** create and deploy applications. Since they must solve problems through parallel computing systems, they are experts in computational solutions in the application domain. Moreover, the **developers** develop the components of parallel computing systems, tuned for exploiting the architecture of a class of virtual platforms. For that, developers are experts in parallel computer architectures and their programming. Finally, the **maintainers** offer the infrastructure of HPC Shelf, on top of which virtual platforms are instantiated. Through contextual contracts, they may specify the architectural features of the virtual platforms they support.

2.3   Architecture

The interests of the stakeholders of HPC Shelf leads to an architecture formed by three elements: SAFe (*Shelf Application Framework*), Core and Back-End.

From SAFe, *providers* derive applications for *specialists*, by accessing the catalog of components of HPC Shelf, where they choose the components of the parallel computing systems that will solve the problems specified by the specialists through the application. Also, they specify how components are orchestrated and how they interact with the application. For that, providers employ SAFeSWL, which is both an architectural description and a scientific workflow language.

The Core manages the life-cycle of components, from cataloging to deployment. Developers and maintainers register components and their contracts through the Core. The applications access the services of the Core for resolving component contracts and deploying the components of parallel computing systems. For that, the Core implements the system of contextual contracts [10].

Each maintainer offers a Back-End to the Core, for the deployment of virtual platforms in their HPC infrastructure. Once deployed, virtual platforms may communicate directly with Core for deploying computations, data sources, connectors and bindings. In turn, these components, and also virtual platforms, may communicate directly with applications through service and action bindings.

2.4   Contextual Contracts

HPC Shelf employs a system of *contextual contracts* for component typing and selection according to application requirements and characteristics of the target parallel computing platforms (*deployment context*) [10].

Contextual contracts are defined from abstract components, which represent sets of components that implement a given concern according to a deployment context. A deployment context is modeled by a *contextual signature*, including a set of *context parameters*, each one typed by a contextual contract (*contractual bound*). A contextual contract is an application of a set of *context arguments* to a subset of the context parameters of an abstract component, where the contextual argument is a contextual contract that is a subtype of the contractual bound.

Each contextual parameter denotes an implementation assumption of an abstract component, related to either an application requirement or an execution platform characteristic. HPC Shelf defines a set of predefined context parameters for representing assumptions about parallel computing platforms they offer, as well as general characteristics of components according to their kinds.

A component declares one contextual contract it implements and a set of contextual contracts it requires (inner component types). In turn, in a parallel computing system, components are indirectly referred by means of contextual contracts. During execution, the contractual resolution mechanism matches contextual contracts and components that implement them.

3   SAFe (Shelf Application Framework)

As stated earlier, SAFe is the application framework of HPC Shelf, from which providers derive applications for attending the needs of specialists in a domain.

The front-end of an application may be a standalone desktop program, a smartphone app, a web browser interface, a web service, and so on. It is only expected that an application implements a collection of domain-specific abstractions that hide the component infrastructure of HPC Shelf from specialists. Using these abstractions, they specify problems that will be mapped onto the parallel computing systems that will solve them. For that, SAFe offers a collection of Java classes and interfaces. An application must be derived from the Application

160   J. de Carvalho Silva and F.H. de Carvalho Junior

class. This class requires the implementation of the method `setServices`, which receives from the framework, as an argument, the *services object*, i.e. an object of the `Services` interface, each time a parallel computing system is deployed, from which the application may connect to the service ports of solution components. This is inspired in CCA (*Common Component Architecture*) [3].

An application specifies both the architectural and the orchestration parts of a parallel computing system through SAFeSWL, which is currently a XML format. The application takes problem specifications produced by the specialist through its interface and maps them onto the XML format of SAFeSWL.

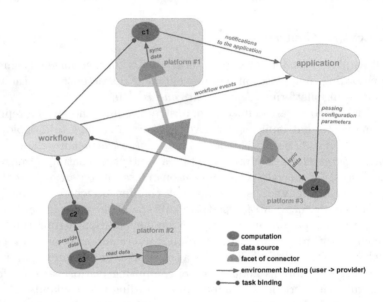

Fig. 1. The view of an hypothetical parallel computing system from SAFe

Figure 1 illustrates how SAFe views a parallel computing system composed by: three *virtual platforms* (**platform#1**, **platform#2**, and **platform#3**); four *computations* (**c1**, **c2**, **c3**, **c4**), two of which (**c2**, **c3**) are deployed in the same virtual platform (**platform #2**); one *data source*, deployed in the same virtual platform of them; one *connector*, for data synchronization among **c1**, **c3**, and **c4**; and *bindings* connecting these components. They are called *solution components*. The labels in the service bindings describe the service they provide. In addition, **Application** is a special component that makes it possible the interaction between the application front-end and the solution components, through service ports. In turn, the **Workflow** component is the *main connector*, which drives the solution components towards the solution. For that, it is connected to the action ports of computation and connector components in the system.

SAFe dialogs with Core for controlling the life cycle of the components in a workflow (parallel computing system), i.e. for their *resolution* (of their contextual contracts), *deployment* and *instantiation*. These operations may be specified explicitly in the orchestration code written in SAFeSWL, by accessing the LifeCycle action ports offered by each component. This is a distinguishing feature of SAFeSWL, as pointed out in Sect. 4.

Notice that service and action bindings must connect remotely the Application and the Workflow components to the solution components. The contextual contract system must guide the choice of the appropriate binding implementations, according to the kind of partners, either local or remote, interface cardinality $(1 \times N, M \times 1$ and $M \times N)$ and characteristics of the platforms where the components are deployed. The choice is transparent for providers when they are specifying workflows. These specifically designed binding implementations, aimed at achieving high efficiency, must be provided by component providers.

3.1 SAFeSWL: Workflow

SAFeSWL is both an architectural description and a scientific workflow language, aimed at describing large-scale and heterogeneous parallel computing systems deployed by applications of HPC Shelf. Despite it has been originally designed for the needs of HPC Shelf, its ideas and concepts may be adopted by other SWfMS with similar requirements. For introducing SAFeSWL, we use two applications:

- Montage [15] is a set of astrophotograph tools for combining astronomical images into a mosaic. It consists of several self-running components that operates on some input files and parameters, generating output files that are input for other components. Each component of Montage is encapsulated as a component of HPC Shelf, where inputs and outputs are implemented as service ports. For their orchestration, components expose action ports with a single action, named go. In what follows, two well-known workflows of Montage have been used as case studies: M101 and Pleiades.
- MapReduce [17] is a model for large-scale parallel computing frameworks aimed at processing large volumes of data. It has been also implemented as a set of components of HPC Shelf. In what follows, a MapReduce computation for counting words in a set of text files (WordCounter) is used as a case study.

3.2 SAFeSWL: Architecture

Using the architectural subset of SAFeSWL, providers may specify the elements of the architecture of parallel computing systems, like the ones in Fig. 1:

1. a set of ***contextual contracts*** that represent the application requirements and platform characteristics that will guide the choice of components in a conversation between the application and the Core, intermediated by SAFe;
2. a set of ***component instances***, each one compliant to a contextual contract;

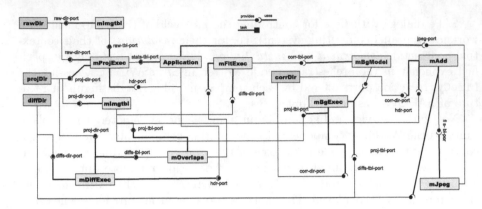

Fig. 2. The M101 architecture (ignoring action ports).

3. a set of **service bindings**, between user and provider ports of interacting components, including both Application and Workflow.
4. a set of **action bindings**, between partner action ports of Workflow, connectors and computations, involved in the orchestration.

Example 1. M101 is a sequential workflow which uses the components of Montage referenced in its architecture, depicted in Fig. 2. Each component has service ports for data transferences between them and a single action port connected to the Workflow component, with a single action named go.

Listing 1.1 shows a SAFeSWL fragment of M101 architecture, declaring the component mImgtbl. The user port dir-port must be connected to a provider port of a repository component that stores raw input images. In turn, the provider port tbl-port provides output information that is passed as input to other components. The action go, of the action port go-port, is activated by Workflow.

```
<computation name="mimgtbl" id="2">
    <uses_port id="33" name="dir−port" id_component="2"/>
    <provides_port id="34" name="tbl−port" id_component="2"/>
    <task_port name="go−port" id="32" id_component="2">
        <action id="321" name="go"/>
    </task_port>
</computation>
```

Listing 1.1. SAFeSWL declaration of mimgtbl

Listing 1.2 exemplifies the declaration of a service binding, which informs to SAFe that there is a connection between the user port u-jpeg-port of the application to the provider port p-jpeg-port of mJPEG. In an analogous way, action bindings (tag tsk_binding) list the action ports of each partner component, by using task_port tags.

```
<env_binding>
    <uses_port id="15" name="u−jpeg−port" id_component="0"/>
    <provides_port id="103" name="p−jpeg−port" id_component="10"/>
</env_binding>
```

Listing 1.2. SAFeSWL declaration of a service binding.

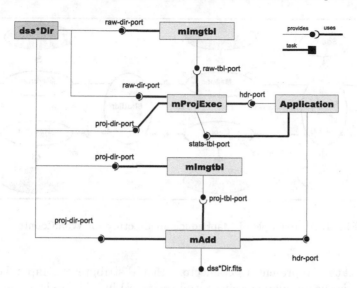

Fig. 3. The Pleiades architecture (ignoring action ports)

In the M101 architecture (Fig. 2), there are *computations*, for representing regular Montage components, and *data sources*, for representing image directories. Through user ports connected to provider ports of data sources, computations retrieve and store images after processing, which will be shared by all components that are connected to the same data source.

Example 2. The next Montage workflow is Pleiades. It runs the same set of computations three times, possibly in parallel, for each color: blue, red and infrared. Each run generates a fits[1] file, merged into a single JPEG file.

Figure 3 depicts the set of computations, data sources and service bindings of a single run of Pleiades. The three runs differ by the data source dss⋆Dir, where ⋆ stands for r, b and ir (blue, red and infrared). Pleiades uses the same computation components of M101.

Example 3. The last workflow in this study is WordCounter, a workflow of the MapReduce application for counting the number of occurrences of words in a large set of files retrieved from a data source. It illustrates the use of contextual contracts, for specifying the *mapping, reduction* and *partition* functions required by a MapReduce computation, as well as the data types of key/value pairs.

Parallel computing systems of MapReduce are built of components from six types (abstract components): Source and Sink, representing the input and output data repositories; Mapper, representing mapper agents that apply the mapping function to a set of input key/value pairs; Reducer, representing reducer agents that apply the reduction function to a set of intermediary key/value

---

[1] Stands for 'Flexible Image Transport System', the standard data format used in astronomy, endorsed by NASA.

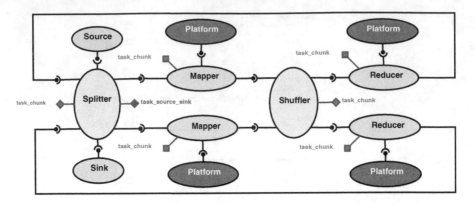

Fig. 4. An example of MapReduce architecture for WordCounter

pairs; `Splitter`, representing connectors that distribute the input key/value pairs between the mappers, receive output pairs produced by reducers and decide on either terminate or redistribute them to start a new iteration; and `Shuffler`, representing connectors that group, by keys, the intermediate key/value pairs produced by the mappers and redistribute them among the reducers.

Figure 4 shows an example of MapReduce architecture for WordCounter, employing pairs of mappers and reducers deployed in distinct virtual platforms. Input, intermediary and output pairs are passed from one component to the next by means of service ports. Also, there are two types of action ports: `task_chunk`, for all computations and connectors, and `task_source_sink`, only for `Splitter`.

```
<connector name="splitter" id="2">
    <uses_port id="31" name="source" id_component="2"/>
    <uses_port id="32" name="sink" id_component="2"/>
    <uses_port id="36" name="collect_pairs" id_component="2"/>
    <provides_port id="33" name="feed_pairs" id_component="2"/>
    <contract>
        <uri>/home/safe-user/contracts/splitter_contract.cc</uri>
    </contract>
    <task_port name="task_source_sink" id="34" id_component="2">
        <action id="341" name="read_source"/>
        <action id="342" name="terminate"/>
        <action id="343" name="write_sink"/>
    </task_port>
    <task_port name="task_chunk" id="35" id_component="2">
        <action id="351" name="read_chunk"/>
        <action id="352" name="perform"/>
        <action id="353" name="chunk_ready"/>
    </task_port>
</connector>
```

Listing 1.3. Declaration of the Splitter connector.

Listing 1.3 presents a fragment of SAFeSWL code declaring `Splitter`. The `contract` tag points to the contextual contract file generated by the application. The `Splitter` component declares two action ports, both having three action names, whose meaning are explained in the next section.

Table 1 presents the context arguments applied to the contextual contracts of the MapReduce architecture presented in Fig. 4. They customize such an architecture for executing the WordCounter workflow. The arguments specify the types of input, intermediary and output key/value pairs, as well as the map and reduction

Table 1. Contextual contracts for the WordCounter workflow.

context parameter name	components	context argument
input_key_type	Mapper Splitter	INTEGER
input_value_type	Mapper Splitter	STRING
output_key_type	Reducer Splitter	STRING
output_value_type	Reducer Splitter	INTEGER
map_function	Mapper	WORDCOUNTER

context parameter name	components	context argument
intermediary_key_type	Mapper Splitter Shuffler Reducer	STRING
intermediary_value_type	Mapper Splitter Shuffler Reducer	INTEGER
reduce_function	Reducer	REDUCESUM

functions. Indeed, the input pair values, of type string, represent file contents, indexed by integer keys. Each application of the map function to an input pair generates a set of intermediary pairs containing a word (key) and its number of occurrences in the file (value). In turn, the reduce function sums the list of integers found by mappers for each word, resulting in the number of occurrences of each word across all the input files.

The contextual contract system may choose **mapper** and **reducer** components specialized for working with the specific types of key/value pairs and functions. However, in the current implementation, generic versions are used. Also, notice that the same MapReduce architecture depicted in Fig. 4 may be used for executing other map/reduce computations only by assigning different contextual contract files to each component, with appropriate context arguments.

3.3   The Orchestration Subset of SAFeSWL

The provider generates the orchestration code of workflows, such as M101, Pleiades and MapReduce, by using the orchestration subset of SAFeSWL, whose abstract syntax is presented in Fig. 5. It is interpreted by the Workflow component, which is connected to action ports of computations and connectors, through action bindings, for driving the parallel computing system. When there are pending activations of a given action by all the components that are partners through an action binding, each computation or connector partner, which is written in a full computational programming language (currently C#), may react by executing an associated computation. For that, they dialog with their action port objects, which implement the `IActionPort` interface. In turn, the Workflow component uses the set of action primitives and combinators of the orchestration subset of SAFeSWL only for specifying the control flow of action activations, i.e. without reacting by executing computations.

Listing 1.4 shows the orchestration code of M101 actions. The `sequence_oper` tag denotes that the enclosing action activations are executed sequentially. When a solution component activates the **go** action, it becomes ready for executing a computation associated to **go** provided that Workflow have also activated **go**.

```
<sequence_oper>
  <invoke_oper action="compute" id="mImgtbl−raw−go.go" />
  <invoke_oper action="compute" id="mProjExec−go.go" />
  <invoke_oper action="compute" id="mImgtbl−go.go" />
  <invoke_oper action="compute" id="mOverlaps−go.go" />
  <!−− other omitted invocations here! −−>
  <invoke_oper action="compute" id="mJpeg−go.go" />
</sequence_oper>
```

Listing 1.4. SAFeSWL orchestration fragment of M101.

TASK ::= **Skip** | **Perform** *action* | **Start** *handle action* | **Wait** *handle* | **Cancel** *handle* |
      Sequence TASK+ | **Parallel** TASK+ | **Repeat** TASK | **Break** | **Continue** |
      Select {*component action*: TASK}+

Skip denotes an empty action. **Perform** denotes a synchronous action invocation, which completes after all component partners, through an action binding, activate the same action. In turn, **Start**, **Wait** and **Cancel** are used for asynchronous action invocations, where an action invocation is started by **Start**. Then, the orchestration task may either wait for the completion of the action, by executing **Wait** for the same handle, or cancel it, by execution **Cancel**. **Sequence** and **Parallel** denote the serial and parallel invocation of a set of tasks, respectively. **Repeat** denotes the iterative execution of a task until the **Break** task is executed. The **Continue** task forces the beginning of a new iteration. Finally, **Select** denotes a choice among a set of tasks, according to the invocation of a set of guard actions.

Fig. 5. Abstract syntax of the orchestration subset of SAFeSWL

Listing 1.5 presents the orchestration code of a single run of the Pleiades workflow. Remember that the three runs, connected to distinct image repositories, are executed in parallel by the Montage application.

```
<sequence_oper>
  <invoke_oper action="compute" id="mImgtbl-raw-go.go" />
  <invoke_oper action="compute" id="mProjExec-go.go" />
  <invoke_oper action="compute" id="mImgtbl-go.go" />
  <invoke_oper action="compute" id="mAdd-go.go" />
</sequence_oper>
```

Listing 1.5. SAFeSWL orchestration fragment of Pleiades.

Listing 1.6 presents the orchestration logic of word counter. Firstly, `splitter` activates `read_source` for reading the *input pairs* delivered by the `input_data` service binding, produced from the `data_source` repository. The stream of input pairs is split into a sequence of chunks of a given size (the chunk size controls the granularity of the parallel computation). Each time a chunk is ready (i.e. the `mapper` may read it through the `input_pairs` service binding), `splitter` activates the `chunk_ready` action. Then, the action `read_chunk` of `mapper` is activated for reading the chunk, and then `perform`, for applying the *map function* to each input pair, producing chunks of *intermediate pairs* that will be read and processed by `shuffler` by using the same `chunk_ready/read_chunk/perform` protocol. Also using this protocol, chunks of intermediate pairs are read and processed (application of the *reduce function*) by `reducer`, producing output pairs that will be delivered back to `splitter`. Finally, `splitter` reads the output pairs and decides whether the computation must either restart or terminate. In restarting (new iteration), the output pairs are fed as input pairs to the `mapper`. In termination, they are are delivered to the `write_sink` repository through the `output_data` binding. A single iteration is necessary for WordCounter.

Using SAFeSWL, non-trivial variants of the basic MapReduce model may be employed, such as: ignoring the map phase (identity map function); applying sequences of distinct mappers and/or reducers in an iteration; using teams of mappers and reducers for large-scale parallel processing, like in Fig. 4; inserting a *combining phase* (`combiner` components) for local reduction of intermediate pairs before shuffling. Also, contextual contracts make it possible the selection of different implementations of the MapReduce components. For example, bindings for communication of KV-pairs with out-of-core capabilitites could be provided.

```
<invoke_oper action="compute" id="splitter.read_source" />
<invoke_oper action="compute" id="splitter.perform" />
<iterate_oper max="-1">
  <choice_oper>
    <select action_id="splitter.chunk_ready">
      <invoke_oper action="compute" id="mapper.read_chunk" />
      <invoke_oper action="compute" id="mapper.perform" />
    </select>
    <select action_id="mapper.chunk_ready">
      <invoke_oper action="compute" id="combiner.read_chunk" />
      <invoke_oper action="compute" id="combiner.perform" />
    </select>
    <!-- same logic for combiner, shuffler and reducer components -->
    <select action_id="splitter.terminate">
      <invoke_oper action="compute" id="splitter.write_sink" />
      <break/>
    </select>
  </choice_oper>
</iterate>
```

Listing 1.6. SAFeSWL fragment of MapReduce orchestration.

4   Related Works and Contributions

The contributions of SAFe may be better evaluated in the context of *scientific workflow management systems* (SWfMS). These systems have been largely applied by scientists and engineers for the design, execution and monitoring of reusable data processing task pipelines in scientific discovery and data analysis [26]. From a systematic study about SWfMS with parallel processing support, we have found Askalon [23], BPEL Sedna [1], Kepler [18], Pegasus [11], Taverna [29] and OSC [19] as SWfMS designs that are worth being compared to SAFe.

The following distinguishing features may be found in SAFe when it is compared to these SWfMS: the compliance with a model of parallel components (Hash); the ability to deploy and orchestrate computational tasks in multiple parallel computing platforms (large-scale parallel processing); a contextual contract system, from which components may be chosen based on functional and non-functional requirements declared by applications; a mechanism to deal with non-functional concerns in general, though component kinds and contextual contracts; the uniform view of software and hardware resources used employed by workflows, viewed as components of distinct kinds; the full control of life-cycle stages of resources (deployment, instantiation, execution, release), by means of explicit SAFeSWL constructors; and a clear separation between the responsibilities and expertises of user categories, specially *specialists* and *providers*.

Askalon provides *activity types* as an alternative to contextual contracts. However, contextual contracts may add restrictions related to application requirements, possibly considering quality of services and monetary costs, to the set of restrictions based on a fixed set of specific platform characteristics used to describe the requirements of *activity types* for selecting *activity deployments*.

The inclusion of non-functional concerns in workflow specification is also a feature of OSC. However, in its current prototype, OSC deals with a specific set of non-functional concerns, including data provenance, fault-tolerance and parallelism, whereas SAFe is naturally extensible. Also, parallelism is intrinsic to the component model of SAFe. In fact, only OSC and SAFe takes the parallelism of components as a concern treated at the level of workflow design.

The incremental instantiation of resources as they are demanded is also supported by Pegasus, through an automatic approach. In turn, SAFeSWL gives to the programmer the ability to specify when components, including parallel computing platforms, are deployed and instantiated during the workflow execution. One might propose automatic tools to help this task, like in Pegasus.

All SWfMS targets scientists and engineers interested in solving problems through computational means. SAFe goes beyond, by distinguish target users in *specialists* and *providers*. Using this approach, only providers need expertise in building computational solutions from the scientific components available in the catalog. In turn, specialists interact with domain-specific interfaces for declaring problems by using abstractions from their domains of expertise. On the other hand, usual SWfMS try to make the composition language simpler for attending users without expertise in computing, compromising its expressiveness.

5   Conclusions and Further Work

This paper introduced SAFe, a CBHPC platform for developing and deploying large-scale component-based parallel computing systems over the HPC Shelf infrastructure (components), serving as a substratum for HPC Shelf applications. For that, it supports SAFeSWL, a language for orchestrating components across a set of parallel computing platforms in long running intensive computations.

SAFeSWL is both an architectural description and scientific workflow language, supporting distinct language subsets for these purposes, respectively. Its prominent characteristics are: the uniform view of software (algorithms and data), hardware (parallel computing platforms) and other kinds of resources needed by applications under the same abstraction of Hash components; the integration with the system of *contextual contracts* of HPC Shelf, aimed at cataloging and discovery of component implementations (resources) based on application requirements and the features of their target parallel computing platforms; the possibility of controlling explicitly the time of deployment, instantiation and releasing of components, allowing the fine control of the use of resources; and a naturally extensible mechanism for dealing with non-functional concerns.

SAFe and SAFeSWL have been validated by means of HPC Shelf application prototypes: Montage and MapReduce. Then, we have discussed the architecture and orchestration of three workflows from these applications: M101, Pleiades and WordCounter. In fact, in the near future, one of our main interests is to implement other HPC Shelf applications on top of SAFe and, by consequence, SAFeSWL workflows, making it possible a deeper evaluation of them.

SAFe, as well as HPC Shelf, is an ongoing project. However, it is now a functional prototype that is ready to be applied in real usage scenarios. Besides the implementation of real case studies for evaluating them in these scenarios, we have worked in some orthogonal projects aimed at extending SAFe with some important features for making it competitive in comparison to mature SWfMS that are currently disseminated and used in practice, such as the formal certification of components and workflows, data provenance, and fault tolerance.

References

1. OASIS Web Services Business Process Execution Language (WSBPEL). https://www.oasis-open.org/committees/wsbpel/. Accessed 23 April 2015
2. Antonopoulos, N., Gillam, L.: Cloud Computing: Principles Systems and Applications. Computer Commmunications and Networks. Springer, London (2011)
3. Armstrong, R., Kumfert, G., McInnes, L.C., Parker, S., Allan, B., Sottile, M., Epperly, T., Tamara, D.: The CCA component model For high-performance scientific computing. Concurrency Comput. Pract. Experience 18(2), 215–229 (2006)
4. Baude, F., Caromel, D., Dalmasso, C., Danelutto, M., Getov, W., Henrio, L., Prez, C.: GCM: a grid extension to fractal for autonomous distributed components. Ann. Telecommun. 64(1), 5–24 (2009)
5. Bell, G., Gray, J., Szalay, A.: Petascale computational systems. Computer 39(1), 110–112 (2006)
6. Blair, G., Coupaye, T., Stefani, J.-B.: Component-based architecture: the fractal initiative. Ann. Telecommun. 64, 1–4 (2009)
7. Church, P., Wong, A., Brock, M., Goscinski, A.: Toward exposing and accessing HPC applications in a SaaS cloud. In: Proceedings of the 2012 IEEE 19th International Conference on Web Services, pp. 692–699. IEEE, June 2012
8. de Carvalho Jr., F.H., Lins, R.D.: Separation of concerns for improving practice of parallel programming. Inf. Int. J. 8(5), 621–638 (2005)
9. de Carvalho Junior, F.H., Rezende, C.A.: A case study on expressiveness and performance of component-oriented parallel programming. J. Parallel Distrib. Comput. 73(5), 557–569 (2013)
10. de Carvalho Junior, F.H., Rezende, C.A., de Carvalho Silva, J., Al-Alam, W.G.: Contextual abstraction in a type system for component-based high performance computing platforms. In: Du Bois, A.R., Trinder, P. (eds.) SBLP 2013. LNCS, vol. 8129, pp. 90–104. Springer, Heidelberg (2013)
11. Deelman, E., Singh, G., Su, M.-H., Blythe, J., Gil, Y., Kesselman, C., Mehta, G., Vahi, K., Berriman, G.B., Good, J., et al.: Pegasus: a framework for mapping complex scientific workflows onto distributed systems. Sci. Program. 13(3), 219–237 (2005)
12. Dimond, R., Racanie Andre, S., Pell, O.: Accelerating large-scale HPC applications using FPGAs. In: 2011 20th IEEE Symposium on Computer Arithmetic (ARITH), pp. 191–192, July 2011
13. Duran, A., Klemm, M.: The intel many integrated core architecture. In: 2012 International Conference on High Performance Computing and Simulation (HPCS), pp. 365–366. IEEE Computer Society, July 2012
14. Fan, Z., Qiu, F., Kaufman, A., Yoakum Stover, S.: GPU cluster for high performance computing. In: Proceedings of the 2004 ACM/IEEE conference on Supercomputing (SC 2004), p. 47. IEEE Computer Society (2004)
15. Jacob, J.C., et al.: Montage: a grid portal and software toolkit for science-grade astronomical image mosaicking. Int. J. Comput. Sci. Eng. 4(2), 73–87 (2009)
16. Laudon, J., Spracklen, L.: The coming wave of multithreaded chip multiprocessors. Int. J. Parallel Program. 35, 299–330 (2007)
17. Li, R., Hu, H., Li, H., Wu, Y., Yang, J.: MapReduce parallel programming model: a state-of-the-art survey. Int. J. Parallel Program. 44(4), 832–866 (2016)
18. Ludäscher, B., Altintas, I., Berkley, C., Higgins, D., Jaeger, E., Jones, M., Lee, E.A., Tao, J., Zhao, Y.: Scientific workflow management and the Kepler system. Concurrency Comput. Pract. Experience 18(10), 1039–1065 (2006)

19. Medeiros, V., Gomes, T.A.: Towards fully configurable support to non-functional attributes in scientific workflows. In: Proceedings of the 8th IEEE International Conference on eScience (eScience 2012) (2012)
20. Mell, P., Grance, T.: The NIST Definition of Cloud Computing. Technical report 800–145, Computer Security Division, National Institute of Standards and Technology, U.S. Department of Commerce, September 2011
21. Mittal, S.: A survey of techniques for architecting and managing asymmetric multicore processors. ACM Comput. Surv. **48**(3), 45:1–45:38 (2016)
22. Post, D.E., Votta, L.G.: Computational science demands a new paradigm. Phys. Today **58**(1), 35–41 (2005)
23. Qin, J., Fahringer, T., Pllana, S.: UML based grid workflow modeling under ASKALON. In: Kacsuk, P., Fahringer, T., Németh, Z. (eds.) Distributed and Parallel Systems, pp. 191–200. Springer, Heidelberg (2007)
24. Rehr, J.J., Vila, F.D., Gardner, J.P., Svec, L., Prange, M.: Scientific computing in the cloud. Comput. Sci. Eng. **12**(3), 34–43 (2010)
25. Sarkar, V., Williams, C., Ebcioğlu, K.: Application development productivity challenges for high-end computing. In: Workshop on Productivity and Performance in High-End Computing (PPHEC 2004), pp. 14–18 (2004)
26. Taylor, I.J., Deelman, E., Gannon, D.B., Shields, M.: Workflows for e-Science: Scientific Workflows for Grids. Springer, Heidelberg (2007)
27. van der Steen, A.J.: Issues in computational frameworks. Concurrency Comput. Pract. Experience **18**(2), 141–150 (2006)
28. Vecchiola, C., Pandey, S., Buyya, R.: High-performance cloud computing: a view of scientific applications. In: 10th International Symposium on Pervasive Systems, Algorithms, and Networks (ISPAN 2009), pp. 4–16. IEEE (2009)
29. Wolstencroft, K., Haines, R., Fellows, D., Williams, A., Withers, D., Owen, S., Soiland Reyes, S., Dunlop, I., Nenadic, A., Fisher, P., et al.: The Taverna workflow suite: designing and executing workflows of web services on the desktop, web or in the cloud. Nucleic Acids Res. p. 328 (2013)
30. Zaspel, P., Griebel, M.: Massively parallel fluid simulations on amazon's HPC cloud. In: Proceedings of the First International Symposium on Network Cloud Computing and Applications (NCCA 2011), pp. 73–78 (2011)

Comparison Between Model Fields and Abstract Predicates

Ke Zhang$^{(\boxtimes)}$ and Zongyan Qiu

LMAM and Department of Informatics, School of Mathematics,
Peking University, Beijing, China
zksms@pku.edu.cn, qzy@math.pku.edu.cn

Abstract. To modularly specify and verify object oriented programs on some abstract level, we need abstraction techniques to hide the implementation details of the classes. *Model fields* and *abstract predicates* are two most important approaches to address the requirements. In this paper, we mainly compare their expressiveness. We develop two translation algorithms, which can translate a program with model fields based specification to one with abstract predicates based specification. We prove that the translation algorithms are correct, and the resulting specifications are well-encapsulated and well-formed. This shows that the abstract predicates technique is more expressive. On the other hand, the model fields based specifications are more user friendly and useful in automatic verification. In addition, we discuss the different characteristics of the two approaches in framing, inheritance, and recursion.

1 Introduction

Object Orientation (abbr. OO) is widely used in software development. Due to the increasing demand on the reliability and correctness, techniques for specifying/verifying OO programs attract more attention recently.

However, to specify/verify OO programs, we have to face the challenges brought by encapsulation, inheritance and polymorphism, which are the core features of OO. Abstraction is the key idea to address these issues. Introducing suitable abstraction mechanisms into the formal notations is helpful to enhance the modularity of OO specification and verification. In addition, these mechanisms are also useful for information hiding and specification re-use. All of these characteristics are crucial in verifying large-scale OO programs.

Researchers have paid much attention to abstraction mechanisms in the OO verification for years. *Model fields* [1] and *abstract predicates* [2] are two important techniques here. Model fields are abstract fields whose values are determined by concrete fields of the object. Abstract predicates are user-defined logic abstractions. Both techniques can specify the program abstractly and support information hiding.

K. Zhang — The work is supported by the NSFC under grant No. 61272160 and No. 61202069.

F. Castor and Y.D. Liu (Eds.): SBLP 2016, LNCS 9889, pp. 171–186, 2016.
DOI: 10.1007/978-3-319-45279-1_12

Model fields and abstract predicates have been studied for years, and both techniques address the similar problems. However, no systematic and formal study has been published on their relationship and advantages/disadvantages. We try to make such a comparison in this paper. We prove that the abstract predicates are more expressive than model fields, by showing: (1) the model fields based specification can be translated into abstract predicates based specification; (2) there exists programs which can only be specified by abstract predicates.

The rest of the paper is organized as follows: Sect. 2 introduces the model fields and abstract predicates techniques and compares them briefly; Sect. 3 presents the translation rules and algorithms, together with some discussion; Sect. 4 summarizes some related work and Sect. 5 concludes.

2   Background

2.1   Model Fields

The *model field* (abbr. MF) technique was introduced in 1990s [3] to deal with data abstraction and data refinement. Syntactically, MF is a kind of field in class declarations which can only be used in the specifications, but cannot be accessed by real code. We use the definition of MF in JML [1]:

Definition 1 (Model fields). *A model field declaration in class C takes the form:*

$$\textbf{model } T \ f \ \textbf{such\_that } R_C(f, \overline{f}, \overline{g});$$

Here T is a type, f is the field name, and the **such_that** *clause introduces a constraint $R_C(f, \overline{f}, \overline{g})$ which must hold in every state. The constraint could mention the model fields $\overline{f}$ and concrete fields $\overline{g}$ of class C.*

Subclass D inherits all the model fields and constraints from its superclass. It can add a new constraint $R_D(\ldots)$ for an inherited model field. Both the inherited constraints and the new constraint $R_D(\ldots)$ must hold in every state.

The official references of JML lack formal semantics, but [4] gives formal semantics for MFs in JML as follows:

Definition 2 (Model field valuator). *Let $\mathcal{S}$ be the set of states, $\mathcal{U}$ be the set of objects, $\mathbb{I}$ be the set of concrete and model fields in classes. A function $M : \mathcal{S} \times \mathcal{U} \times \mathbb{I} \to \mathcal{U}$ is called a* model field valuator *iff:*

For every state $s \in \mathcal{S}$, every field $x \in \mathbb{I}$ and every model field $o.f$ with constraint ψ (ψ denotes the conjunction of all the constraints which $o.f$ must conform to):

- *The type of object $M(s, o, x)$ is a subtype of the declaration type of field $o.x$,*
- *$\psi[\overline{M(s, o, f)/o.f}] = \textbf{true}$ in state s.*

Here $[M(s, o, f)/o.f]$ means replacing $o.f$ with $M(s, o, f)$. Taking model fields into account, specifications are always meant to hold for every possible valuator.

```
class Rec : Object{
    int x1, y1, x2, y2;
    invariant x1 ≤ x2 ∧ y1 ≤ y2;

    model int width such_that width = x2 − x1;
    model int height such_that height = y2 − y1;

    Rec() ⟨⟩⟨width = 1 ∧ height = 1⟩
    {x1 := 0; y1 := 0; x2 := 1; y2 := 1; }

    void ScaleH(int factor)
    ⟨0 ≤ factor⟩⟨width = old(width) × factor/100⟩
    modifies width, x2;
    { x2 := (x2 − x1) × factor/100 + x1; }
}
```

Fig. 1. *Rec* specified by MFs

For example, a MF method specification (pre and post-conditions) $\langle\phi\rangle\langle\psi\rangle$ specifies $C.m()$, iff for every possible valuator M, the concrete fields based specification $\langle\phi[M(s,o,f)/o.f]\rangle\langle\psi[M(s,o,f)/o.f]\rangle$ specifies $C.m()$.

If the method specifications only depend on MFs, an abstraction boundary is formed which separates the real code (and concrete fields) from the specification. The constraints of MFs serve as a bridge to connect the specification and the implementation. To express this idea, we have the following definition:

Definition 3 (Well-encapsulated). *If the method specifications (pre and post-conditions) in a class do not mention any concrete field, we call it a* well-encapsulated specification *or an* abstract specification *of the class.*

Notice that we do not forbid the invariants to mention concrete fields in Definition 3, because the invariants are always treated as conditions to constrain the valid object states. In the view of modular programming, those invariants should not be concerned by other objects. In fact, the example in Fig. 1, which comes from literature on MF [5], uses concrete fields in its invariant. Thus we allow the invariants to mention concrete fields in Definition 3.

Figure 1 shows a class *Rec* specified by model fields. *Rec* uses the coordinates of two opposite corners to represent a rectangle, and declares model fields *width* and *height* as the abstraction of the concrete fields.

In the class, the method *ScaleH* scales the rectangle horizontally, which is specified using the model field *width*. In addition, the **modifies** clause lists all the (concrete and model) fields modified by the method, which is useful when reasoning about frame properties of the method.

2.2 Abstract Predicates

The *abstract predicate* (abbr. AP) technique is proposed when researchers apply Separation Logic [6] to OO languages [2]. Basically, they are user-defined predicates in class declarations.

class Rec : **Object**{
    //*concrete fields and method bodies are the same as* **Fig. 1**
    define $rec_{Rec}(\textbf{this}, w, h) :$ $w = x2 - x1 \wedge h = y2 - y1;$

    $Rec()$ $\langle\rangle\langle rec(\textbf{this}, 1, 1)\rangle$

    void $ScaleH(\textbf{int } factor)$
    $\langle(0 \le factor) \wedge rec(\textbf{this}, w, h)\rangle\langle rec(\textbf{this}, w \times factor/100, h)\rangle$
}

Fig. 2. Rec specified by APs

Definition 4 (Abstract predicates). *An abstract predicate definition in class C takes the following form:*

$$\textbf{define } p_C(\textbf{this}, \overline{v}) : \psi;$$

The predicate has a name p, parameters $(\textbf{this}, \overline{v})$, and a definition ψ which is a separation logic assertion. The definition could mention any object o which is accessible from class C, and also the predicates of o (i.e. the predicates whose first parameter is o).

    Subclass inherits all the abstract predicates from its superclass, and it can also override the definition of inherited predicates.

The predicates with same name (but in different classes) form an *abstract predicate family*. Paper [7] defines its semantics as follows. Briefly speaking, when a predicate family $p(o, \overline{v})$ is used in the specification, its definition $p_C(o, \overline{v})$ is chosen according to the dynamic type of o.

Definition 5 (Assumption context). *We define an assumption context Δ, which is a set including the following formulas:*
    For every class C, predicate p, parameters o and $\overline{v}$,

$$(1)\ o : C \Rightarrow (p(o, \overline{v}) \Leftrightarrow p_C(o, \overline{v})) \quad (2)\ \frac{\textbf{define } p_C(\textbf{this}, \overline{v}) : \psi;}{p_C(o, \overline{v}) \Leftrightarrow \psi[o/\textbf{this}]}$$

$$(3)\ p(\overline{v}) \Leftrightarrow \exists w \cdot p(\overline{v}, w) \qquad (4)\ p() \Leftrightarrow \textbf{true}$$

When the type of o is C, denoted as $o : C$, we can translate the family to a specific entry for class C. In addition, the entry for class C is equivalent to its definition in class C. The last two rules allow us to change the arity of predicates.

    Taking APs into account, specifications are always meant to hold within the assumption context Δ.

For example, if the proof obligation of a concrete specification ψ is $\Gamma \vdash \psi$, where Γ denotes the static environment, then the proof obligation of an AP specification ψ' is $\Gamma, \Delta \vdash \psi'$.

We can also use APs to specify the class Rec abstractly, as shown in Fig. 2.

2.3   Preliminary Comparison

Both MF and AP are commonly used techniques in OO verification. Here we briefly compare their ideas and applicabilities, and leave the comparison of expressiveness to the rest of the paper.

In common, MF and AP assertions can both be easily translated into assertions on the concrete fields. We can either unfold MF references by their constraints, or unfold AP invocations by the predicates' definitions. The real code must satisfy the unfolded assertions. On the other hand, outside the encapsulation, we only use the abstract specification for reasoning.

MFs are just names referring to some values derived from concrete fields, thus it is a relative simple and easy-to-use mechanism. In addition, since the values of MFs are constrained by concrete fields, their values can be really implemented and automatically updated in the verification or static/dynamic analysis. It makes MFs useful in the automatic verification or analysis. Both JML [1] and Spec# [8] integrate MFs into their specification languages to express the abstract specifications of classes and interfaces.

On the other hand, the close connection between MFs and concrete fields restricts the way to define MFs and the flexibility of specifications, especially for subclasses and overridden methods.

The power of APs comes from their structure. Predicates may have arbitrary parameters, which can be instantiated in invocations, or be used to connect different parts of specifications. Besides, recursive APs can be naturally defined, which makes it easy to handle recursive data structures. Furthermore, APs decouple the specification from implementation details more thoroughly, since it describes the properties instead of the values of the program states. The definitions of the predicates are almost arbitrary even in the presence of inheritance, which provides enough expressiveness. Due to these advantages, verification frameworks like VeriFast [9], implement AP technique as its abstraction mechanism.

However, the developers need more logic training before using APs. In many cases, they must carefully design appropriate predicates to ensure the correctness of the specifications, especially when inheritance and overridden methods are involved. In addition, the AP specifications cannot be automatically verified.

In conclusion, both abstraction techniques have their own merit, thus neither of them is superior to the other in practical applications.

3   Expressiveness

Considering the importance of the abstraction techniques in OO verification, we are interested in comparing the expressiveness of MFs and APs. As an example, Sect. 2 shows that *Rec* can be specified by both techniques respectively. Although it is just a particular case, it gives us some clues for the study.

We notice that each MF holds a value and a constraint binding it to some concrete fields (directly, or indirectly via other MFs). Correspondingly, AP is also able to describe a value by adding a parameter, and the definition of the predicate can describe any constraints between this value and the concrete fields. Thus, it seems that MF is a special case of AP. But we still need to consider their scope rules and their different ways to deal with frame properties.

Following this basic idea, we develop a set of rules and two translation algorithms, which can translate the MF specification into AP specification. It indicates that the AP is not less expressive than MF. We prove the correctness and termination of the translation algorithms, and we also show a program which can only be specified by APs.

3.1 Translation Rules

In this subsection, we introduce our translation rules and an algorithm. We take a sequential subset of Java. The AP specification is written using separation logic [2], and MF specification uses a subset of separation logic (without separating conjunction/implication). Before translation, the program is specified by MFs. After translation, we will obtain the same program specified by APs. However, during the translation, the specification may contain both kinds of notations. In such cases, we define the semantics as follows:

Definition 6. *Suppose ψ is an assertion with both MF and AP notations, and s is a state. ψ holds in s iff for each possible model field valuator M, the AP based assertion $\psi[M(s, o, f)/o.f]$ holds in s.*

We introduce some notations at first:

- $spec_1 \Longrightarrow_t spec_2$ denotes that we translate specification $spec_1$ into $spec_2$;
- B and C are classes, φ and ψ assertions;
- $\mathsf{model}(C, \overline{f_i}), \mathsf{concrete}(C, \overline{g_j})$ state that $\overline{f_i}, \overline{g_j}$ are all the MFs and concrete fields of class C, respectively. We assume the set $\{\overline{C.f_i}\}$ unchanged even after these MFs are translated into APs.
- $\mathsf{fresh}(\overline{r_j})$ means that $\overline{r_j}$ are fresh variables, and $\mathsf{inh}(C, f_k)$ denotes that f_k is also defined in the superclass of C.

The rules are listed in Fig. 3. Here are some explanations.

Rule [H-PPRE] says that, we introduce a predicate $pri_C(\mathbf{this}, r_1, \ldots, r_n)$ for each class C, to assert all the concrete fields of the class. This predicate serves as a safeguard to prevent these fields from being exposed in the abstract specification.

[H-MPRE] shows how we translate a MF definition into an AP definition. The last premise indicates the existence of the definition for the MF f_k in class C. We translate the MF definition into an AP definition p_C^k with the same number k. If $p_C^k(\mathbf{this}, v)$ holds, then the value of v equals a possible value of the MF f_k.

In [H-MPRE], we do not handle those $\overline{f_i}$ in the constraint. Those MF appearances will be translated by the rule [H-TRANS] below.

Subclasses are allowed to strengthen the constraints of the inherited MFs [1,5], thus an inherited MF should satisfy not only the constraint defined in C, but also the ones inherited from the superclasses of C. Rule [H-MINH] translates

$$[\text{H-PPRE}] \quad \frac{\text{concrete}(C, \overline{g_j}), \quad \text{fresh}(\overline{r_j})}{\Longrightarrow_t \textbf{define } pri_C(\textbf{this}, \overline{r_j}) : \ \bigwedge_j \textbf{this}.g_j = r_j}$$

$$[\text{H-MPRE}] \quad \frac{\begin{array}{c} \text{model}(C, \overline{f_i}), \ \text{concrete}(C, \overline{g_j}), \ \text{fresh}(v, \overline{r_j}), \ \neg\text{inh}(C, f_k), \\ \textbf{model } T \ f_k \textbf{ such\_that } R_C^k(f_k, \overline{f_i}, \overline{g_j}) \in C \end{array}}{\begin{array}{c} \textbf{model } T \ f_k \textbf{ such\_that } R_C^k(f_k, \overline{f_i}, \overline{g_j}) \Longrightarrow_t \\ \textbf{define } p_C^k(\textbf{this}, v) : \ \exists \overline{r_j} \cdot pri_C(\textbf{this}, \overline{r_j}) \wedge R_C^k(v, \overline{f_i}, \overline{r_j}) \end{array}}$$

$$[\text{H-MINH}] \quad \frac{\begin{array}{c} \text{model}(C, \overline{f_i}), \ \text{concrete}(C, \overline{g_j}), \ \text{fresh}(v, \overline{r_j}), \ \text{inh}(C, f_k), \\ \text{super}(C, B), \quad \textbf{model } T \ f_k \textbf{ such\_that } R_C^k(f_k, \overline{f_i}, \overline{g_j}) \in C \end{array}}{\begin{array}{c} \textbf{model } T \ f_k \textbf{ such\_that } R_C^k(f_k, \overline{f_i}, \overline{g_j}) \Longrightarrow_t \\ \textbf{define } p_C^k(\textbf{this}, v) : (\exists \overline{r_j} \cdot pri_C(\textbf{this}, \overline{r_j}) \wedge R_C^k(v, \overline{f_i}, \overline{r_j})) \wedge p_B^k(\textbf{this}, v) \end{array}}$$

$$[\text{H-MOLD}] \quad \frac{\langle \varphi \rangle \ m(\ldots) \langle \psi \rangle, \quad \textbf{old}(o.f_k) \text{ appears in } \psi, \quad \text{fresh}(d_k)}{\langle \varphi \rangle \langle \psi \rangle \Longrightarrow_t \langle \varphi \wedge p^k(o, d_k) \rangle \langle \psi[d_k/\textbf{old}(o.f_k)] \rangle}$$

$$[\text{H-TRANS}] \quad \frac{\begin{array}{c} \psi \text{ is not an invariant}, \quad \text{fresh}(\overline{v_i}, \overline{r_j}), \\ o_i.f_i, o_j'.g_j \text{ are all the model/concrete fields in } \psi \end{array}}{\psi \Longrightarrow_t \exists \overline{v_i}, \overline{r_j} \cdot \psi[v_i/o_i.f_i][r_j/o_j'.g_j] \wedge \bigwedge_i p^i(o_i, v_i) \wedge \bigwedge_j pri(o_j', \overline{=}, r_j, \overline{=})}$$

$$[\text{H-INV}] \quad \frac{\begin{array}{c} \psi \text{ is an invariant in class } C, \quad \text{model}(C, \overline{f_i}), \quad \text{fresh}(\overline{v_i}), \\ B \text{ ranges in the superclasses of } C \text{ (inclusive)} \end{array}}{\psi \Longrightarrow_t \exists \overline{v_i} \cdot \psi[v_i/f_i] \wedge \bigwedge_k \bigwedge_B R_B^k(v_k, \overline{v_i}, \overline{g_j})}$$

Fig. 3. Translation rules

the inherited MFs, where $\text{super}(C, B)$ says that B is the immediate superclass of C, and p_B^k is the AP in class B which p_C^k inherits. Clearly, p_C^k should also conform to the definition of p_B^k.

[H-MOLD] deals with the $\textbf{old}(o.f_k)$ in method specifications, where $o.f_k$ is a MF. Here $\langle \varphi \rangle \ m(\ldots) \langle \psi \rangle$ means that φ and ψ are the pre and post-conditions of method m. In programs with MF specification, $\textbf{old}(o.f_k)$ can be written in the post-condition, to denote the value of $o.f_k$ in the pre-state. Rule [H-MOLD] declares d_k explicitly for the value of $o.f_k$ in the pre-state, then we can use d_k to substitute all the $\textbf{old}(o.f_k)$ in the post-condition. Furthermore, the pre-condition after translation is equivalent to the original one. Since the constraints of model fields must be satisfiable, i.e. there surely exists a value d_k which equals to $o.f_k$ in the pre-state, [H-MOLD] does not strengthen the pre-condition.

[H-TRANS] translates assertions in the program except the invariants (i.e. the pre and post-conditions of methods and the definition of predicates). Here the AP $p^i(o_i, v_i)$ asserts that v_i has the same value as the MF $o_i.f_i$, then the substitution of all the $o_i.f_i$ to v_i does not modify the semantics of the assertions. The $pri(o_j', \overline{=}, r_j, \overline{=})$ means that the parameter corresponding to $o_j'.g_j$ is r_j, and we do not care about the value of other parameters.

[H-INV] translates a MF invariant into a concrete fields based invariant. Without the ownership [10] technique, the MF invariant can only mention the model and concrete fields defined in the same class. Thus we can just unfold the constraints and substitute the MF appearances by fresh variables within the scope of the existential quantifiers. The ownership technique will be considered in Sect. 3.5.

Based on the rules in Fig. 3, we present an algorithm to translate a program with MF specification to the same program with the corresponding AP specification:

Algorithm 1. *We translate a program by 4 steps:*

- *For each class, use rule* [H-PPRE] *to encapsulate all the private fields;*
- *For each MF definition, use* [H-MPRE] *or* [H-MINH] *to translate it into an AP definition;*
- *For each* **old**(·) *appearance in assertions, use rule* [H-MOLD];
- *Use* [H-INV] *to translate all the invariants, and use* [H-TRANS] *to translate all the other assertions.*

We can use this algorithm to translate the specification of all the classes and client code. In this and the next subsections, we will prove several useful properties of the algorithm.

Theorem 1. *For a program S with MF specification, using Algorithm 1, we can obtain a program T with AP specification. In addition, the specification of T is well-encapsulated.*

Proof. The second step will remove all the MF definitions, and the fourth step will remove all the MF appearances in assertions. Thus T has an AP specification (and we will prove that it is a well-formed specification in the next subsection). Besides, we can see that all the concrete field appearances in the method specifications are substituted by the AP *pri* in the fourth step. Thus, the resulting specification is well-encapsulated.   □

Theorem 2. *If a program S with MF specification is well-encapsulated, we can modify the rules to simplify the translation algorithm:*

- *Delete the rule* [H-PPRE] *and delete the first step in Algorithm 1;*
- *In other rules, unfold the AP pri*(...) *or pri$_C$*(...) *to its definition.*

If we obtain a program T from S using the simplified algorithm, then the specification of T will still be well-encapsulated.

Proof. We can prove it by induction. If the method specifications in S do not mention concrete fields, no matter which rule we use, the method specifications in T would not mention concrete fields.   □

Example 1. The specification of *Rec* in Fig. 1 is well-encapsulated. According to Theorem 2, we can translate it using the simplified algorithm. The result is shown in Fig. 4.

```
class Rec : Object{
    int x1, y1, x2, y2;
    invariant x1 ≤ x2 ∧ y1 ≤ y2;

    define width_Rec(this, v) :  v = x2 − x1;
    define height_Rec(this, v) :  v = y2 − y1;

    Rec()
    ⟨⟩⟨∃v, v′ · v = 1 ∧ v′ = 1 ∧ width(this, v) ∧ height(this, v′)⟩

    void ScaleH(int factor)
    ⟨(0 ≤ factor) ∧ width(this, d)⟩⟨∃v · width(this, v) ∧ v = d × factor/100⟩
}
```

Fig. 4. *Rec* translated into abstract predicates

3.2 Well-Formedness of Translation Result

Both MF and AP frameworks provide some scope rules about: (1) the locations in specifications where a MF or an AP can be mentioned; (2) the concrete fields that a MF or an AP can depend on. These rules can be found in the related work [7, 11].

Most of the scope rules are stated in Definitions 1 and 4. Besides, MFs can be mentioned in the invariant of the same class, but APs cannot be mentioned in any invariant. Based on the scope rules, we define:

Definition 7 (Well-formed). *If the MF or AP specification does not violate the corresponding scope rules, it is called a* well-formed *specification. A program with well-formed specification is called a* well-formed *program.*

Theorem 3. *If a program S with MF specification is well-formed, we translate S using* Algorithm 1 *and obtain T, then T is well-formed.*

Proof. We prove the two requirements of the scope respectively.

(1) An AP can be used anywhere (syntactically), except the invariants. Due to [H-INV], the invariants in T do not mention any predicate. Thus T meets the first requirement.
(2) Since S is well-formed, the MFs in S only depend on the (model and concrete) fields in the same class. Thus the APs in T only depend on the fields in the same class, which is allowed by Definition 4. Therefore T meets the second requirement.

From (1) and (2), we can conclude that T is well-formed.   □

3.3 Framing

Framing is an important problem in verification. It requires us to specify the boundary of memory locations modifiable/modified by the methods. For example, we must be able to prove that *ScaleH* does not modify *height* in Fig. 1; and *ScaleH* does not modify the validity of *height*(this, v) in Example 1.

```
class SRec : Object{
    int x1, y1, x2, y2, scale;
    model int width such_that width = (x2 − x1) × scale;
    model int height such_that height = (y2 − y1) × scale;
    void ScaleH(int factor)
    ⟨0 ≤ factor⟩⟨width = old(width) × factor/100⟩
    modifies width, x2;
}
```

Fig. 5. Another implementation of *Rec* with model fields based specification

Several solutions are proposed to deal with the frame problem. Literature on MF often uses a **modifies** clause to declare the fields possibly modified by the method, while the other fields will not be modified. Thus in Fig. 1, we are sure that *ScaleH* does not modify *height*.

Specifications based on AP use separation logic to describe the frame properties. In Example 1, since predicates $width_{Rec}$ and $height_{Rec}$ are separated, we know that *ScaleH* does not modify *height*.

Since MF and AP techniques use different strategies to deal with the frame problem, we need to present another algorithm to translate the **modifies** clauses into separation logic assertions.

The example in Fig. 5 illustrates the main difficulty of the translation. Class *SRec* includes a concrete field *scale* as the scale factor of the rectangle, and both MFs *width* and *height* depend on this field.

Due to the **modifies** clause of *ScaleH*, we can still prove that it does not modify *height*. But after we translate this program using Algorithm 1, we cannot use frame rule to prove that $height_{SRec}$ is not modified by *ScaleH*, since the predicates $width_{SRec}$ and $height_{SRec}$ are not separated.

This example suggests us to merge the predicates which are not separated. Firstly we introduce some notations:

- In order to distinguish the new rules from those rules in Fig. 3, here we use $spec_1 \Longrightarrow_f spec_2$ to denote that $spec_1$ is translated into $spec_2$.
- α denotes a sequence of numbers, and $\alpha :: k$ is the sequence which appends k at the end of sequence α. $\alpha[i]$ denotes the i-th number in the sequence.

We begin from a simple case without inheritance. All the new rules are shown in Fig. 6.

[P-MRG] merges two APs into a "big" AP. The superscript α records that the "big" AP is merged from which predicates, the order of elements in α is the same as the order of parameters.

[P-SBST] uses the "big" AP to substitute for the predicates in specifications. If p_C^{α} is merged from p_C^k and other predicates, then all the $p^k(o, v)$ in specifications can be translated to $p^{\alpha}(o, \bar{=}, v, \bar{=})$, which means the first parameter is o and the $(i + 1)$-th parameter is v, and we do not care about other parameters.

$$p_C^\alpha, p_C^k \text{ are not separated,}$$

[P-MRG] $\dfrac{\textbf{define } p_C^\alpha(\textbf{this}, v_1, \ldots, v_n) : \psi_\alpha, \quad \textbf{define } p_C^k(\textbf{this}, v) : \psi_k}{\begin{array}{c}\textbf{define } p_C^\alpha \ldots; \ \textbf{define } p_C^k \ldots \Longrightarrow_f \\ \textbf{define } p_C^{\alpha::k}(\textbf{this}, v_1, \ldots, v_n, v_{n+1}) : \psi_\alpha \wedge \psi_k[v_{n+1}/v]\end{array}}$

[P-SBST] $\dfrac{\begin{array}{c}\textbf{define } p_C^\alpha(\textbf{this}, v_1, \ldots, v_n) : \text{-}, \\ \mathsf{type}(o) = C, \quad k = \alpha[i], \quad p^k(o, v) \text{ appears in } \psi\end{array}}{\psi \Longrightarrow_f \psi[p^\alpha(o, \overline{\text{-}}, v, \overline{\text{-}})/p^k(o, v)]}$

[P-MTHD] $\dfrac{\begin{array}{c}\langle \varphi \rangle\, C.m(\ldots) \langle \psi \rangle, \ m \text{ is not a constructor, } \mathsf{fresh}(v), \ \mathsf{type}(o) = C, \ k = \alpha[i], \\ \textbf{define } p_C^\alpha(\textbf{this}, v_1, \ldots, v_n) : \text{-}, \quad p^\alpha(o, \ldots) \text{ appears in } \langle \varphi \rangle\langle \psi \rangle, \\ o.f_k \text{ does not appear in the } \textbf{modifies} \text{ clause of } m()\end{array}}{\langle \varphi \rangle\langle \psi \rangle \Longrightarrow_f \langle \varphi \wedge p^\alpha(o, \overline{\text{-}}, v, \overline{\text{-}}) \rangle\langle \psi \wedge p^\alpha(o, \overline{\text{-}}, v, \overline{\text{-}}) \rangle}$

[P-MDF] $\dfrac{}{\textbf{modifies} \ \ldots \Longrightarrow_f}$

Fig. 6. Translation rules about **modifies** clauses

[P-MTHD] deals with method specifications. If a "big" AP $p^\alpha(o, \ldots)$ appears in the pre or post-condition, but model field $o.f_k$ does not appear in the **modifies** clause ($k \in \alpha$), then we need to explicitly declare that the corresponding parameter of the "big" AP is not modified.

The resulting specification of [P-MTHD] can usually be simplified. For example, $p^\alpha(o, a, \text{-}) \wedge p^\alpha(o, \text{-}, b)$ can be reduced to $p^\alpha(o, a, b)$ due to the definition of p^α.

The last rule [P-MDF] simply deletes the **modifies** clause. Based on these rules, we define the translation algorithm as follows.

Algorithm 2. *For a result of* Algorithm 1, *i.e. a program with AP specification and* **modifies** *clauses, we translate the* **modifies** *clauses by 4 steps:*

- *For each class, use rule* [P-MRG] *to merge its APs until all the "big" APs are separated from each other; (If we cannot judge whether two APs are separated, we just merge them.)*
- *Use* [P-SBST] *to translate all the assertions until there are only "big" APs in them;*
- *For each method, for each "big" AP $p^\alpha(o, \ldots)$ appears in the pre or post-condition, for each $k \in \alpha$, if $o.f_k$ does not appear in the* **modifies** *clause, use* [P-MTHD] *to declare that it is not modified;*
- *Use* [P-MDF] *to delete all the* **modifies** *clauses.*

Theorem 4. *Suppose program S has MF specification and* **modifies** *clauses. We use* Algorithms 1 *and* 2 *to translate S and obtain a program T, then the frame properties provable in S are also provable in T.*

Proof. In program S, suppose a model field $o.f_k$ is not modified by a method $C.m$. We will prove the corresponding frame property in program T:

(1) If $k \in \alpha$ and the AP $p^\alpha(o, \ldots)$ appears in the pre or post-condition of $C.m$, then [P-MTHD] would declare that the corresponding parameter of the "big" predicate remains the same in the pre and post-conditions;

(2) If $k \in \alpha$ but the AP $p^\alpha(o, \ldots)$ does not appear in the pre or post-condition of $C.m$, since $p^\alpha(o, \ldots)$ is separated from the other "big" APs, we can use frame rule to prove that the parameters of p^α are not modified.

So we can conclude that all the frame properties provable in S are also provable in T.   □

Example 2. After using Algorithms 1 and 2 to translate the class *SRec* in Fig. 5 (with some simplification), the result is:

> **define** $widthHeight_{SRec}(\textbf{this}, v1, v2)$:
> $\quad v1 = (x2 - x1) \times scale \land v2 = (y2 - y1) \times scale;$
> $SRec()\ \langle\rangle\langle widthHeight(\textbf{this}, 1, 1)\rangle$
> **void** $ScaleH(\textbf{int}\ factor)$
> $\langle 0 \leq factor \land widthHeight(\textbf{this}, d, v')\rangle\langle widthHeight(\textbf{this}, d \times factor/100, v')\rangle$

Then we take the inheritance into account. Notice that a subclass can add new constraints for the inherited MFs, thus after translation, two separated APs in the superclass may be not separated in the subclass. To keep the behavioural subtype relation, we also need to merge them in the superclass. Thus, the requirement of [P-MRG] that

$$p_C^\alpha, p_C^k \text{ are not separated}$$

should be modified to

$$\exists D <: C \cdot p_D^\alpha, p_D^k \text{ are not separated.}$$

That is to say, if two APs are not separated in one of C's subclasses, we need to merge them in C. This rule needs to check all the subclasses of C, thus it is not modular. The other rules remain unchanged.

We prove the correctness and termination of both translation algorithms. The proof can be found in our technical report [12].

Theorem 5 (Correctness). *If $S \Longrightarrow_t T$ or $S \Longrightarrow_f T$, then program S satisfies its specification iff program T satisfies its specification.*

3.4 Further Investigation

Previously, we have proved that APs are not less expressive than MFs. Here we show an example which can only be specified by APs, therefore, APs are strictly more expressive than MFs.

When dealing with recursion data structures, APs are more expressive than MFs. For the length of linked lists, we can define a recursive AP:

> **define** $len_{Node}(\textbf{this}, v)$: $(\textbf{this}.next = \textbf{null} \Rightarrow v = 1)$
> $\quad \land(\textbf{this}.next \neq \textbf{null} \Rightarrow len(\textbf{this}.next, v - 1));$

However, using MFs (without the ownership mechanism), we cannot define the length recursively. Since the constraints of MFs are invariant-like properties (they must hold in all the program states), MFs cannot depend on the fields of other objects. Thus, methods like "append a node to a linked list" cannot be specified by MFs.

Even in the presence of the ownership mechanism, MFs have more restrictions on recursion than APs. In a typical setting [5], the constraint of the MF $o.f$ could only mention the fields of o, and the fields of the representation fields of o. Thus, to allow the MF *len* depending on *next.len*, each node must own the next node. But this design will prevent us from looping through the list[1].

In conclusion, APs are strictly more expressive than MFs.

3.5 Ownership

Since MFs can only depend on the fields of the same object, they can hardly describe the properties of aggregate objects. To solve this problem, [1,5,13] introduce the ownership [10] mechanism into MF approaches. With this mechanism, a MF declaration in class C takes the form:

$$\textbf{model } T \ f \ \textbf{such\_that } R_C(f, \overline{o.f}, \overline{o.g});$$

Here o ranges in all the objects which are (transitively) owned by **this** object, including **this** itself.

On the other hand, since APs can already mention other objects in its definition, [14] states that AP technique do not need the ownership mechanism to describe the properties of aggregate objects.

When we take the ownership mechanism into account, the MF specification except the class invariants, can still be translated. However, the translation rules need to be revised for a little bit, since the constraints of MFs can depend on other objects now. Take [H-MPRE] as an example, we modify the premise "$\overline{f_i}$ are model fields of **this**" to "$\overline{o_i.f_i}$ are model fields of **this** and the objects **this** transitively owns", and replace "$\overline{f_i}$" with "$\overline{o_i.f_i}$" in the rule. Other rules can be revised similarly.

But the invariants cannot be directly translated, since AP specification does not allow multi-object invariants. To solve the problem, we translate the invariants into method specifications, as suggested by [14].

We define a predicate for each class:

$$[\text{H-INVD}] \quad \frac{\textbf{invariant } \psi_i; \text{ are all the invariants of class } C}{\textbf{invariant } \psi_i; \Longrightarrow_t \textbf{define } inv_C(\textbf{this}): \ \bigwedge_i \psi_i;}$$

---

[1] In literature on ownership, the nodes of a list do not own each other, instead, they have a same owner. If we define that each node owns the next node in JML, we cannot loop through the list and modify its elements, since it violates the *owner-as-modifier* discipline; in Spec#, we cannot even loop through the list since the owner of a variable must be kept unchanged in a loop.

And its definition needs to be translated by [H-TRANS]. This AP is true iff all the invariants of class C holds. Then, suppose $\overline{o_i}$ are the objects owned by o, we assert that $inv(o)$ holds on the entry and exit of every public method of $\overline{o_i}$:

$$[\text{H-INVM}] \frac{o : C,\ \overline{o_i} \text{ are all the objects owned by } o, \text{ including } o \text{ itself}}{\langle\varphi\rangle\, C.C(\ldots)\langle\psi\rangle \Longrightarrow_t \langle\varphi\rangle\, C.C(\ldots)\langle\psi \wedge inv(\text{ret})\rangle;\ \langle\varphi\rangle\, o_i.m(\ldots)\langle\psi\rangle \Longrightarrow_t \langle\varphi \wedge inv(o)\rangle\, o_i.m(\ldots)\langle\psi \wedge inv(o)\rangle}$$

Here ret denotes the return value. When reasoning about the aggregate object (o together with $\overline{o_i}$), the multi-object invariant can be proved using [H-INVM][2]; when reasoning about the other objects, the multi-object invariant can be proved using frame rule.

Notice that if the behavioural subtype relation holds in the original specification, then it holds in the translating result, since we just add a same predicate to all the pre and post-conditions of non-construction methods.

In conclusion, considering the ownership mechanism, the MF specification can still be translated into AP specification. However, the invariants need to be translated into method specifications.

4   Related Work

The concept of *model fields* was proposed by Leino in his PhD thesis [3], where it was called *abstract fields*. In the thesis, MFs are used to specify/verify data refinement. However, the work almost ignores information hiding, and requires MFs to be uniquely determined by the constraints.

Müller *et al.* [13] presented a modular technique for specifying/verifying frame properties using MFs. It also uses the ownership technique to deal with aggregate objects. However, the work does not fully support the inheritance.

Leino and Müller presented a modular verification methodology for MFs [5]. In this work, the MF $o.f$ is updated only when o is in valid states. It is tightly combined with the ownership technique, thus it can deal with the frame properties of aggregate objects modularly, and fully supports the inheritance.

There are some other applications of MFs. MFs are used to express the abstract specifications in JML [1], to write and check *design by contract* assertions [15], and to achieve information hiding in the specifications for interfaces [16].

The concept of *abstract predicates* was proposed by Parkinson and Bierman [2] in developing an OO program verification system based on separation logic. More recently they take inheritance into account [7], and introduce static/dynamic specifications for each method, to avoid restricting subtypes' behaviors or re-verifying inherited methods.

---

[2] In fact, different encapsulation disciplines (e.g. *owner-as-modifier* in JML, *dynamic ownership* in Spec#) lead to different proof obligations of the invariants. Here [H-INVM] needs to generate all the proof obligations of the invariants, according to the adopted encapsulation discipline.

Liu *et al.* proposed an OO verification framework in [17], whose abstraction technique is similar to Parkinson's. It can deal with the inheritance by using simpler notations, where each method only need one specification and re-verification is avoided as well. Qiu *et al.* extend the framework for interfaces [18], and give a solution to the problems brought by multiple inheritance.

There are some other abstraction techniques for OO verification, e.g., pure methods [19] and data groups [20]. The *pure methods* are side-effect-free methods, thus they can be invoked in specifications to hide implementation details. *Data groups* can help information hiding in decribing frame properties. Each data group represents a set of variables, and it can be used in the modifies clauses to announce the modifiability of its members.

Although many papers focus on MF or AP based techniques, a systematic comparison between them is lacking. Burgman [21] proposed a comparison between JML and Separation Logic in verifying multi-threaded Java programs. But the work does not focus on the abstraction mechanisms.

5 Conclusion

In this paper, we compare two important abstraction techniques for specifying/verifying OO programs, the *model fields* and the *abstract predicates*.

By developing the translation rules and algorithms, we demonstrate that any program with MF specification can be translated into one with AP specification. The translation is still correct in the presence of inheritance, recursion, or even the ownership technique.

We prove that the resulting specification obtained from the translation is well-encapsulated, well-formed and correct. A program satisfies its MF specification iff it satisfies the resulting AP specification. In addition, we demonstrate the existence of programs which can only be specified by APs, which indicates that APs are more expressive.

On the other hand, MFs have its own advantages like user friendliness and supporting automatic verification. Our conclusion is, the seeking for the powerful and easy-to-use OO abstraction techniques has not come to the end. As a future work, we plan to investigate the other abstraction techniques and compare them, and try to develop better specification techniques or specification patterns for OO programs.

References

1. Leavens, G.T., Baker, A.L., Ruby, C.: Preliminary design of JML: a behavioral interface specification language for java. SIGSOFT Softw. Eng. Notes **31**(3), 1–38 (2006)
2. Parkinson, M., Bierman, G.: Separation logic and abstraction. In: POPL 2005, pp. 247–258. ACM (2005)
3. Leino, K.R.: Toward reliable modular programs. Ph.D. thesis, California Institute of Technology (1995)

4. Bruns, D.: Formal semantics for the java modeling language. Diplomarbeit, Universität Karlsruhe, June 2009
5. Leino, K.R.M., Müller, P.: A verification methodology for model fields. In: Sestoft, P. (ed.) ESOP 2006. LNCS, vol. 3924, pp. 115–130. Springer, Heidelberg (2006)
6. Reynolds, J.C.: Separation logic: a logic for shared mutable data structures. In: LICS 2002, pp. 55–74. IEEE CS (2002)
7. Parkinson, M.J., Bierman, G.M.: Separation logic, abstraction and inheritance. In: POPL 2008, pp. 75–86. ACM (2008)
8. Barnett, M., Leino, K.R.M., Schulte, W.: The Spec# programming system: an overview. In: Barthe, G., Burdy, L., Huisman, M., Lanet, J.-L., Muntean, T. (eds.) CASSIS 2004. LNCS, vol. 3362, pp. 49–69. Springer, Heidelberg (2005)
9. Jacobs, B., Piessens, F.: The VeriFast program verifier. CW Reports (2008)
10. Clarke, D.G., Potter, J.M., Noble, J.: Ownership types for flexible alias protection. In: OOPSLA 1998, pp. 48–64. ACM (1998)
11. Leavens, G.T., Poll, E., Clifton, C., Cheon, Y., Ruby, C., Cok, D., Müller, P., Kiniry, J., Chalin, P.: JML Reference Manual (2008)
12. Zhang, K., Qiu, Z.: Comparison between Model Fields and Abstract Predicates. Technical report, School of Math., Peking University (2016). https://github.com/fm-pku/mf-ap/blob/master/mf-ap.pdf
13. Müller, P., Poetzsch-Heffter, A., Leavens, G.T.: Modular specification of frame properties in JML. Concurrency Comput. Pract. Exp. 15(2), 117–154 (2003)
14. Parkinson, M.: Class invariants: the end of the road. In: International Workshop on Aliasing, Confinement and Ownership, vol. 23 (2007)
15. Cheon, Y., Leavens, G., Sitaraman, M., Edwards, S.: Model variables: cleanly supporting abstraction in design by contract: research articles. Softw. Pract. Exp. 35(6), 583–599 (2005)
16. Leavens, G.T., Müller, P.: Information hiding and visibility in interface specifications. In: ICSE 2007, pp. 385–395. IEEE CS (2007)
17. Liu, Y., Hong, A., Qiu, Z.: Inheritance and modularity in specification and verification of OO programs. In: TASE 2011, pp. 19–26. IEEE CS (2011)
18. Zongyan, Q., Ali, H., Yijing, L.: Modular verification of OO programs with interfaces. In: Aoki, T., Taguchi, K. (eds.) ICFEM 2012. LNCS, vol. 7635, pp. 151–166. Springer, Heidelberg (2012)
19. Darvas, Á., Leino, K.R.M.: Practical reasoning about invocations and implementations of pure methods. In: Dwyer, M.B., Lopes, A. (eds.) FASE 2007. LNCS, vol. 4422, pp. 336–351. Springer, Heidelberg (2007)
20. Leino, K.R.M.: Data groups: specifying the modification of extended state. In: OOPSLA 1998, pp. 144–153. ACM (1998)
21. Burgman, R.: Specifying multi-threaded Java programs (2010). http://referaat.cs.utwente.nl/conference/12/paper

Erratum to: A Monadic Semantics for Quantum Computing in Featherweight Java

Samuel da Silva Feitosa[1]([⊠]), Juliana Kaizer Vizzotto[1], Eduardo Kessler Piveta[1], and Andre Rauber Du Bois[2]

[1] Universidade Federal de Santa Maria, Santa Maria, Brazil
{sfeitosa, juvizzotto, piveta}@inf.ufsm.br
[2] Universidade Federal de Pelotas, Pelotas, Brazil
dubois@inf.ufpel.edu.br

Erratum to:
Chapter 3 in: F. Castor and Y.D. Liu (Eds.)
Programming Languages
DOI 10.1007/978-3-319-45279-1_3

In the initially published contribution the name of the author Samuel da Silva Feitosa was incorrect. The correct name is as follows: Samuel da Silva Feitosa.

The updated original online version for this chapter can be found at 10.1007/978-3-319-45279-1_3

© Springer International Publishing Switzerland 2016
F. Castor and Y.D. Liu (Eds.): SBLP 2016, LNCS 9889, p. E1, 2016.
DOI: 10.1007/978-3-319-45279-1_13

Author Index

Printed in the United States
By Bookmasters